Praise for *HEAD STRONG*

"Scott Fedor's journey from adversity to advocacy is a testament to the notion that we help ourselves by helping others. On page after page of this truly gripping and inspiring memoir are gems of hard-earned wisdom from which we can all learn–real-life examples of the power of choosing purpose and service over fear and doubt. What a gift Scott has given the world by courageously committing to share his story!"

– Jeff Bell, author of *When in Doubt, Make Belief*

"An intimate and honest journey through one man's traumatic injury– one that permanently damages his body yet perpetually intensifies his will. His story is an informative, clear-eyed examination of what it takes to fight back from personal tragedy, with grit, humor and hope. His resolve will challenge the limits of your own life."

– Lisa Fenn, author of *Carry On: A Story of Resilience, Redemption, and an Unlikely Family*

"Scott Fedor was living the American dream, but one sunny July afternoon, his life turned into a nightmare. *HEAD STRONG* is a book written by a man who should be dead, and if not dead, nowhere near as alive as he is today. His story will make you laugh, cry, wince, smile, take a deep breath, and thank God that you are alive. And if you don't believe in God, you might after reading this book."

– Rev. Damian J. Ference, author of *The Strangeness of Truth: Vibrant Faith in a Dark World,* priest of the Diocese of Cleveland

"*HEAD STRONG* takes you on an inspirational journey, full of trials and tribulations, and ultimately a renewed sense of strength and purpose."

– Jon Gordon, best-selling author of *The Energy Bus* and *The Seed*

"Scott Fedor's inspiring story is a reminder that life as you know it can change in an instant and with the right attitude we can all learn to embrace change. Sometimes our biggest hurdles teach us that helping others is the best way to heal ourselves."

– Hogan Gorman, author of *Hot Cripple*

"Scott Fedor's story is one that we can all learn from. It's a testament to how fleeting life can be and how to look death in the face and say, 'No, not today.' We all face moments that challenge us, Scott is an inspiration on using passion and strength to overcome times of adversity and never take one day for granted."

– Freddie Kitchens, Cleveland Browns Head Coach

"Very few understand what challenges individuals living with a spinal cord injury go through both physically and mentally on a daily basis. Sucking it up and developing an Iron Will is priority one. The power of the human spirit and the resilience that one's psyche can build is truly amazing. Scott W. Fedor's book *HEAD STRONG* is a must read for young and old. After reading this book YOU'LL want to do a huge gut check!"

– Patrick Rummerfield, motivational speaker,
first quadriplegic to complete Hawaii IRONMAN

# HEAD STRONG

# HEAD STRONG

## HOW A BROKEN NECK STRENGTHENED MY SPIRIT

***

**SCOTT W. FEDOR**

Published by Coyote Crest, LLC
Westlake, Ohio



Library of Congress Control Number: 2019905404

ISBN: 978-1-7330810-1-6 (paperback)
ISBN: 978-1-7330810-2-3 (hardcover)
ISBN: 978-1-7330810-0-9 (ebook)

Printed in the United States of America

*Cover design by Vanessa Mendozzi*
*Front cover photography by Eric Mull*
*Back cover photography by Jurgen Dopatka*

scottwfedor.com

1 3 5 7 9 10 8 6 4 2

First Edition: July 2019

*For Dad, Mom, and Lindsey*

"What saves a man is to take a step. Then another step. It is always the same step, but you have to take it."

– Antoine de Saint-Exupéry, *Wind, Sand and Stars*

# CONTENTS


| | | |
|---|---|---|
| | *Foreword by Kate Voegele* | xv |
| | *Prologue: I'm Going to Die* | xix |

## PART ONE

| | | |
|---|---|---|
| 1: | Gonna Fly Now | 3 |
| 2: | Escape to the Mountains | 13 |
| 3: | You Only Live Once | 23 |
| 4: | Your Ship Has Come in | 31 |
| 5: | English Customs | 39 |
| 6: | Best Friends | 48 |
| 7: | I'm Going to Marry That Girl | 65 |
| 8: | Priorities | 73 |
| 9: | Oh, the Places You'll Go | 80 |
| 10: | Keys to the Kingdom | 86 |
| 11: | Independence Day | 94 |

## PART TWO

| | | |
|---|---|---|
| 12: | There's Been an Accident | 109 |
| 13: | Hell Doll | 119 |
| 14: | Do You Want to Live? | 127 |

15: Streets of Worryville 134
16: Why Me? 142
17: Him Again 151
18: Thanksgiving 162
19: New Neighbors 175
20: Revelation 182
21: Plateaued 190
22: What If? 198
23: Breakthroughs 207
24: Her Again 216
25: Getting Back Up 220

## PART THREE

26: Broken 229
27: Acceptance 241
28: God Bless You 250
29: New Tomatoes 260
30: Thank You 265
31: Wants and Needs 270
32: I'm Going to Live 279

*Epilogue: My Story* 290
*Acknowledgments* 293
*If You Would Like to Help* 295
*Suggested Reading* 297
*About the Author* 299

# FOREWORD

Scott Fedor and I share many of the same passions. Among them are Cleveland sports, a fat glass of red wine, a long list of ’70s singer/songwriters, and an unquenchable zest for far-off travel. I first met Scott in 2010 at one of my hometown concerts in Cleveland. As a recording artist born and raised in the birthplace of rock ‘n’ roll, I always looked forward to my hometown shows more than anything on my tours. It was always such a respite from the vagabonding road lifestyle to be among my family and friends, and to get the chance to meet fellow Clevelanders. There’s something about the Northeast Ohio sensibility–a fiercely unpretentious goodwill and genuineness–that truly tethers you to the region and the people in the community, even if they’re strangers, wherever you go.

Earlier in the tour my dad had told me a bit about his new friend Scott over the phone while our tour bus hurtled through cornfield-lined roads toward home, and I was incredibly moved hearing about his story. In fact, it’s impossible not to be moved hearing just even a snippet of Scott’s story. In addition to finding Scott and his story incredibly inspiring, I also found him to be hilarious and a generally awesome person who quickly became a great friend.

As the years passed, our friendship continued to grow and I always so looked forward to catching up over those aforementioned fat glasses of red at holidays, family and friend gatherings, and my hometown gigs. Seeing Scott in the audience at my Cleveland shows is a huge highlight of any tour for many reasons, one in particular being that he is undoubtedly as serious a music fan as anyone I've ever met. I'm always honored that a guy who counts Bruce Springsteen and James Taylor as favorites also enjoys my shows and has been cool enough to let me send him sketches of new songs over the years and ask for feedback. If Scott is digging the new material, I know I'm doing something right.

Though I already knew we shared a passion for discovering far-flung places, I loved reading about Scott's deep love for international travel and his global adventures in this book. When my husband and I decided to pick up and fulfill our bucket list dream of moving to France last year, I thought often of Scott and his "you-only-live-once" approach. I never knew about most of the items on his bucket list detailed in the book, and was equally impressed and entertained reading about everything from his bull-riding adventures to his many treks across China and how he determinedly got to work at a young age to start knocking down the items on his list one by one.

Before I met Scott, I'd never known anyone with a spinal cord injury. I couldn't possibly fathom the unique struggles my friend faced every day or imagine what it was like to go through the myriad of battles he's had to fight. What was overwhelmingly apparent, however, was his steadfast determination to live his life as fully and wholeheartedly as possible, despite the immeasurable adversity he'd experienced.

We all grow up seeing common wisdom like "live your life to the fullest" and "appreciate each day" and "have an attitude of gratitude" on everything from classroom posters with bad fonts to our Instagram feed, and yet the message often falls flat. It doesn't sink in until there is real humanity behind it. What amazes me about Scott and about this book is his ability to bring these fundamental truths to life in a way that not only hits home, but goes a step beyond that. Scott's story is one of unbelievable courage and the power of faith, attitude, and choice.

I've often heard Scott say that being called an "inspiration" isn't his goal. I get it. Or at least I think I do in the best way I can. It's easy for people to meet someone like him, who has been to hell and back and overcome immense obstacles, and place them into a tidy box as "such an inspiration" with a bunch of other random stuff. It can feel trivial and somewhat empty. In the greater scheme of the work that Scott is doing with the nonprofit he founded and built, Getting Back Up, the scope of the difference he makes and the work he is determined to do in the world goes far beyond simply existing as a human embodiment of inspiration. Of course, in the literal sense of the word, I myself consider Scott to be a massively inspiring person with a massively inspiring story. And I know you will too, especially as you read this book. But as I thought about it, I realized the way the word relates to Scott's story needs a reframe.

The word "inspiration" as we regularly use it comes from the Latin "inspirare," which became "inspiratio" and eventually, in Middle English, inspiration. The Middle English definition of the word is simple: *divine guidance*. This strikes me as incredibly significant as it relates to Scott and his story. Whether you're a person of any type of faith or not, I believe you will be extremely moved by Scott's recounting of how his strong faith pulled him out of despair time and time again along his journey. He speaks often of the power of prayer and how it kept him going in the most trying of times, and there are many points in his story during which he describes experiencing a strong sense of God's hand at work, both emotionally and physically. As a deeply spiritual person myself, reading his story I have no doubt that there were and still are larger forces at play on Scott's road to recovery. Is Scott an inspiration? Absolutely. But maybe it's more accurate to say that in addition to *being* an inspiration, Scott has a faith that has opened him up to receive tremendous amounts of it in the form of true divine guidance.

One of the most inspiring parts of Scott's journey is the charitable work he does through Getting Back Up. Reading about his intensive mission to provide continuing therapy for those living with spinal cord injuries, you can't help but be greatly moved by his capacity and deep desire to give back after everything he's experienced himself. Having already provided aid to over one hundred people, Scott and GBU truly demonstrate the extraordinary power of serving others and the healing it brings.

Ultimately, this book is the story of my friend who made the incredibly courageous decision that he was going to live. And not only live, but thrive. He made the conscious choice to face his adversity head-on, despite a harrowing road full of seemingly insurmountable obstacles. I'm grateful to know him and incredibly honored to be a part of this story in some small way. Scott is a true fighter, a profound voice, and a headstrong force for good who has transformed an unthinkable challenge into a powerful tool to serve. Enjoy this book and savor its wisdom, wit, and heartbreakingly beautiful story. I can't wait for you to get to know my friend Scott and his amazing journey.

Kate Voegele
Recording artist, songwriter, and actress
Los Angeles, 2019

# PROLOGUE

# I'M GOING TO DIE

*I'm going to die.*

The words invaded my mind as quickly as the feeling that immediately engulfed my body and rendered me useless milliseconds after I hit the water. I tried to move my arms, though I already knew what I'd done.

This was bad.

Playing high school sports, I had pinched some nerves that left me with a numbing sensation throughout my arm, making it uncomfortable and awkward to move it. This was different, though.

There was no tingling sensation.

There wasn't even any pain.

There was nothing.

# PART ONE

# ONE

# GONNA FLY NOW

Sitting still has never been easy for me.

Growing up I had an abundance of energy and was always eager to tackle whatever adventure lay in front of me. I wouldn't classify myself as hyper, but I never had a problem finding the energy needed to make it through the day, regardless of what was in store. I imagine the only time I took a nap was when I was put into a "time out" or the babysitter needed a break.

I was born and raised in Cleveland, a gritty Midwestern town with a quiet confidence, a bit of an edge, and a strong backbone, where my parents raised me to reflect those same characteristics. A product of Catholic education, I was disciplined when needed, but praised even more, taught to believe in myself, to work hard, and to remember that life was unfair and didn't owe me a thing.

Fortunately for my sake, and probably more for theirs, my parents discovered a way for me to harness all the energy I exhibited as a child. As soon as I could walk and talk, I participated in some athletic endeavor or another. Not to boast, but I was recognized as "Athlete of the Year" at the conclusion of the school year. Sure, it was kindergarten, but I did get an awesome medallion to commemorate my achievement.

Throughout most of my schooling and into my early college years, my school day was usually followed by some sporting activity. Often, I would not get home until early evening, which barely left time to eat dinner and finish any homework before I headed to bed. However, I always completed what needed to be done.

On plenty of occasions, I made my mother rush me across town to different libraries to check out the books I needed to finish an assignment. It drove her nuts to find out the project wasn't due for another two weeks.

Yeah, I was a little neurotic at times. Patience was never my strong suit.

Although my compulsive need to get everything done right away drove my parents crazy, they'll be the first to admit my grades never suffered due to my extracurricular activities.

At the tender age of two, I was enrolled in swimming lessons at the local YWCA. For the next fourteen years, I swam on a regular basis. Most of those early years were spent listening to the *Rocky* soundtrack in the car as my father drove me to my lessons. My favorite song on the tape was, "Gonna Fly Now," the main theme song from the movie.

My dad encouraged me to close my eyes and visualize the goal in front of me. In this case, it was in the pool, executing the front crawl with the precision of an Olympian. I'll be the first to admit I was the furthest thing from the next Michael Phelps, but all the visualization and lessons took hold enough that I eventually became an instructor at the same YWCA facility where I learned to swim. Many an afternoon was spent teaching younger kids the same basic techniques I had learned and how to correctly execute each stroke.

I also taught them the proper form needed to dive into the water.

Along the way, I received my lifeguard certification, a piece of paper that didn't just make it possible for me to earn extra cash during the summer, but also held me accountable for the safety of others.

My real passion was baseball. Some of my fondest childhood memories were of throwing the ball around with my father in a game of catch in the front yard. His uniform of choice was usually a business suit, sans the jacket, with the tie loosened and the sleeves rolled up. Not because he was more comfortable in slacks than in jeans, but because I waited on the porch, glove in hand, and ambushed him as soon as his car pulled into the driveway, pleading for a game of catch.

My dad worked for himself in the insurance industry, and after a long and tiring day, I'm sure he looked forward to relaxing once he arrived home. However, he never turned down my requests for a game of catch, and we'd usually throw the ball until Mom called us for dinner, or the setting sun made it too dark to continue.

I couldn't get enough baseball.

My summers were packed with ball games from Memorial Day to Labor Day. I played in local recreational leagues, on traveling teams in different cities, on my grade school and high school teams, and into my early college years.

Several summers were spent at the Ohio University baseball camp in Athens, Ohio. Some summers I played on multiple teams, which left me without a single day that did not involve a game or practice. My father even set up a batting cage in the basement of our home, where I spent countless hours honing my swing as I hit a ball tethered to a pulley system into a net.

All the practice and preparation paid off.

When I was sixteen years old, I tried out for the Continental Blue Streaks, a traveling baseball team based out of Stow, Ohio. I was fortunate enough to play second base on the team. Every day I drove more than forty-five minutes each way for practice. That summer with the Blue Streaks I played over one hundred games across the state of Ohio, as well as tournaments in Michigan, Indiana, and Tennessee. As the summer wound down, the Blue Streaks were playing at a high level.

We won the district tournament, then the regional tournament, and eventually the state tournament, which qualified us for the 16-Year-Old World Series. A week later a bunch of pubescent baseball players flew to Laredo, Texas to compete in the Continental Amateur Baseball Association World Series.

Laredo was as much fun off the field as it was on it. During the day, we played against some of the best teams from across the United States and Puerto Rico. At night, we walked across the bridge over the Rio Grande River and into the Mexican border town of Nuevo Laredo.

Once in Mexico, it seemed like we were in a different world. Although we could still spot the Howard Johnson, our home for the week, across the river, we might as well have been 1,000 miles away. It was the Wild West, and quite an adventure for this wide-eyed sixteen-year-old who enjoyed a few sips of local tequila and bargain-basement pricing on a slew of souvenirs.

One night after we returned from a south-of-the-border jaunt, some impromptu horseplay broke out in my room with my teammates. One of them inadvertently knocked over the table lamp, which revealed an opening in its base that hid a sandwich-sized plastic bag of marijuana.

I had never seen drugs up close, and the baggy of weed looked like a Hefty-sack of grass to me. I was nervous that Pablo Escobar, or some other drug kingpin, might bust down the door any moment to claim the goods he'd stashed in my room.

I wasn't the only one who thought Pablo was hot on our trail, and after a little deliberation, we decided to hand the pot over to the hotel staff. A group of us, scared and giddy at the same time, crammed into the elevator and rode it down to the lobby, where we exited and promptly walked over to the front desk to hand over the contraband.

"Okay, thank you," they said casually, as if it were a routine occurrence.

To this day, whenever I think back to the experience of playing in the CABA World Series against future major leaguers, the first thought that comes to mind is the bag of drugs stuffed inside a Howard Johnson hotel lamp. I used to wonder what might have happened to the dope, but as I've grown older, I've concluded that those clerks probably had a fun evening thanks to some Midwestern boys with down-home family values.

A few days later, the tournament and our season were over, and we flew back to Ohio after finishing seventh out of the twelve-team field. The opportunity to play in the World Series was one of those "once-in-a-lifetime opportunities" that every little-leaguer dreams about, and I appreciated each moment of it and realized its magnitude at the time.

I was a true believer in the notion of appreciating every encounter that came my way. That was indeed the case with another "once-in-a-lifetime opportunity" I enjoyed the following year while playing high school football for the Saint Ignatius Wildcats.

In the state known as the birthplace of the National Football League, Saint Ignatius football reigns supreme. Saint Ignatius, an all-boys Jesuit high school in the heart of Cleveland, is synonymous with both academic and athletic excellence.

Especially when it comes to football.

Heading into my senior season in 1993, Saint Ignatius was the defending state champion and ranked number one nationally in the preseason *USA Today* and ESPN high school football polls. In addition to having won the state title in 1992, the school had also won the state championship three of the four previous years, as well as a national championship in 1989.

Each weekend we took the field to defend our title knowing we would get the best from every team we played. A team could lose all the games it played, but if they beat Saint Ignatius its season would be considered a success. My teammates and I knew that there was no such thing as an easy week. We were the bull's-eye on everyone's schedule.

Our weekly preparation paid off, and we made it through the

regular season undefeated, including a win over our archrival, Saint Edward, in a thrilling triple-overtime game, considered by many to be one of the greatest Northeast Ohio high school football games of all time. After winning the next three playoff games, we once again found ourselves in the position to play for another state title.

It was the first weekend in December, and earlier that morning before I headed to school, I snuck behind the bar in the basement of my house while my parents slept. I emptied half a bottle of orange Gatorade down the sink and then filled the half-empty bottle to the top with vodka and stashed the bottle in my duffel bag. Several of my teammates had mentioned packing celebratory beverages to enjoy on the ride home after what we hoped would be a sweet victory. At worst, it might take the sting off a tough loss.

After our traditional pregame mass, the team boarded the charter buses for the sixty-mile trek down to Paul Brown Stadium in Massillon. The mixtape I made to get me pumped and in the right frame of mind included some of my favorite rock songs and classic motivational tunes, including my childhood anthem, "Gonna Fly Now."

As I sat on the bus, head propped against the window, headphones in my ears, staring out at the highway and visualizing a victory, one thought kept replaying itself in my mind.

*Unbelievable–we are playing for the state and national championships!*

All the summer workout sessions, grueling conditioning programs, and long practices had prepared us for this moment. For me, it seemed like more of a culmination of the previous six years. Before Saint Ignatius, I had played football at Incarnate Word Academy in the seventh and eighth grades and in two seasons I had only experienced victory twice. Back then, I didn't know what it was like to win.

At Saint Ignatius, I didn't know what it was like to lose.

Over the previous four years, my class had played forty-three games, winning them all. However, the game we were about to play, our forty-fourth, was undoubtedly the biggest. My football career as a defensive back at Saint Ignatius reinforced the fact that hard work, preparation, and perseverance yield amazing results.

Before we took the field, Coach Chuck Kyle gathered us in the locker room. It would be the final time we would huddle together for one of his passionate pregame pep talks.

"You cherish every second of every play. You cherish it!" He told us.

Those powerful and profound words have remained with me throughout much of my life. Cherish the joyous moments of your life because they will be gone before you know it.

After his pep talk, we stormed onto the field and proceeded to defeat Cincinnati Archbishop Moeller High School, another state powerhouse. We had done it. My teammates and I had achieved our goal. We were champions. We had won the Ohio High School Football State Championship and in doing so secured the number one ranking in the country!

I still have a picture of me and my dad that was taken on the field shortly after the game ended. It was a very proud moment for both of us, as well as my mother and sister, Lindsey. The victory was also the culmination of the sacrifices they too had made along the way throughout my football career.

As our buses traveled back to Cleveland, we were greeted by a police escort when we crossed into Cuyahoga County. It felt cool to pass other cars and roll through red lights as the police sirens flashed, signaling we were some critical convoy, although, I must admit I still find it a little comical when I think about the fact that a bunch of underage high school students who were sneaking sips of booze received a police escort back to their school.

The opportunities I was fortunate enough to experience while playing sports helped make me the person I am today.

I am a firm believer that children, if given a chance, should participate in some athletic endeavor. Regardless of whether they choose to partake in an individual sport or a team sport, the lessons acquired from competition can prove to be as valuable as those learned in the classroom.

Those lessons have not only helped me through many challenges in my life but have also helped forge my character.

To be successful in any sport, one must put in the effort and time to develop the appropriate skills needed to compete. Whoever is willing to work hard, persevere, and improve on his or her shortcomings will find success both on and off the field. I was fortunate to experience many positive moments and victories in the sports I played.

I also experienced my share of defeat and physical setbacks.

During my freshman football season at Saint Ignatius I suffered a herniated disc in my back. It wasn't severe enough to sideline me, but it bothered me throughout most of the season. Once football season ended, I jumped right into the wrestling season. During a wrestling practice, I further injured my back and that's when I experienced my first stinger.

A stinger is a spinal injury that is caused by restriction of the nerve supply to the upper arm via the brachial plexus, which innervates the upper arm as well as some muscles in the neck and shoulder. It often occurs when the nerves are stretched too far from the head and neck. The injury often leaves one with the feeling of temporary paralysis, unable to move the upper part of one side of the body.

The stinger hampered me to the point that I stopped wrestling. For several months before and after school, I attended physical therapy sessions at the Cleveland Clinic. Luckily, I was able to repair myself enough to play second base on the Saint Ignatius baseball team that spring.

Injury is a part of the game, but the fear of getting injured should not deter someone from participating in a sport. That is why you prepare yourself through conditioning programs that are designed to help prevent injury. Unfortunately, it's impossible to totally remove risk from anything, but if someone plays with fear, often they will get hurt. I never worried about getting hurt. I always focused on the fun.

When you stop having fun and only focus on the difficulty that may arise, it's time to stop playing.

The same can be said about life.

Make no mistake about it, sports can also cause heartbreak. Heartbreak can certainly build character, but it sucks. Even if you are just a spectator, heartbreak is still unavoidable–unless you're a New York Yankees fan, since the Yankees seem to always win. If you want to know real heartbreak, try being a Cleveland sports fan, which is an extreme exercise in character building.

Mention "The Drive" to any Browns fan, and they will immediately cringe. My dad and I were in Municipal Stadium to witness John Elway orchestrate a comeback for the ages, which sent the Broncos to the Super Bowl and the Browns into another long off-season.

Leaving the stadium that evening I was in tears. My dad reminded me that you win some, and you lose some. But life goes on.

It's tough to argue with that.

A little more than two years later my father and I sat perched in the last row of the Richfield Coliseum and shuddered with disbelief as Michael Jordan hit what Clevelanders refer to as "The Shot" at the buzzer to beat the Cavaliers in an epic showdown.

Two of the most iconic moments in the history of professional sports, "The Drive" and "The Shot," and I had the inauspicious honor of being on hand to experience both. Yet each year I returned to cheer my teams on despite impossible odds. If that doesn't build character, then I don't know what does.

My father and I saw the good, the bad, and the ugly that sports offered. We sat in the grandstands of Daytona International Speedway and hugged each other when Dale Earnhardt finally won the Daytona 500. Three years later we shared heartache when he crashed and died in the same race. His death reinforced a valuable life lesson.

The world doesn't owe you anything. And sometimes, life can be very unfair.

In 2009, my wife Kristy and I watched from the Churchill Downs grandstands as Mine That Bird won the heralded Kentucky Derby. I had placed a win wager on the 50-1 longshot, and we celebrated into the early morning hours in downtown Louisville. It helped ease the heavy hearts we endured a year earlier when we sat in those same grandstands and witnessed Eight Belles be euthanized after she suffered compound fractures in her ankles at the finish line.

Sports have taught me some of life's tough lessons.

You can never give up because you don't know when that victory might occur. It doesn't matter if it's a Cleveland sports team or an obstacle in your life. Breakthroughs can happen. Sports have also instilled in me the fact that no matter how earth-shattering things may seem at the time, it will get better, and you will emerge a stronger individual because of it.

That philosophy would be put to the test years later.

# TWO

# ESCAPE TO THE MOUNTAINS

The excitement I experienced on the playing field was matched in the endeavors I undertook off the field. My early education was cultivated through a multitude of other pursuits besides academics and athletics.

One afternoon, shortly after my freshman year of high school had concluded, my friends and I decided we wanted to go to Huntington Beach, a favorite summer hangout along the Lake Erie shore. It was a perfect day for the beach, but we had no way to get there. We were only fifteen years old (except for one of us who was fourteen). However, we weren't going to let a little detail like not having a car or driver's license stop us. And so, my friend had the wonderful idea to "borrow" his grandmother's car.

Around noon I left my house, walked to the four-way stop along the parkway our house was situated on, and waited a few yards deep in the woods until I saw a rusty Oldsmobile slow to a halt. I recognized the car immediately since we'd taken it for a spin a few days earlier. I hustled from the woods and hopped in the front seat.

The four of us were filled with giddy excitement as we headed to Huntington Beach. We just had to make sure we were back before our parents arrived home from work.

I rode shotgun so I could help with the necessary turns. The turn signal lever was busted, so we used a screwdriver as a makeshift lever. Whenever the driver needed to turn, he blurted out, "Turn signal," and I handed him the screwdriver to jam into the place where the real lever should have been so he could signal we were turning. My other important duty was to ensure the radio worked. Each time the car hit a bump the radio shorted out, and the others shouted, "Radio." I'd punch the glove compartment to start the music again. Not sure how the wiring was configured to allow for this to work, but it did, so we were happy.

My friend wasn't the most experienced behind the wheel, and plenty of mistakes were made that could have landed us in serious trouble. He drove the wrong way on a one-way street and didn't realize it until the oncoming traffic confronted us. He misjudged the speed when we pulled into a gas station, popped the car's wheel onto the concrete island, and smacked into one of the fuel pumps. Luckily, nothing blew up. And he bumped the car in front of us as he slowed to stop at a red light. The four of us held our breath as we waited for the driver to emerge from the car. I don't know what we would have done, but fortunately, for some reason, the driver never got out.

Eventually, we made it to Huntington Beach. We felt like the kings of Cleveland as we strutted along the beach, smiling at all the beautiful girls. If they knew the ordeal we'd gone through to make it there, they'd probably want to hang out with us. At least, that's what I told myself.

After a few hours, we left, as it was imperative to get the car back before anyone knew it was gone. We all feared how awful the rest of the summer would be if our parents grounded us. What we didn't realize was that my friend's grandmother, who supposedly never left the house, decided to run an errand that day. When she didn't see the car in the garage, she called the police and reported it as stolen. His mother hurried home after she received a call at work that the vehicle had been stolen. However, knowing her son all too well, she trusted her instinct, which told her he had taken the car for a joy ride and called off the cops.

My buddies dropped me off where they had picked me up, and I walked home feeling smug with what we had pulled off. My mom was waiting for me at the front door, and she wasn't happy. She immediately sent me to my room and threatened to tell my dad what I had done. I was both shocked and grateful she hadn't yet told him. Lucky for me, my mom covered for me quite a bit throughout my adolescent years, sparing me the wrath of my father. However, it didn't take long for word to spread about what had happened, and the phone rang off the hook that night. My friends wanted to hear all the details, which I was happy to relive over and over.

For me, it was a great day.

At the age of fifteen, it was easy to feel exempt from accountability and responsibility. Although I had a penchant for mischief, I'd like to think I was a good kid. That was certainly the case when it came to my grades, as I took school very seriously. My parents instilled in me the importance of a good education. I knew good grades mattered and I worked diligently to achieve them.

My father stressed how important it was to read to improve one's education. He gave me his *Sports Illustrated* magazines and encouraged me to read about the fantastic endeavors that took place on the playing fields. The magazine also ran a lot of human-interest pieces that appealed to me. There was one story that affected me in an incredibly profound way.

The December 14, 1992 issue of *Sports Illustrated* ran a feature entitled, "He Has the Strength." The article chronicled the story of Dennis Byrd, a football player for the New York Jets who had broken his neck and suffered a devastating spinal cord injury during a game two weeks earlier. The injury left him paralyzed on the football field, unable to move, and forced him to look up at the expressions of fear that blanketed his teammates' faces.

The article detailed the type of individual that Dennis was and the way in which he chose to live his life. He was a profoundly religious man who had always trusted in God's will. After his injury, his faith was certainly put to the test. In the article, the author, Peter King, mentioned the Biblical verse written in black marker on white cardboard that hung from the ceiling of Byrd's hospital room:

"For I reckon that the sufferings of this present time are not worthy to be compared with the glory that shall be revealed in us. – Romans 8:18."

Byrd spoke of how he drew strength from the Scripture each morning when he opened his eyes. It was the first and last thing he saw each day. When he was in heavy sedation just after his injury, someone scrawled the verse on the cardboard and hung it in his room.

As I lay on my bedroom floor and flipped through the pages of the story, I found myself overcome with strong emotions. I read the verse over and over, and eventually sat down behind the typewriter at my desk, typed it out onto a piece of paper, and tucked it away in my wallet. I referred to it often throughout my life, especially during challenging times, to remind myself to always trust in the Lord.

I enjoyed the stories in *Sports Illustrated* about the athletes who overcame the odds and achieved success. However, there were two things that I enjoyed reading about more, both of which developed into obsessions.

The first was Mount Everest. The second was the Navy SEALs.

I had a voracious appetite for both subjects and devoured as much material as I could unearth. The idea of overcoming an insurmountable challenge fascinated me, and plenty could be gleaned from studying the tendencies of the brave individuals who conquered Mount Everest or became Navy SEALs. Something inside me yearned for the opportunity to take on a challenge like Everest. It was the tallest mountain in the world, and only an exclusive fraternity of individuals had been to its summit. I was spellbound by the incredible commitment needed to scale its peak successfully.

Throughout my life, I told anyone who listened that one day I would climb Everest. I researched the cost of an expedition, the type of equipment it required, the training needed, and the success rate for reaching the summit. I read about the exploits of Sir Edmund Hillary, the first documented person to stand on its peak. I studied maps that highlighted the different routes, comparing the southeast ridge to the north ridge. I decided my attempt would be from the southeast ridge since it was less technical than the north ridge. Growing up in Ohio, my mountain climbing experience was limited.

In May of 1996, eight people died on the mountain in one day, its deadliest day ever. Details of the day's events surfaced in books, magazines, movies, and TV interviews. As the survivors recounted their tales, I felt as if I had climbed the mountain with them. I knew all the different places along the peak that were mentioned. I knew about those who died, left on the mountain because it was too difficult to carry them down.

Later, when I wrote my bucket list, climbing a mountain was near the top. There wasn't any doubt in my mind that I would one day attempt to reach the summit. That was a claim that only a quarter of those who tried to climb it could make. For me, it simply wasn't a matter of "if" but entirely a matter of "when." Little did I know that the day would come when I'd be forced to push my physical and mental well-being to its limit to achieve near impossible odds. It just wouldn't be on Mount Everest.

The other, and equally neurotic, fascination I had was with the proud group of men who call themselves Navy SEALs. I used to sit in the family room of my home and watch TV shows about the SEALs. With awe, I watched the stress the candidates went through in hopes of being selected to join the Teams, as the SEAL units were called. Just like my need to swallow every morsel of information about Mount

Everest, I felt an overwhelming desire to learn all I could about the SEALs. I especially enjoyed reading the books written by former SEALs, which served to further propagate my appreciation for these remarkable warriors and their incredible will.

I developed an infatuation with "Hell Week," a part of their training that consists of six days of cold, wet, and brutally difficult exercises on fewer than a couple hours of sleep. Hell Week tested physical endurance, mental toughness, pain, cold tolerance, teamwork, attitude, the ability to perform under high stress, and sleep deprivation. It wasn't fun, nor was it supposed to be. Similar to summitting Everest, only a quarter of SEAL candidates made it through the week. It took a tremendous amount of determination and desire to achieve either feat.

Unlike climbing Mount Everest, though, I didn't plan to ever be a Navy SEAL. I had the desire to be an Army guy. Toward the end of my junior year, I began the arduous application process to attend the United States Military Academy at West Point. This was in stark contrast to what I told the guidance counselor several months earlier when I sat in her office with my parents and declared I wanted to pursue a career in Hollywood.

"Tell me, Scott, how much acting experience have you had?" she politely asked.

"None," I said.

"So how do you expect to be an actor?"

"I don't know. I guess I'll meet someone like Tom Cruise and ask him to show me the ropes," I said with a straight face as my parents did their best to contain their amusement.

To this day, my dad still laughs about the exchange I had with the counselor. I'm quick to remind him that she also told him *Sports Illustrated* wasn't exactly advanced reading. However, I'm still glad he pushed me to read it.

The first step in the West Point application process was a Candidate Questionnaire that ranked me against other potential candidates in the areas of academics, athletics, and leadership. After that had been submitted, I obtained two congressional nominations from U.S. Senator Howard Metzenbaum and U.S. House of Representatives member Eric Fingerhut. The next step was to complete two different tests, both important measurements of the candidate's potential, and both of which produced memorable results for me, albeit for different reasons.

The first test was the Physical Aptitude Examination, or PAE, whose objective was to measure my physical fitness level. The test consisted of four events: pull-ups, a basketball toss from a kneeling position, a 300-yard shuttle run, and a standing broad jump. That year I set the record for the best jump among the Northeast Ohio candidates. I also managed to bang out twenty-two pull-ups, the third highest in Cuyahoga County. I had the grades, the nominations, and an outstanding PAE. An appointment looked like a realistic possibility. The only thing left was to complete the medical exam administered by the Department of Defense Medical Exam Review Board.

Despite my history of neck and back problems, I didn't foresee the medical test as a hurdle. I was a year-round athlete with less than eight percent body fat, and I wasn't happy unless I was breaking a sweat. However, I had a history of asthma that required the use of an inhaler and I had been hospitalized for an asthma-related breathing problem during the fall of my junior year. Once West Point got its hands on my medical history, things went south real fast.

I was informed that because of my asthma I might not be eligible for an appointment. The Captain of Admissions told me several cadets had asthma; however, the recent Gulf War, Desert Storm, proved to be an issue for the soldiers with asthma due to the desert sand. It caused the Army, especially West Point, to reevaluate its acceptance policy on asthma-related illnesses. My hopes for admission were doomed.

However, my hospitalization wasn't entirely due to asthma. The evening before I was admitted, I had felt a bit under the weather and took some cough medicine and other antihistamines. Later that night, I went to a party where I drank alcohol and smoked cigarettes. Sometime the following afternoon I awoke with what felt like a ton of bricks on my chest, barely able to get enough air in my lungs. My mother drove me to the ER where doctors administered an IV to dilate my bronchial tubes. I never mentioned anything about the previous night, and the doctors attributed everything to an asthma attack. There would be no appointment to West Point, and I learned a hard lesson about the ramifications of careless actions.

Not too long after the hospitalization I once again found myself breathing heavy. This time it wasn't from any ill-advised behavior, but rather from hiking deep into the Allegheny National Forest. It was the day after Thanksgiving, and I embarked on a wilderness retreat, along with two dozen other Saint Ignatius students. All students were required to go on a retreat, and I chose the outdoor option known as "Escape to the Mountains." For three days and nights, we camped under the stars and participated in activities designed to strengthen our relationship with Christ.

Each night we packed our food in a garbage bag wrapped in mesh netting, tied a rope to one end, and hurled the other end over a sturdy tree branch so it could be hoisted several feet off the ground. It was late November, and the animals we shared the forest with were hungry. Hanging the food in a tree prevented them from raiding our stash. It was also imperative that we didn't spill food on the ground or on our clothing; otherwise, an ammonia spritz spray would be needed to eliminate the alluring odor.

One of our evening meals was a dish called "Turtles," a concoction of ground beef, steamed carrots, and roasted mushrooms. I inadvertently tipped the paper plate against my body and spilled grease down the front of my flannel shirt and jeans. Unfortunately for my tent mate, I smelled like ammonia the rest of the night. Sometime during the night, I abruptly awoke to loud tweets from the whistles we wore around our necks in the event of an emergency. I sprang from my sleeping bag, gathered myself, and tried to make sense of the screams from outside my tent.

"Bear! Bear! Bear!"

It took a split second for the words to register.

I scrambled to put my boots on and hurried out of the tent to join the others by the smoldering fire. They all pointed at my tent. I focused my eyes in the night and saw the large silhouette that lumbered just a few yards behind it. A Pennsylvania black bear had wandered into our camp and was frighteningly close to where I had slept. I heard the twigs snap beneath the bear's feet with every step it took. However, it was the low and deep moan the bear made that scared the shit out of me. To make matters worse, I had gone to bed in the same grease-drenched flannel shirt from earlier to keep as warm as possible in the cold mountain environment.

Black bears are common in the Allegheny National Forest, and we had been taught was to do should we cross paths with one. Although typically afraid of humans, it is possible they might venture near a camp, especially late in the year in search of food.

We all started to scream and shout at the animal as we had been instructed.

"Bears suck! Bears suck! Go away! Bears suck!"

Of course, we didn't think bears sucked. We just tried to make a lot of noise and secrete the hormones from our adrenal glands, which were supposed to scare away the big, furry creatures. It worked, and after several minutes, somewhat of an order was restored to our camp. I didn't sleep another wink that night!

The following morning, we resumed the scheduled activities, including something known as a Witness, an extremely personal account of an individual's life and relationship with the Lord. Four retreat leaders each gave a Witness: God of Sky, God of Fire, God of Earth, and God of Water. Each was profoundly moving and emotional for the individual who delivered it, and in most cases, brought him to tears. Several of the other retreat participants also had to wipe away the tears from their eyes. I was so affected by what I saw and heard, the following year I helped lead a retreat and gave my testament about my relationship with Christ through my God of Sky Witness.

A large portion of the account I gave touched on my relationship with my mother. As an adolescent, I developed quite a temper and many times my poor mom was on the receiving end. I spoke from the heart and gave a very cathartic and overdue narrative about our relationship. When I was finished, I was utterly drained, and don't think I could have shed another tear no matter how hard I tried. Others were equally moved by what I had delivered. I felt clean and free like I had been baptized again. I prayed intensely for God's forgiveness, as well as my mother's forgiveness. In the end, I felt a renewed sense of strength.

To this day it is still one of the proudest and most rewarding moments of my life.

# THREE
# YOU ONLY LIVE ONCE

Growing up I was consumed by the desire to live the most fascinating and adventurous life I could imagine. I'm not sure where the obsession came from or what spawned my sense of adventure, but I always sought to accomplish things that I felt justified a well-lived life, such as climbing Everest or becoming a SEAL.

Regardless of the adventures or milestones I experienced, I never seemed to reach a place where I was content with everything I'd done. I constantly tried to one-up my latest adventure by doing something even more extreme.

As with the stories of personal triumph I read in *Sports Illustrated*, inspirational sayings and motivational quotes fascinated me, whether it was a maxim passed on by my father or a famous Zen Master. I scribbled the passages down on pieces of paper and tacked them to my bedroom walls or folded them up and tucked them away in my wallet. Scores of Post-it notes decorated my bedroom walls ready to provide some wise advice.

Other kids my age looked at *Playboy*, but I amassed a collection of motivational, self-help, and "How To" publications vast enough to fill a bookshelf. When I was in high school, my mom gave me a copy of *Life's Little Instruction Book*, by H. Jackson Brown Jr. to add to my library. Within the pages of the plaid-covered paperback were 511 suggestions the author wanted to pass on to his son to help him lead a happy and rewarding life.

I read the book a dozen times over the next several years and wrote down a new tidbit each time to stuff into my wallet along with all the others. I had about ten personal favorites I referred to regularly, but none made more of an impact on me than #435:

"Make a list of twenty-five things you want to experience before you die. Carry it in your wallet and refer to it often."

Simple. Powerful. Life-changing.

However, at the time I made my list, I had no idea how much the concept would influence my life, not by doing things on my list, but by living with the philosophy that if I wanted to do something, I needed to find a way to do it. In a roundabout way, my list served as a primer to remind me never to give up or stop trying, because you never knew which attempt might be successful.

I wrote my bucket list long before it was ever a movie or a catchy term that came to be used in everyday vernacular. Although I was a teenager and my mind was focused on experiences that provided immediate and personal gratification, I still wrote down items I believed, if accomplished, would help me live a fulfilled life and find the contentment I always sought.

On a small piece of lined yellow paper, I wrote out the following:

Twenty-Five Things I Want to Accomplish Before I Die

Travel across country in a car.

Visit/hike the Grand Canyon.

Climb a mountain.

Visit Sweden.

Visit Australia.

Skydive.

Play in a Major League Baseball game.

Sleep behind the Hollywood sign.

Visit the Field of Dreams.

Become a father.

Build a house in Montana.

Spend some time in California.

Camping excursion in Alaska.

Go on a safari (observation).

Own a tiger.

See the Northern Lights (Aurora Borealis).

Own two horses.

Ride a bull for 8 seconds.

Write a novel.

Visit Easter Island.

A tremendous amount of thought went into the list, and it was based on things that were important and relevant in my life at the time. Although it only entailed twenty initial accomplishments, I knew I would come up with more endeavors to add at a future date. I was also convinced I would most likely exceed the allotted twenty-five that Mr. Brown suggested.

I never considered that I might one day run out of time to check off each item.

While I was a senior in high school, I came across a poster on the back of the door in the Campus Retreat office that struck me the moment I laid my eyes on it. It was a worn and wrinkled poster of a man diving off a cliff, arms outstretched and silhouetted by the sun. The quote on the poster read:

"You only live once, but if you live right once is enough."

I immediately knew I had just found the perfect summation of how I planned to live my life and convinced the Retreat Director to give me the poster. Years later when I traveled to China, I had a calligraphy made of the quote in Chinese characters. The artist who did the writing asked my permission to use the quote in some of his future calligraphies. I guess it had an impact on him as well.

Throughout my childhood, my adventures were mostly limited to getting lost in the woods behind our house, or dressing up as a ninja, equipped with foam nunchucks, to sneak up on the family dog. Each time I got close the dog growled, part in fear, but mostly out of annoyance. My parents called out from the adjoining room to stop teasing the dog. I was astonished they knew I was nearby; after all, when you're a ninja your survival relies on the art of stealth. Mine needed some work, but that didn't stop me.

As I grew, both physically and mentally, so did my exploits. My quest for an adrenaline fix no longer relied on my ability to sneak up on the dog. I was in search of bigger things, and I usually found them.

I enrolled at Lehigh University in Bethlehem, Pennsylvania in the fall of 1994. Since West Point was no longer an option, I wanted to attend a school with a stellar academic reputation, as well as one that would afford me the opportunity to continue my baseball career.

The summer after my freshman year I was in the best shape of my life. I joined a local fitness gym and worked out at least three days a week. My workout partner was my high school friend Mike, also home from college. Each workout we pushed one another to achieve more than the previous workout and we kept journals to record the reps we did. Weeks rolled by, and the weight increased, along with my confidence. I was in the zone and felt invincible.

During one of our workouts, the subject of skydiving came up, something we had both given thought to on previous occasions, but never seriously pursued. We successfully recruited another friend of ours to join us for a day at Cleveland Skydiving Center, a nearby drop zone in Garrettsville. The night before, we gathered in our friend's basement for a few hours, where we drank beer and watched skydiving movies. They pulled into my driveway in a convertible, top down, bright and early the next morning, and the three of us headed toward

Garrettsville all donned in wife-beater tank tops, bandannas, and sunglasses. We found out that another group who made a jump that day remembered us passing them on the road and could tell where we were headed. Where else could we be going dressed like that!

The first order of business was to sign the release form that absolved the facility of any injury, including death, which might arise from the "risky activity" we chose to undertake. The training commenced and lasted more than six hours since we decided against a tandem jump and opted for solo jumps. We wanted the maximum adrenaline rush and decided to take on the responsibility of safe passage to the ground ourselves. Anyone could do a tandem jump, we told ourselves, but not everyone was brave enough to sign up for a solo jump, especially for their first leap.

Skydiving centers seek to minimize any risk of calamity and don't offer actual solo jumps to first-time participants. Novices must settle for the next best thing–static line jumping, which consisted of a long, fixed cord attached to one end of the airplane and the other end to the parachute harness. Once the jumper fell the appropriate distance, the line became taut, pulled the harness, and deployed the chute. There was still plenty of risk associated with a static line jump.

Most of the training focused on what to do in the event of a dreaded malfunction. Different types of malfunctions were explained and how to address each of them. In each case, the final resolution was to cut away the main chute and deploy the backup. I listened intently but fully expected a smooth experience that would allow me to walk away in one piece.

The remainder of the training focused on how to exit the aircraft, which involved a careful climb from the plane onto a tiny platform step, followed by a reach for the sway bar, which attached the wing and fuselage. We were told to grip the sway bar tightly then step off the platform into nothing and allow our body to dangle in space. Basically, hang off the plane's wing for dear life, but look cool while doing it. The last part was the easy part–let go.

After training, we got dressed in our jumpsuits. They gave us a plastic hockey helmet to wear, but I'm not sure what purpose it would serve if I were to fall thousands of feet from the sky and smack into the ground. Nonetheless, I picked out a blue one and boarded the white and red Twin 125 Cessna airplane, which wasn't much larger than the inside of the convertible that brought us there.

Finally, it was time to jump.

The Cessna rumbled along the grass runway and lifted into the sky. Ten minutes later we reached the proper altitude, and a game of rock-paper-scissors determined the jump order. I would be second.

Once it was my turn to take the plunge, I went through my checklist with the pilot and exited out onto the ledge and grabbed the sway bar. Our training repeatedly stressed that it was imperative that we look back at the pilot for the "all clear" signal before we let go of the sway bar.

I forgot to do that.

I grabbed the sway bar, paused for half a second, and then pushed away and fell backward into the great below. That was the first thing that didn't go according to plan. The second thing was much more serious.

A few moments after my fall, the static line tightened, and I felt the force of the chute rip from my backpack and jerk my body upward. I heard a loud, flapping noise, looked up, and quickly saw something I never hoped to encounter. My chute hadn't fully deployed and fluttered in the wind.

All hope was not lost, most of it had fully opened. However, my mind frantically raced ahead and contemplated whether to deploy my backup. Every second I spent figuring out what to do in the sky, was a second closer to splattering on the approaching ground. A voice crackled over the one-way radio receiver attached to my suit.

"It looks like you've got some line twists, Scott. You need to start kicking out of them."

Line twists, one of the potential malfunctions we learned about a few hours earlier, occurred when the parachute twisted around the vertical access on its deployment and only partially opened. Imagine being turned in circles on the playground swing, twisting the metal chains attached to the seat until they became tightly intertwined. The same thing had happened to my chute. And like a playground swing, to get out of it I had to kick in the opposite direction and swing my body around until the lines were untangled.

It worked. My chute fully opened, caught the air, and allowed me to enjoy the descent to the ground. Once on the ground, I gathered my parachute and joined my friend while we waited for the last of our trio to land. They had all heard what had gone wrong with my jump through their receivers and were thrilled that catastrophe had been avoided. So was I.

While I hadn't panicked and I'd maintained my composure throughout the whole ordeal, my legs shook like a baby's rattle from the adrenaline surging through my body. I had successfully achieved the rush I wanted, but my legs were so shaky I could barely walk. Back in the main office, the owners informed us we could make another jump for half price. Everyone else was satisfied with the safe jump they already had under their belts, so the three of us were the only ones who decided to have another go at it and headed back up for another jump.

That afternoon spent in Garrettsville with two of my high school buddies proved to be one of those moments that I look back on and always smile about. It also allowed me to cross off the first item from my bucket list.

A month after my skydiving adventure I found myself on another plane. This time it was a commercial flight to Bangor, Maine. A girl I had become friends with at Lehigh invited me to spend a week with her family on Moosehead Lake, the largest body of water east of the Mississippi contained in one state.

The week was full of fishing, hiking, boating, canoeing, rock climbing, and white water rafting on the Kennebec River. We even spent a day looking for moose and managed to see one up close. I was amazed by the size of the animal, which appeared to glide across the ground as it walked. I had fun trying to replicate the unique calls the moose made, although I'm not sure the others found as much humor in it as I did.

My friend's father invited me to join him on an upcoming fishing expedition in Denali National Park in Alaska. As he described it, the salmon swam so thick through the river that you could shoot them with a gun. The plan was to fly to a remote part of the park, set up camp, and fish for several days. It was the trip of a lifetime, and another chance to mark something off my bucket list. However, I declined the invitation.

This is probably one of the biggest regrets I have. I don't know if I will ever have the chance to visit Alaska and I still wonder if my reason for not joining him was justified. The trip was planned for early September, which would have caused me to miss the first week of classes at Lehigh. I was concerned that if I missed a full week, I would have to play catch-up most of the semester. Whether that would have been the case, I'll never know. One thing I do know, though, is had I missed that first week of classes I might not have had the opportunity to adjust my course schedule the way I did when I arrived on campus.

It was an adjustment that impacted my life in a way greater than I ever would have imagined.

# FOUR
# YOUR SHIP HAS COME IN

A woman in her early forties wearing gray sweatpants set next to me on the small commuter plane from Bangor, Maine to Newark, New Jersey. I admit it's easy to underestimate people by how they are dressed, and that's what I did with my seatmate, Virginia Kamsky.

Little did I know that by the time we finished talking she would plant a seed in my mind that would send my life down a path completely unforeseeable a few hours earlier

Ginny, as she liked to be called, was on her way home to New York City. As we talked, I learned she was the founder of Kamsky Associates, Inc. and now served as the Chairman and CEO. Having played a significant role in China's economic opening to foreign business and investment, she was highly regarded as the premier expert in navigating the opportunities and obstacles of China's business world.

Throughout our conversation, we shared many personal details. She told me she started to learn Chinese at the age of ten and later majored in East Asian Studies. She had been an interpreter for President George H. W. Bush on his visit to China. I was fortunate enough to see him speak in person during a 1992 campaign stop in

Strongsville, Ohio, but this woman had spoken for the man and translated his words for the Chinese heads of state!

"If you want to be successful, learn to speak Chinese," she advised me.

Sound advice from someone whose career was based on business in China and was a Trustee for the China Institute in America, as well as someone *Newsweek* chose as one of "America's Top 25 Asia Hands."

Once our plane had taxied to the gate, Ginny invited me to join her in her limousine for a cruise around New York City since I had never been to the Big Apple. I finally had the chance to tour the city and to do so with someone of her stature. I thanked her for the invite but declined the offer. It was the second time in less than twenty-four hours I turned down an amazing opportunity because I did not want to deviate from my schedule.

Planning things out to every detail would evolve into a major theme of my life, and I would eventually discover that things don't always go to plan.

Instead, we exchanged handshakes and contact information at the gate and went our separate ways. I had taken our conversation to heart and the first thing I did back on Lehigh's campus a week later was enroll in a course called Beginner Chinese I.

In high school I studied Latin, but Mandarin Chinese, considered one of the toughest languages to learn, was remarkably different and had its challenges. I spent several nights pulling my hair out trying to speak and write the elegant Chinese characters. Chinese is a tonal language, and the slightest inflection in one's voice could translate into something unintended. Constant repetition was vital. One of my speaking partners was Tucker Quayle, another Lehigh student, and the son of Dan Quayle, the former Vice President of the United States. The two of us met a few nights a week and practiced speaking while a Secret Service agent lurked a short distance away.

A serendipitous moment occurred when I came across a flyer for "Lehigh in China," a full immersion program where students could live and study in China. I immediately signed up. It had been a year since my encounter with Ginny, and I now had the chance to travel to China.

For six weeks my days consisted of Economics, International Relations, and Chinese language classes in the mornings, followed by afternoon field trips to business entities and cultural landmarks. The purpose of the program was to gain insight into China's transition from a command economy to a market economy.

My time in China presented me with the opportunity to further learn the language as well as gauge how well I spoke it. I also learned several choice phrases from the taxi drivers, after my classmates and I asked them to teach us what we would never learn in the classroom. I still remember a lot of them.

The first week of the program was spent in the capital city of Beijing. Our group of twenty-five students and three instructors bunked up at a local university that also operated as a hotel. On our third day we headed to Tiananmen Square, the fourth-largest city square in the world, which encompassed 109 acres in the center of Beijing. Any chance to explore the sites of Tiananmen Square and The Forbidden City offers a surreal experience. However, the day we took in the sights was anything but ordinary.

It was June 4, 1996, the seventh anniversary of the Tiananmen Square Massacre, when Chinese troops with assault rifles and tanks had inflicted casualties on unarmed protesters who tried to block the military's advance toward the Square. The horrific events were fresh in everyone's mind, and the government had put the military on high alert to quell any potential uprising.

Walking through the Square as an American college student, I could sense the strange aura in the air, and while I never felt in danger, I also never felt like I roamed free. The military presence was constant, especially as I waited in line to view Chairman Mao's body as he lied in state inside the mausoleum of Mao Zedong. If I had to guess, I think it would be something akin to a visit to Ground Zero on the anniversary of September 11th.

Beijing was a fascinating city full of cultural significance. When we weren't busy with classes, we visited historical sites. Museums, monasteries, and temples, the most famous being The Temple of Heaven, were all part of the agenda. Additionally, I had the once in a lifetime opportunity to walk along The Great Wall of China.

Talk about feeling small!

The Great Wall stretches for 5,500 miles, covering a vast part of the country. I felt like an ant on a never-ending journey as a classmate and I jogged along it trying to see as much of it as we could during our allotted time. In some areas, the steps were more than two feet high and handrails were needed to maintain balance.

It's not something to be done in a wheelchair.

One of the more memorable visits in Beijing occurred when we visited the US Embassy to meet with some of the top US diplomats in China. The meeting's objective was to learn about the current state of affairs between the two countries. I sat at attention, dressed in a shirt, tie, and cowboy boots as I listened to several experts predict where things were headed with China. It was a remarkable opportunity to pose questions to some of the most knowledgeable minds in the world when it came to America's relationship and foreign-policy with the Far East.

After the meeting, a few Marines escorted us through the embassy on a guided tour. They pointed out some of the building's various nuances, including a "quiet room" that was soundproof and swept several times a day for listening devices so that it was safe to discuss confidential matters within its walls. It seemed like something straight out of the Tom Clancy novels I devoured throughout college.

The Marines invited us to join them later that evening at a TGIF party to end the week. A small group of us hopped in a taxi and headed to the Embassy to party with the US Marines. It was a wild and crazy night, and at one point I danced atop a pool table with a huge Marine to the rap song "Baby Got Back" by Sir Mix-A-Lot.

I had the opportunity to see a great deal of the Chinese countryside, perhaps more than most people do since we traveled through the country by train. I endured a twelve-hour train ride to Shanghai. It wasn't glamorous by any means. There were four tiny sleeping platforms to each compartment. I chose to sleep on the top level, figuring it would be quieter. Unfortunately, I was situated next to a tiny speaker that played Chinese music nonstop the entire trip. By the time we arrived in Shanghai I desperately craved some Sir Mix-A-Lot, or anything but the sounds of stringed fiddles, fretted lutes, and bamboo flutes.

My residence in Shanghai was the Shanghai International Studies University, which also doubled as a hotel. One of the first visits was to the Shanghai Stock Exchange, where we visited the trading floor. My Finance class at Lehigh had visited the New York Stock Exchange trading floor, and I could now boast that I had walked the floor of two major stock exchanges separated by over 7,000 miles.

There was a lot to do in Shanghai and the days were packed with activities. So were the nights. Every evening a group of us headed out to the local bars, our favorites being Shanghai Sally's and Malone's, popular hangouts for American ex-pats who lived in China.

A taxicab ride in Shanghai was a harrowing experience. Every driver had one hand glued to the wheel and the other to the horn, which provided a never-ending blare of car horns as vehicles crisscrossed lanes with no regard for traffic signals or pedestrians. It was best to just strap on the seatbelt and hope for an accident-free journey, and I was lucky enough to avoid any mishaps.

I spent a few days in the outlying cities of Suzhou and Wuxi. Two beautiful cities steeped in Chinese history, especially Suzhou, referred to as the "Venice of the East" because of its array of canals, stone bridges, and meticulously designed gardens. It was also where I first tried “gou rou,” otherwise known to Westerners as dog meat.

I grew up in a family that always had a dog who we treated as one of our own. Eating one was not something I planned on, but I discovered I had done just that when I asked our server about the tough and greasy dish we were served. She answered in Chinese. Being the only one at the table who had a command of the language, my classmates asked me what she said.

“Some kind of beef,” was all I said at the time. I didn’t feel like watching people throw up.

It didn’t take long to discover that authentic Chinese food is nothing like the American version of Chinese food and it wasn’t always easy to get used to it. However, one of the best meals I’ve had in my life was on our last night in Shanghai when my roommate and I stopped for a bite at a rickshaw vendor on the sidewalk. After the strangers ahead of us finished their meals, the vendor took their plates and chopsticks, rinsed them in a dirty tub of cold water, and handed them to us. He then proceeded to pile mounds of dumplings and noodles onto our plates. We took our seats on the milk crates that had been set out and ate the most delicious meal in the world by moonlight in Shanghai. The entire feast cost a total of $1.50 for the two of us.

The next morning, I boarded the train for a twenty-hour ride to Guangzhou, a city that is about as far south in China as you can go. Upon arrival in the southern town, we settled at an outdoor bar until we boarded for the next leg of our trip, which was a nine-hour boat ride along the Pearl River into Hong Kong Harbor. The boat we traveled on was a shipping barge that had been converted to accommodate ferry passengers. It certainly wasn’t first-class travel, but it did have a karaoke bar. It was late at night by the time we boarded and set sail for Hong Kong. After I had belted out tunes for hours in the karaoke lounge, it was time to retire for the night.

The beds we slept on consisted of a sheet thrown over a two-inch-thick foam pad, a far cry from Westin's heavenly bed. My roommate and I got the crazy idea to sleep on the deck of the barge. We found a spot near the front of the boat and positioned our mattresses in the most strategic place we thought would provide shelter from the strong winds. It didn't matter. The wind was intense and loud, and neither of us slept for more than five minutes.

However, it was a small price to pay for the view that greeted us in the early hours of dawn. As the sun awakened and began its upward ascent, the ship made its way into Hong Kong Harbor. We stood against the front rail of the freighter and marveled at the city skyline stretched across the horizon, drenched in the amber morning light. Sunlight reflected off the mirrorlike finish of the Hong Kong high-rises, creating a breathtaking sight to behold. I could even see the reflection of our ship in one of the buildings as if the harbor city had beckoned out to me, "Your ship has come in!"

Our time in Hong Kong lasted only a week. But it was memorable. The city was so vibrant, congested, and full of energy that it made New York City look like Buffalo. It's known as an Alpha city due to its importance in the global economy. While there we had a meeting with banking executives from the region on one of the top floors of the Bank of China Tower, which overlooked Hong Kong Island. Looking back, it reminds me of a meeting I once had in New York City with Goldman Sachs in one of the World Trade Center towers that overlooked lower Manhattan.

I spent a night gambling in Macau, which was still under Portugal's rule at the time. The island was seedy and decadent, a South Pacific juxtaposition that was reached by way of a one-hour hydrofoil ride across the South China Sea. That night I lost more money than I won, but that wasn't the point.

The penultimate night spent in Hong Kong was the Fourth of July, my favorite holiday. Although I was far away from home on the other side of the world, I had a fantastic time as I celebrated in the Far East.

In an international city like Hong Kong, it's easy to find other Americans, and a few of my classmates and I rode the Mass Transit Railway into the heart of the city and partied with other patriots well into the night.

On one of the evenings there we enjoyed dinner and drinks with a Kraft executive in his luxurious Kowloon residence. That night further reinforced my desire to pursue a career in international business. I was drawn to the intoxicating allure of international travel and big-city business and wanted to fill my future with it.

After another year at Lehigh, I had the opportunity to do just that.

# FIVE
# ENGLISH CUSTOMS

As I waited in line to clear Customs at London Heathrow airport, I looked around at the other weary travelers who had just arrived in England.

*Why have they come to London?*

*How long did they travel to get here?*

*Have any of them ever been kicked out of the country before?*

My thoughts turned back to my current situation, and I grew anxious wondering how Customs officials would treat me this time around.

*Will I be allowed entry or turned around, kicked out, and sent back to the United States on the next available flight?*

I hoped it was the former. I didn't want to go through the latter again.

Two weeks prior I had found myself in the same line after I traveled through the night. My body should have been tired since I hadn't slept on the plane, but I didn't feel tired. I was wide awake, full of adrenaline, and looked forward to the challenge that awaited me that summer.

On the final day of my junior year at Lehigh University, I received a phone call that I'd been offered a job with Siebe, a diversified engineering firm headquartered in Windsor, England. The company's CEO was a Lehigh alum who offered a current Finance student an opportunity for a paid internship in the Treasury department of Siebe. I interviewed on campus and had been fortunate enough to get the position. My summer would be spent in Windsor, a suburb of London, while I learned the ins and outs of corporate finance in an international setting.

Things moved fast, and I was wanted in London as soon as possible. I left Lehigh's Pennsylvania campus and drove home to Cleveland to pack my bags. A few days later, I hopped on a flight across the Atlantic to the United Kingdom. To say I was excited to embark on the adventure was an understatement.

The previous summer in China had heightened my hunger for international travel and my desire to experience different cultures. I was scheduled to graduate from Lehigh next year with a degree in Finance and a concentration in Mandarin Chinese. An internship with Siebe would be a nice feather to stick in my cap.

Once I stepped off the plane, I retrieved my luggage and then queued in the Customs line. An agent motioned for me to approach her station. I dropped my bags and presented her with my passport.

"What brings you to London?" she asked.

"I'll be working here for the summer."

"I need to see your papers."

I produced the Siebe offer letter that outlined the duration of my internship and the rate at which I'd be compensated. The events that transpired were nothing short of disastrous. She studied the document for an unusually long period and then asked me to produce my student work visa.

"I don't have one of those. That letter is all I have."

Boy, was that the wrong answer! She immediately summoned her supervisor, who after a short conversation with her, instructed me to pass through the gates and proceed toward the Customs office, and not in the direction the other passengers were headed.

Various officials questioned me for hours and wanted to know why I didn't have a work visa given the fact I had clear documentation that stated a paying job awaited me in London. By now, this was the same question I had for the folks at Siebe, who it was apparent to all of us in the room, had dropped the ball. A call was made to the company to inform them of the situation.

The Siebe CEO knew I spoke Chinese and tried to arrange a flight to China for me where I could work at one of the company's subsidiaries while my work visa was processed. Unfortunately, this was not allowed by the Customs officials, and they decided that I would not be allowed entry into the UK. I was ordered to return to the States on the first flight out the following day. My passport was confiscated, along with the offer letter, and I was issued a temporary visa that expired in twenty-four hours.

A man from Siebe by the name of David arrived at the airport and transported me to a local hotel where I spent the night. We both laughed at my predicament, dumbfounded by the colossal mistake someone at Siebe had made. Unbeknownst at the time, David and I would develop a friendship that lasted for several years.

I took a quick shower at the hotel and then met Sharon in the lobby for a brief introduction. She was the woman I had agreed to rent a flat from for the summer. Afterward, I was treated to a dinner in nearby Eton by David and another gentleman from the company. The dinner tasted terrible and lent credence to the stereotypes I had heard about the boring and bland English food. On my plate was a cold, wet chicken dish that resembled a thick, pink piece of meat toast with chunks of olives in it. It looked less appealing than the dog meat I had in China. However, I still enjoyed the evening with the others as we made light of the day's events. They were both impressed by my positive attitude and ability to roll with what had happened. Honestly, what could I have done? It wasn't like I had a choice.

After a long day and a meal with my future coworkers, I collapsed into bed for some sleep. A few hours later I was awakened by the sound of the alarm clock. I showered once again, got dressed, and met David in the lobby for a ride back to Heathrow airport. Less than thirty-six hours after I had left Strongsville, Ohio, I was back home and asleep in my own bed.

A fortnight later I once again stood in the Customs line at Heathrow airport.

"Next," the Customs Agent shouted in my direction.

I stepped up to the counter, handed my passport and work visa over, and in my most pleasant voice asked the agent how he was doing. He was all business. It didn't take him long to rifle through my passport to the exact page where a dark black "X" was affixed over the English stamp which signaled I was "persona non grata" in the country to which I now sought entry. He asked what happened, and I explained the situation as best I could. He looked at my work visa again and then stared back at me.

"Okay," he said, and stamped my passport and handed it back to me.

And just like that, in an uneventful fashion, I was welcomed into the United Kingdom and finally able to commence with the five-month internship that had brought me there in the first place. As it turned out, the whole fiasco ended up being the best thing that could have happened. My ordeal created such an uproar and embarrassment that the CEO came down hard on the Treasurer for whom I would be working. It was apparent that not a lot of planning had gone into my arrival, and the CEO instructed him to put together a detailed work plan for me.

When I finally showed up for my first day on the job, I was informed that in addition to the experience I would gain in the Treasury department, I would also get a sampling of what some of the other departments did. The sampling included visits to multiple subsidiaries in Germany and Italy, where I enjoyed dinners in castles situated on the banks of the Rhine and in the foothills of the Alps. I even had the chance to experience the legendary Autobahn. Despite repeated urging, I couldn't convince the taxi driver to do more than 120 km/h, roughly 75 mph. In hindsight, that was probably a good thing.

I was appreciative and thrilled to be able to experience as much of England and parts of Europe as I did that summer. Besides taking in the traditional sites of London, I also took part in some of the more local customs. I saw the musical *Smokey Joe's Café* on the famed West End, London's version of Broadway. During an afternoon lunch break, I wandered over to Windsor Castle and stood along its driveway and waved to Queen Elizabeth II and Prince Charles as they departed for the annual Royal Ascot horse races. I even queued for tickets at Wimbledon.

It turned out that a Delta Tau Delta fraternity brother of mine, Alex, had an internship that summer in Brussels, Belgium and we arranged to spend a weekend together. I met him at the train station in Windsor on a Friday evening, and we headed to the Vansittart Arms, a local pub, affectionately known as The Vance, which had become my regular watering hole. We laughed all night as we enjoyed several pints of Guinness and other local favorites. When closing time came, we coerced the owner into selling us a bottle of wine to take with us.

We stopped along the sidewalk and purchased a bag of English French fries, known as "chips," and then strolled over to Windsor Castle, where the queen lived. The Castle is a magnificent fortress that sprawls across an area that encompasses more than thirteen acres. Its grounds are equally impressive, highlighted by a double lined avenue of trees over three miles long known as The Long Walk. It was along that path, a stone's throw from the Castle, that Alex and I plopped ourselves down under one of the trees to enjoy our feast of wine and chips.

I'm not sure how long we were asleep, but we both passed out after we had finished the wine. When we awoke, it was eerily quiet, the dead of the night, and not a soul could be seen or heard. We stumbled to our feet, gathered our senses, and headed back toward town. However, the problem was that I wasn't exactly in the clearest frame of mind and couldn't figure out how to get us back home. We wandered the empty streets until we came upon an Army barracks.

Since my navigational expertise had malfunctioned, I came up with the brilliant idea to ask the soldiers for directions. We approached the barracks and were suddenly startled by a loud bang.

I froze in my tracks.

Alex took off sprinting down the road. We were both unsure what was going on, but positive we had just been shot at. A few long seconds later we realized the loud clang we heard was a metal garage door that had been flung open so the soldiers could stand outside and puff on their cigarettes.

Alex and I approached the soldiers coolly and explained that we needed directions. We told them we were Americans, as if it wasn't evident by the way in which Alex and I spoke. It was apparent that we were also tipsy. They got a chuckle out of the two of us and were very cordial, offering us not just a cigarette each, but also a ride home. We piled into the back of a jeep with a few other soldiers and rode along as they conducted their patrol rounds before dropping us off at the flat where I lived. In the wee hours of the morning Alex and I finally arrived back at the house, passed out, and got a few hours of rest before we woke to the sounds of Sharon and her kids. After breakfast with Sharon and her children, James and Hannah, Alex and I walked into town and hopped a train for a day trip to Oxford University.

England was one of the best summers of my life, and I've had some memorable summers.

The previous summer, a few days after I arrived home from China, my girlfriend and I had traveled across the country in her car. I had always wanted to see America the beautiful through the front windshield, which is why I made it a goal of mine when I wrote my bucket list. We headed out to Montana, and along the way made several stops, including a visit to the annual Sturgis Bike Rally in South Dakota and the actual "Field of Dreams" in Iowa, where I walked through the mystical cornfields. I didn't disappear as they did in the movie, but the visit did allow me to cross one more item off my list. There were several other adventures along the way: the Mitchell Corn Palace, Mount Rushmore, and the world's most massive Jolly Green Giant statue in Minnesota. We camped out in the Badlands, Yellowstone National Park, Arches and Canyonlands National Park, and various places in Montana. Unfortunately, we ran out of money on our way to the Grand Canyon and had to head back home.

The time I spent in England not only rewarded me with substantial work experience, adventurous travel, and plenty of wonderful moments, but it also afforded me the opportunity to meet some remarkable people and experience their English customs in an intimate way. Sharon welcomed me into her family and her home, which was situated directly under the flight path of the British Airways Concorde jet. On many an evening, I watched the supersonic airplane cruise overhead. Earlier that year the Concorde had crossed the Atlantic from London to New York in its fastest time ever. A few guys from the office had flown on the jet. Unfortunately, it wasn't one of the duties of my internship. Sharon also invited me to share in her family's vacation to The New Forest, a place where wild horses run free. I was almost attacked by one when I got too close to her foal for a picture. We took a day trip to see Stonehenge, one of the most famous ancient structures in the world, and a trip to the City of Bath, which was founded by the Romans around 60 A.D.

James and Hannah, Sharon's children, shared every weekday morning with me. After breakfast, we danced in the living room to the Spice Girls and Dire Straits before they left for school and I headed off to work. When I arrived home in the evening, Sharon would join us, and we would all take, Gemma, the family dog, for a walk. Often, we stopped by the pub for a drink and a bite on our way home. I celebrated the Fourth of July with her, even though it was an insignificant day as far as the Brits were concerned. It was a big day for me, though, and the second year in a row I celebrated it on foreign soil. Our celebration consisted of cheap fireworks and cheap champagne that made for a fun, yet subdued affair.

However, it seemed extravagant compared to the somber event that occurred three days earlier. That was the day that, after a reign of ninety-nine years, England transferred sovereignty over Hong Kong back to China. I sat in the living room alone and watched the ceremony on the telly. The previous summer, I witnessed firsthand the eager anticipation the Chinese had for this day. An obscenely large countdown clock hung from the side of a government building in Tiananmen Square that counted down the seconds until China ruled Hong Kong. Now it was a year later, and I shared in the melancholy spirit that pervaded the English citizenry.

My work colleagues were just as hospitable as Sharon's family. One of the girls I became friends with invited me to her wedding and I had the chance to witness another English custom: naked men in kilts. I attended the wedding with a few women from Siebe and afterward headed to one of their homes for a late-night swim. When we arrived at the woman's country estate, I thought it was a hotel. It was a beautiful, old stone dwelling surrounded with high bushes that provided a very private setting. She offered me one of her husband's bathing suits so I could take a dip in the pool. Lucky for me it was not a Speedo, as most

Europeans were accustomed to. We drank wine, ate pizza, swam, and laughed long into the night.

The night before I left England to head back stateside for my senior year at Lehigh, a large group of work colleagues gathered at The Vance to send me off in proper English style. We all imbibed our fair share of pints, sang songs, and exchanged gifts until the place shut down. I flew out the next morning, not knowing if I would ever see any of them again.

I was fortunate enough to have that opportunity a couple of years later.

# SIX
# BEST FRIENDS

My course had been charted.

After two summers abroad I was convinced I wanted to pursue a career in international business. I had earned my Bachelor of Science degree in Finance as well as a minor in Mandarin Chinese. I also minored in Communications, which I figured would serve me well in the business world.

Upon graduation from Lehigh I accepted a position as a financial analyst at Delphi Packard Electric Systems in Warren, Ohio, a suburb of Youngstown. While in China I had the opportunity to visit one of the company's Far East operations and discovered its world headquarters was in Ohio. I saw Delphi as a unique opportunity that would afford me a chance to work in finance, as well as offer me the potential for an international assignment.

I relocated to the nearby town of Niles to embark upon the next phase of my life.

***

I'm willing to bet that Youngstown isn't the first place that pops into people's heads when they think of cowboys, bulls, and rodeo. However, as with anything, you'd be surprised what you find when you open your eyes and look. And so, on the outskirts of an abandoned steel town in Northeast Ohio I learned to ride a bull.

It didn't take long for me to develop a reputation as a wild and free-spirited individual among my fellow coworkers. One afternoon I mentioned that I had always wanted to ride a bull. The last thing I expected was that someone knew a way to hold me to it. A woman who was an avid horse rider informed me she knew of a place that hosted Friday night bull-riding sessions. The gauntlet had been thrown down, and now I had to prove my mettle. Truth be told, I was excited for the chance since it was on my bucket list.

Man versus beast–a classic confrontation that has existed throughout history, and precisely what I envisioned when I added the daring feat to my bucket list in the first place. Was there anything rawer and manlier than to pit oneself against a large, wild animal and try to control it? At the time, I didn't think so. Strapped to the back of 2,000 pounds of pure force and testosterone, with nothing to hold me in place except a rope and sheer will, I welcomed the adrenaline-laced contest.

There was no hesitation.

The following weekend I drove to Double L Rodeo Productions, a ranch in Kinsman, Ohio, thirty miles from Youngstown. I had no idea what to expect. The ranch was more of a massive barn with a fenced-in pen, bleachers, and a concession stand. A far cry from the large arenas associated with the Professional Bull Riders events I watched on TV on Sunday afternoons. It was early December, and my car got stuck in the muddy parking lot. Not a good start.

Every Friday evening, the Double L hosted Jackpot Buck-Outs, where each contestant rode bulls twice and the highest combined score won. After the Jackpot was over, there was an open ride session where anyone brave enough could hop on a bull and have at it. All that was required was a signed waiver that released the ranch from liability. Another release form. I was getting used to those.

I got a kick out of the fact that it cost ten dollars to watch the event, but only five dollars to participate in it. I saved money by choosing to ride! Anyone off the street could show up and take a chance at riding a wild beast that could kill you for a fin and a signature. Sign me up!

The girl at the gate asked me if I had ever ridden before.

"Nope."

"Okay," she said, "Find another rider and ask if you can borrow their equipment."

"What about training? I'd like to avoid getting hurt if possible," I told her.

"Ask another cowboy to show you what to do. Good luck."

Maybe I was naïve, but I expected that there would be some kind of lesson offered to first-timers like myself. No such luck. The cowboy stereotype of being mellow and of few words was true. However, I needed to seek out someone with experience to show me what to do; otherwise, I could get seriously injured.

I spotted my coworker and her husband in the bleachers and said hello. They brought a video camera to record everything, which could either be good or bad depending on the result. I headed behind the chutes where others psyched themselves up as they waited their turn. Bull riders possessed a certain type of cockiness that was on full display. Each was eager to prove their bravado, and it didn't take long before I struck up a conversation with a few of them. They were excited it was my first time and happy to show me the ropes, literally.

One of the most important things that separated a successful ride from a disastrous one was the proper rope set-up. The art of a good ride was part skill and part strength. The only thing to grab on the back of a bull was the rope wrapped across the animal's back. The makeshift handle was all you had to keep upright as the bull spun, jumped, and kicked. I had neither a rope nor a pair of spurs, but others offered to share their equipment with me and provided their own two cents about what to do once I climbed over the chute. One of them summed it up best and said, "Just squeeze tight and hold on with every muscle". The rest would just happen. Easy enough. Yeah, right.

Three of us congregated behind the chute where my bull, Hobo, was loaded. He was an older bull with a beautiful brindle color and a twisted set of horns. He weighed almost a ton. Before that evening, what scared me the most was the idea of being impaled by a bull's horns. I was wrong. When I grasped how massive, swift, and agile the magnificent animals were, I realized being trampled would cause a lot more damage than a poke from a horn. A hoof to the chest packed hundreds of pounds per square inch and could easily smash my internal organs.

They gave me a vest that was lined with hard plastic, akin to a bulletproof vest but without the Kevlar. Again, the same thought I had about my parachute helmet rattled around in my skull. People put a lot of faith in plastic when it comes to protecting your life.

I put the vest on and tucked my mouth guard into one of its pockets. A vest, a mouth guard, and the athletic cup I wore were all that protected me. However, I did have my cowboy boots on, so at least I looked like I knew what I was doing. I fastened a pair of borrowed spurs to the heels of my boots.

My nerves started to kick in as the reality of what was about to happen dawned on me. My heart beat fast in my chest, in unison with the country music blaring over the house speakers. I slid a leather glove on my left hand, which would be strapped into the rope. My right arm served as my "trim tab" and would help maintain my balance. The chute behind me clanged open, and another bull and rider sprang from the gate. The bull spun around a few times and launched its rider into the air like a ragdoll. The poor guy barely lasted two seconds, well short of the eight-second qualifying ride, which may not seem like a lot but feels like an eternity when you are getting tossed around like a jockstrap in the dryer.

It was my turn.

I climbed up and over the chute and placed my left foot squarely on the back of the bull. The animal didn't even budge. It was like I wasn't even there. I reached across to grab the rail on the other side and slid my body down onto Hobo.

Wow! I felt a sudden rush as I sat on the back of a ton of muscle that could trample me like an ant and not think anything of it. My legs shook from another incredible adrenaline surge that pumped through every part of my body.

"Take a deep breath, Scott," one of the guys said when he noticed my legs.

I slid my left hand under the rope's handle and inched my body up along the animal's spine until the back of my hand was now firmly pressed against my crotch. Bad mistake to wear the cup. I could have gotten another inch closer had I not worn it. The closer you are to your hand the more likely your shoulders will be lined up to help maintain the center of gravity. I needed all the help I could get.

A cowboy reached over the rail and pulled on the rope, which tightened around the animal's torso to keep me as secure as possible. Hobo shifted his weight to let me know he was aware of what was about to happen, and what I hoped to accomplish.

Man versus beast.

I wrapped the end of the rope around my wrist, across my palm, and secured it with a closed fist. I pounded my wrist with my right hand a few times to pack it tight, then pulled up on the rope with my left arm as my right arm held the rail.

*Remember, Scott, don't squeeze him with your spurs until the chute opens.*

I forgot the instruction I'd been given, again, and squeezed my spurs into the bull. Hobo's thick hide felt like I'd dug into a brick wall, and he lurched in the stall, a dangerous maneuver that could land someone on the ground in the chute. If that happened, kiss your ass goodbye since there was nowhere for the bull to go except to stomp up and down all over you.

*Shit, I wasn't supposed to do that!*

Fortunately, Hobo was a seasoned bull, and it didn't take him long to settle down. I'm pretty sure he knew I was a rookie and decided to cut me a little slack.

*Okay. Now I'm ready.*

"Okay boys," I yelled as I nodded my head, the universal sign to swing the gate open.

The gate swung open, and Hobo immediately turned to his left and shot out into the arena. No turn, no jump, a straight sprint across the packed mud. I held on as tight as I could and squeezed with my legs. I made it forty feet before the first buck.

That was all it took. The rope loosened, and I shot off his back like a bottle rocket from a coke bottle. My body flew a few feet up into the air before I crashed to the hard ground and landed on my head like a lawn dart. I scrambled to my feet, made a beeline for the fence, and climbed up on it. Hobo calmly retreated to an open area through which he exited.

My ride was over.

Three seconds. Barely a third of how long I hoped for. But I had done it. I rode a bull.

A natural high remained as I headed back to the chutes where the guys waited for me, smiles on their faces. They were quick to congratulate me and offer a few words of advice and encouragement. A few other cowboys came over to celebrate my initiation. I handed the vest back to one of them, and he noticed my mouthguard in its pocket. In all the excitement, I forgot to wear it.

Another rider invited me to join the group for a beer back behind the chutes. I was so amped up, my mouth so dry from the adrenaline rush, I drank it in about six seconds. I couldn't even last eight seconds with a beer!

Everything happened at warp speed, but something had awakened inside of me. I knew it had not been a one-time thing. The feeling I experienced caught hold of me like a fire, and I couldn't extinguish its flames. The urge was too strong. I was addicted and had to ride again.

Soreness set in as I drove home, and my groin muscles throbbed. My head raged, and my neck was sore. I also felt nauseous and figured it was due to the rush I'd experienced. A good night's rest would sort me out. However, I still felt foggy a few days later, and my mind processed everything slower than usual. By midday on Monday, I could barely keep my eyes open as I sat at my desk.

After work, I drove myself to the ER where the doctor ordered a CAT scan. The nurse had to wake me up when it was over since I had fallen asleep. The doctor told me I had a medium grade concussion and asked if I knew what might've caused it. I was hesitant to admit that I had face-planted into the ground after being tossed from a bull and told him I fell in the shower. I was afraid my insurance wouldn't cover a risky activity like bull riding. The doctor didn't buy it and he eventually got the truth out of me. He sent me home with a stern warning that I should not ride any more bulls.

Two weeks later I was back at the Double L for another crack at Hobo. He won the first round, but I was determined to even the score. Fresh off a concussion, I successfully rode Hobo a full eight seconds and crossed another accomplishment off my bucket list.

I had brought a friend with me who was impressed and wasn't surprised when I told him I wanted to ride again.

Next up was a bull named Knot Head.

The chute gate swung open, and Knot Head spun. I stayed with him, but he got antsy and worked himself into a corner between the fence and open gate. He smashed me hard against the fence, and I had no choice but to hop off. I didn't get away clean and instead fell to the ground a few feet from him, the worst place I could have landed. One of his hooves smashed squarely against the side of my chest, just missing my heart. The force was powerful enough to split the flannel shirt I had on. The shirt still hangs in my closet as a reminder of how powerful an animal can be.

I slowly gathered myself, got to my feet, and staggered behind the chutes. My friend waited for me and steadied me as I collapsed into his arms. I immediately took a knee and tried to catch my breath.

"Dude, are you hurt?" he asked me.

I glanced up at him with an "I-can't-believe-you-just-asked-that" look.

"Sorry. Stupid question," he said.

This time around I brought some adult beverages, and we drank a few beers as we watched other guys ride. On the way home I shoved a few between my thighs to ice my muscles.

That spring I rode over a dozen bulls and traveled with other cowboys to various Buck-Outs in Ohio. One of them rode on the Midstates Rodeo circuit, and I had the opportunity to tag along and ride a few bulls along the way. I never won any money, but I still had a blast. I purchased my own pair of spurs, chaps, rope, and a vest. I joked that the stars on my blue and black chaps were a reminder of the stars I saw after my rides. There was some truth to that. After a year of the whole cowboy thing, all I had to show for it was a few concussions, a separated shoulder, a torn calf muscle, and a damaged rotator cuff.

And one ripped flannel shirt.

***

I was in my Delphi plant office in Warren when I called my English friend, David, to finalize our plans for a summer trip to Ireland. I had hoped to visit the Emerald Isle during my initial time in England, but the opportunity never presented itself. However, I had been back home in America for almost two years and I was anxious to travel. Ireland would be perfect.

During my time in England, I formed two solid bonds that eventually led me back to the British Isles. The first attachment was a lasting affinity for Guinness. The other connection was the friendship I developed with, David, strengthened over the many pints of Guinness we shared.

Davey, as I called him, was the first person I met in England, when our paths first crossed at Heathrow. I spent most of my Friday nights with him and his mates at The Vance, and it didn't take long for our group to be recognized as a mainstay by the other locals. Occasionally, David's wife joined us for a drink, but most of the time it was just us boys. We had a proclivity for loud laughter and ample amounts of Guinness. I once claimed to Davey that I could drink the stuff all night. It wasn't but an hour later that the stout had gotten the better of me, and I required his help to balance, lest I ended up on the pub floor.

David was your classic English chap. Quiet and reserved when he needed to be, but at other times mischievous and ornery. He was mostly bald, with a thick British accent and a wonderful personality and kind demeanor. It was impossible not to like the guy. It wasn't long after I returned to America that we made plans to reunite for some old-fashioned revelry.

That summer I caught a direct flight from Cleveland to Gatwick Airport, about thirty miles south of Central London. Once again, I was asked questions about the obtrusive black mark in my passport. Satisfied with my answers, the Customs officials admitted me into England. David picked me up at the airport, and we drove back to his flat for the evening. After a lovely dinner with his wife and daughter, we headed to The Vance for a few pints. It felt great to be back at the pub. Two years later, and the owner still remembered me and called me by the affectionate moniker he gave me, "Yank!"

The next morning, we flew to Dublin for a week of travel across the heart of Ireland. We arranged to travel with a tour group that offered a package called "The Celtic Knot," which took us from Dublin to the western shores of Galway, with stops at several towns and villages along the way.

Our tour guides were two Irish dudes who reminded me of the guys I played rugby with at Lehigh. They dressed in khakis and T-shirts and looked like they had just rolled out of bed five minutes earlier. They were extremely knowledgeable of the region and sites we saw, probably from having done the tour a hundred times. And they were fun to party with, as was the rest of the gang, an eclectic mix of Australians, Canadians, and Europeans. I was the only American. Everyone was eager to engage in conversation with one another, which made for a pleasant experience.

The extended travel across the country allowed me to experience all the beauty typically associated with Ireland. Lush, green rolling hills, sprinkled with timeworn rock formations, dotted the landscape in all directions. History lessons were imparted to us by our guides, complemented by the many stops we made along the way, which included Birr and Bunratty castles, the seaside town of Kilkee, and the famed Cliffs of Moher. However, I came to discover the real history and culture of Ireland existed in its pubs.

Ireland lives in its people, and their culture was on full display each time we popped in for a pint somewhere. My best memories are filled with the evenings we spent singing, laughing, and engaging with residents in "the craic," their term for fun, entertainment, and enjoyable conversation. In other words, loud talk and braggadocio. I became an expert in the art.

I made it known to my tour mates that my goal was to beat an Irish man in a true test of manliness–a drinking contest. A common stereotype associated with the Irish is that they have a knack for imbibing large quantities of alcohol. I was determined to measure my worth against the best. Now I am not glorifying the use of alcohol, nor have I ever thought of myself as having a problem with it. However, I did like to enjoy a good pint–especially when it came to Guinness. I could swallow sixteen ounces of the black stuff in less than ten seconds. Thus, I felt that qualified me as an aficionado, able to hold my own with the best of them. By the time our group reached Banagher, about halfway between Dublin and Galway, I was more than eager to put my talents to the test.

That evening we stumbled upon JJ Houghs Singing Pub, a wonderful place full of rich character. Its cozy confines felt like the inside of a house you might find in, Middle-earth, the enchanted land in the J. R. R. Tolkien novels. The chairs were nothing more than empty kegs with cushions on them, positioned around large oak tables. The main centerpiece was a massive stone fireplace that warmed the entire place. It was the middle of the summer, but the fire seemed utterly appropriate. It was known as the singing pub for a reason. There was plenty of traditional Irish music sung by many of the regulars, as well as some more contemporary ballads that were belted out by several members of our contingent. I also took a turn at a melody; however, I couldn't carry a tune if it had handles.

As the night progressed and we became friendly with the locals, word had spread that I was looking to challenge a real Irishman at his unofficial pastime. It wasn't long before a willing participant surfaced.

The rules were simple: the first one to drink three pints of Guinness would be declared the winner. I even went so far as to boast that I could complete the feat in thirty seconds. Half a dozen pints were brought to the table and placed in front of us. Most of the crowd on hand was gathered around our table to watch the spectacle. My opponent was more than twice my age, an older gentleman in his fifties, good-natured with rosy cheeks. He seemed confident in his ability to make quick work of the forty-eight ounces that lay before him.

We raised our glasses. *Sláinte!*

I immediately hurried the first glass to my lips and drank its contents as fast as I could. I was so focused, I didn't notice how gingerly he sipped his pint. After about nine seconds I slammed the glass on the table and reached for the second. That's when I noticed his slow and deliberate pace.

"You're doing great," he chided me.

I finished my second at a slower rate and proceeded to let out a huge belch. Bloated, I reached for the final glass. My competitor was barely halfway through his first glass. I realized he had no intention of rushing through his three pints. After all, why would he? It was a foolish challenge that only led to an uncomfortable feeling.

"You win, but you need to finish," he said.

Everyone laughed, and I realized I had been set up.

"I'm going to enjoy these," he said with a wink.

The bloke had outsmarted me. I tried to drink as much beer as I could, as fast as I could, while he enjoyed his and watched me make a fool of myself. I eventually finished my last pint–but it took an hour!

We arrived in Galway the following afternoon. Galway is the fourth-largest city in Ireland, and it's known as "Ireland's Cultural Heart" due to its vibrant lifestyle and numerous festivals, celebrations, and events. It was the Fourth of July, so of course, I had to celebrate. And while it's not a holiday in Ireland, there were plenty of Americans celebrating in the pubs we visited. That evening I hung out with a group of American students, enjoyed more Guinness, and sang the national anthem over and over. It was the third time in the past four years I celebrated Independence Day in a foreign country. I also met a beautiful Irish girl that evening who had me singing the praises of Irish women for months after I returned home.

Our group spent the night at a hostel that I didn't make it back to until after midnight. The alarm clock rang at 4 a.m. It was Guinness time. Situated on the mouth of the River Corrib and surrounded by harbors, Galway was once a booming fishing village, and many fishermen could still be found around town. Since most of them brought their catch ashore in the early morning, many of the pubs were open to serve them. Before the sun came up, a few of us made our way to the pub for an early-morning toast. Of course, I ordered a Guinness. In hindsight, I should have opted for a much lighter lager. The late-night revelry and lack of sleep left my stomach a bit uneasy, and the last thing it needed was another pint of Guinness Stout. I only drank half of it but was able to rally and enjoy some famous Irish whiskey a few hours later during a tour of the Kilbeggan Distillery, the oldest licensed distillery in Ireland.

A few days later the tour concluded back in Dublin. Unfortunately, by the time we got off the bus, it was too late to take a tour of St. James Gate, home of the Guinness brewery. However, Davey and I headed over to where it was located. I walked up to the main gate and knocked on it.

No one let me in.

We spent our final evening in the famous Temple Bar district of Dublin before we caught a flight back to England the following morning. Once again in Windsor, I was able to visit with Sharon, my gracious host from two years earlier. There was a final trip back to The Vance, and then it was back to Cleveland. After dinner with my family, I drove back to my apartment in Youngstown.

It would only be my home for another three months.

***

In the fall of 2000, I relocated to Toledo, Ohio and assumed the role of Senior Financial Analyst for Calphalon, a division of Newell Rubbermaid.

Delphi Packard Electric Systems had ceased its Fellowship Program that offered select individuals the opportunity to pursue an MBA at a top-tier business school. It had also scaled back its international relocation program. These two issues, combined with my constant want for a challenge, motivated me to seek other opportunities.

My experiences at Calphalon would be life-changing.

Not long after I started at Calphalon, I applied to the University of Michigan Business School. It has consistently been ranked as one of the nation's top business schools and is less than an hour's drive from Toledo. It was also the only school I applied to. I am a diehard Ohio State Buckeyes fan, but the opportunity to receive a degree from a top business school like Michigan was something I could not pass up. Several evenings a week after work I drove the fifty-five miles from Toledo to Ann Arbor to attend classes, which lasted until 10 p.m. On most nights, I barely arrived home before midnight, a routine that continued for three and a half years, until I graduated in December of 2004.

At the time of my graduation, the University of Michigan's Ross Business School was ranked as the top school in the country according to the *Wall Street Journal*. Graduating was one of the greatest achievements of my life due to the sacrifice and commitment that was needed to stay the course and balance a high-profile job with a demanding course load.

I certainly don't miss those long days, especially the ones that began in the early morning at the chiropractor's office to receive physical therapy for the chronic neck and shoulder pain that had plagued me since high school. The thousands of sleepy miles I logged traveling back and forth to Ann Arbor did nothing to help my back, but all the sacrifice was worth it.

On graduation day I wore an Ohio State Buckeyes necktie and walked across the stage as I gripped a Buckeye in my hand. One hand clenched a poisonous nut as the other shook the Dean's hand and received my diploma noting my accomplishment. Sure, the tie might have been a bit obnoxious, but it was par for the course considering that my Lehigh graduation cap was adorned with a large number 3 in honor of Dale Earnhardt.

Prior to my MBA, I had already embarked upon a marketing career. A year and a half after I began working at Calphalon I was approached by its president, Kristie Juster, with an exciting and challenging opportunity. Calphalon, a manufacturer of high-end cookware, needed to broaden its reach in other markets, and Kristie wanted me to lead the company initiative to establish a market presence in the cutlery arena. My entire career had been spent in finance and operations roles, yet Calphalon had confidence in my ability to not only create a new product category but, more important, lead a team of fellow employees to achieve success.

I eagerly accepted the challenge. I was confident in my ability to deliver results, but also respectful of my lack of experience in building a new product category. What I did not lack was grit and determination, resourcefulness, and perseverance. There wasn't a doubt in my mind that I could achieve success if I worked for it. Those traits, along with the tremendous effort of the others on my team, proved instrumental.

The vision and planning my team implemented vaulted Calphalon into a market leadership position within the cutlery industry. We managed to capture over seven percent market share in our first two years, and more than ten percent market share by the end of our third year. I was granted both utility and design patents on the knife designs I invented, and my designs were recognized by several leading trade publications as the best new consumer products of the year.

The national accolades were appreciated, but even more meaningful was the recognition by my peers when my team received the company's inaugural Breakthrough Leadership Award, as well as Newell Rubbermaid's Breakthrough Marketing Award. I took tremendous pride in leading my team toward a shared vision of excellence. Receiving recognition for that was something special.

Without a doubt, though, the highlight of my time at Calphalon was the friendships I formed with my fellow employees. Most of us were close in age and often found ourselves involved in activities outside the office, which also included the company softball, volleyball, and dodgeball teams I competed on. We had a penchant for hijinks and were adept at the whole "work hard, play hard" adage, even if some of the "play" took place on company time.

During a leadership conference in Virginia Beach, an impromptu dance contest broke out aboard a ferry on the James River. As a child, I garnered an appreciation and love for breakdancing that stayed with me well into early adulthood. Along the way, I incorporated a Michael Jackson dance routine into my regimen. Showcasing my skills (I use the word "skills" loosely) had become somewhat of a tradition at Calphalon's leadership meetings. At a company meeting in Keystone, Colorado, I was partaking in a late-evening putting contest when I was summoned from the golf course to the clubhouse because Kristie needed to see me immediately. As I entered the building, Michael Jackson music began to play, and everyone clapped in unison.

There was only one thing to do. I moonwalked into the center of the floor and broke out into a crazy dance routine. I was the only person I'm aware of who had grabbed his crotch and thrust himself in the direction of our president and got her to laugh about it. The crotch grab, done while I simultaneously swung a bent knee wildly in front of me, was a classic "King of Pop" move. I also included the worm and a few backspins in my routine for good measure. I once even performed after hours during the week of the International Housewares Show at our Culinary Center in Chicago while dressed in a brand-new Hugo Boss suit.

My routines weren't just limited to Calphalon business meetings. I also had a reputation for breaking into crazy dance at wedding receptions. I was a groomsman in two different employee weddings, and true to script, I performed at them as well. One wedding was for

Brent, who worked for me on the Cutlery team. The other was for Eric, whose wife was the Human Resources Manager. Both would later also serve as groomsmen at my wedding, along with Kevin, another former Calphalon employee.

Some of my lifelong friendships were formed with my coworkers at Calphalon. I especially became great friends with Eric, whose wife had helped recruit me to Calphalon. Eric worked the night shift as a supervisor for UPS, but we still managed to get together at least twice a week. The two of us loved to compete against one another, especially when it came to golf and bowling. Eric usually had my number on the links, but I laid claim to the hardwood lanes and once bowled a 222 to claim the "World Champion" title between us. We shared a mutual love for Kid Rock, NASCAR, and Slim Jim beef jerky, and attended several Kid Rock concerts and NASCAR races over the years together. Somehow, we always found a way to make each experience more memorable than the last.

Eric was someone I could always count on to be there for me, no matter what the situation. His friendship and dependability were not something I took lightly. The same could be said for Kevin. They are two of the greatest friends anyone could ask for. However, one summer evening would ultimately change my world forever.

That was the evening I met my best friend.

# SEVEN
# I'M GOING TO MARRY THAT GIRL

I met Kristy Costell on June 23, 2005, in Maumee, Ohio, a suburb of Toledo.

A work colleague had left the company, and several employees gathered that evening at BW3s to wish him well. That night also happened to be Game 7 of the NBA Finals between the San Antonio Spurs and the Detroit Pistons, the adopted team of many in Toledo due to the Motor City's proximity. The place was packed, loud and lively. Our group had gotten there early enough to secure a prime table right in the center of the room.

It was well into the evening when my life changed forever.

A colleague nudged me to get my attention. He wanted me to take notice of the hot blonde that stood a few feet from our table. I looked over in the direction he referred to and immediately locked eyes with her. Without hesitation, and for some unknown reason, I motioned for her to come to me with my finger. It was something I typically wouldn't do, but for whatever reason felt compelled to do in that moment.

Kristy's eyes met mine, and she saw me signal for her. At first, she seemed a bit hesitant, but then slowly began to walk toward me. We met at the bar a few feet away from our friends. It was just us. And right from the beginning, we hit it off. We talked for over an hour, completely oblivious to our friends and everyone else in the bar. She explained that her great-aunt had died earlier that evening and her friends coerced her to join them to get her mind off things. I was glad she had listened to her friends and I offered my ear as support.

We talked about a variety of things throughout our conversation, including our faith and religious beliefs. We were both raised Catholic, firmly rooted in our core belief in God, and were not afraid to talk openly about it to each other. I showed her the picture of Jesus, worn and wrinkled, that I carried in my wallet, as well as the typed-up verse, Romans 8:18, that had been there since I put it in my wallet ten years earlier. I knew I was experiencing the most magical moment of my life.

If there was one word to describe Kristy that night, it was "striking." Her inescapable beauty radiated across the room and filled my heart the moment I first laid eyes on her. She had a calming presence about her that made me feel relaxed and at ease. Her green stilettos with sequins made her just a few inches shorter than me. She looked gorgeous. She seemed shy, but as we talked more, the shyness transformed into an innocence that left me with the feeling that I was right where I was meant to be. Although I wanted to, I had never believed in love at first sight. I'd had some long-term relationships in my life, but none that ever took hold of me in such a way that I never wanted it to end.

With Kristy, it was love at first sight.

It wasn't just her looks that had drawn me in, but her demeanor. She was like a hardy, yet fragile flower that I wanted to bring home, place on my windowsill, and care for every day. I wanted to take care of that girl and I felt like I had been put on earth to do just that.

The hour we spent talking seemed like only minutes. Before we parted I handed her my business card and hoped to impress her further. But that was not the way to impress Kristy, who was simple and real, not one to make a big deal over titles or status or even money. She accepted my card with a smile and then commandeered my cell phone. As she keyed in her number, she informed me that it was under the name "Kristy." At that point, I realized I had called her Kristen throughout our entire conversation. She had seen no need to correct me or call attention to my mistake. Instead, she just ignored it and chose to let us both enjoy and embrace the magical time that took place between us.

Kristy was the purest human being I had ever met, and as I walked away to rejoin my friends, an enormous smile spread across my face. I approached one of my friends and with a matter of factness stated to him, "I'm going to marry that girl!"

A few days later, as I sat in the Toledo airport parking lot fresh off a flight from a business trip, my phone rang. Kristy had returned my call. We talked for some time before I finally started my car and drove home. Later that night, during a seven-hour phone conversation, neither of us were ever at a loss for words, and we both found it easy to talk to the other, something that would continue well into our relationship many years later.

Kristy laughed when I told her how my friend and I referred to her as the "smoking hot" girl in the green dress that night. She proceeded to tell me how she and her friends discussed the "awesome arms" the guy in the blue shirt had. I had worn the blue shirt.

Our relationship was destined for excitement and exploration from the beginning. Always up for anything, we quickly took advantage of doing just that. There was a card game, Living Life, designed to challenge someone to live life to the fullest. The game consisted of thirty cards that listed "feel good" adventures to experience, such as contacting an old friend, taking a day trip, or finding your "mojo." The game had sat idle on my bookshelf and waited for the moment I felt inspired enough to dust it off. Finally, it was the perfect time to remove the cards and begin each meaningful To Do with a worthy partner to share in the adventures.

The first adventure listed on Card One was to watch a sunrise, so not long after we began our relationship, we found ourselves sprawled across a blanket in a local park. Kristy and I had stayed up all night watching movies, including my all-time favorite, *Joe Versus the Volcano*, a movie about a hypochondriac who learns what it means to truly live while on a journey to a tropical island where he plans to sacrifice himself to the island's mystical volcano. The only sacrifice we made that night was to forgo sleep and greet the new day with the rising sun.

En route to the park in the wee hours of the morning, we stopped at the grocery store for orange juice and cheap champagne. Mimosas at sunrise seemed like not only the perfect way to start the day but also an appropriate way to kick off our journey together. We sat on a blanket in the middle of the open field and watched the sun come up, while we laughed endlessly and told each other stories. Inevitably, nature soon called, and our only option was a Porta-Potty permanently placed next to the parking lot.

If you want to know someone, observe how they handle a dilapidated and disgusting public restroom. For me, and probably most guys in general, it's no big deal. For a beautiful woman who wants to maintain her sexiness, it can be a daunting task. However, it was that moment when I was first introduced to Kristy's resourcefulness as she produced the roll of toilet paper she snagged from my apartment before we left. She was fully prepared for the moment and emerged from the plastic potty house with a smile across her face. That smile served to reinforce the feelings I had of being fully prepared to move through life with her by my side.

It was summer, and there was much to take advantage of. We both had an appreciation for the outdoors and relished the fresh air and sunny days. Since Kristy loved butterflies, one of our first dates was to the Butterfly House in nearby Whitehouse, Ohio. I swallowed my pride, picked her up, and drove us out to spend an afternoon with the butterflies. It was easy to swallow my pride when it came to Kristy. Even something like butterflies perched atop my head seemed completely natural with her.

I was smitten. And it didn't take long before I polled my friends on how long I should wait before I proposed to her. My friends were eager to dispense their sound advice. One told me to wait at least three months. Another said we needed to go through a calendar year to see how the change in seasons and weather affected our relationship. A former coworker told me not to place any time frame on it, and just do what felt right.

Everything felt right with Kristy. Even the butterfly kisses we gave each other. The only reason I didn't propose a few weeks after we first met was so others didn't mistake our love for some newfound infatuation. Kristy and I knew it was something much more than that.

Kristy invited me to spend the Fourth of July with her family at their cottage on Coldwater Lake in Coldwater, Michigan. Unfortunately, I had already made plans to spend the holiday with my friends at Put-In-Bay, a small group of Lake Erie islands near Catawba, Ohio. For several years, a group of us got together for an annual boys' weekend there. My friends would not let me live it down if I skipped out on the trip. Especially for a girl. I called her from a patio bar on the Fourth as she watched the fireworks with her family. I wished I could have been there with her to celebrate my favorite holiday at her side. I couldn't wait to get back to Toledo. A few days away from her felt like an eternity.

Several weeks into our relationship I found myself in the aisles of a large craft store looking for the perfect pad of stationary. I purchased a fifty-page notepad, went home to my apartment, and proceeded to write something I loved about Kristy on each piece of paper. By the time I had finished, there were fifty folded sheets of paper that each listed a different quality she possessed. I stuffed each of them into a wooden box. A day later, the two of us lay in my bed as she unfolded each of the little love notes. The smile on her face filled me with a happiness I had never felt before. I repeated the gesture on our first wedding anniversary since paper was the symbolic gift to celebrate one year of marriage.

We shared several interests, especially our love of the water. Kristy is an Aquarius, and I am a Pisces. A fish in the water. Two things that belonged together.

Shortly after the Fourth of July, Kristy once again invited me to the lake house for the weekend to meet her parents, brother, and sister. That Saturday morning, I hopped in my GMC Jimmy and drove the hour and a half to Coldwater Lake. In my mind, I knew that I was meeting my future in-laws. Kristy introduced me to everyone. Her parents, Gary and Karen. Her sister, Angie, who was my age, and her husband, Sean. They had three kids: Avery, their newborn daughter; and Colin and Ryan, eight and four. I was also introduced to her older brother, Rob, and his fiancée, Amanda. Everyone made me feel comfortable and at home with them, and from that moment on, there would never be a point at which I felt uncomfortable among any of them.

We spent the weekend boating, swimming, sitting around the fire, playing with her niece and nephews, and falling more in love with each other. Sunday afternoon Kristy drove back with me to Toledo so we could attend the Silvertide concert later that evening.

The two of us had nicknames for each other that we had taken from the book *Hope for the Flowers*, by Trina Paulus, which I had read to Kristy over the phone one evening. On the surface, it is a love story between two caterpillars, Stripe and Yellow, who become butterflies. However, at its core, it is an allegorical novel about leaving behind the safe things in life to discover that which makes you happy and alive. Its central theme is resurrection, faith, and finding your place in life.

I was Stripe. She was Yellow. We were two butterflies who had found each other.

As I drove Kristy home after the concert, I put in a CD that included the song, "Yellow," by Coldplay. There's a line in the song's chorus that goes, "You know I love you so." Each time that line was repeated, I turned up the radio. It was my not-so-subtle way of telling Kristy that I loved her.

We finally had the chance to tell each other we loved one another a short time later when she accompanied me to Buckeye Lake in Hebron, Ohio for the weekend. My aunt and uncle, Jo and Jim, had a house situated on the lake. Every summer I tried to spend a weekend there. It was a fun retreat with plenty to do. Usually, I brought along someone to spend the weekend with me at their house. They had met all my girlfriends over the years and were never shy to share their opinions, and I looked forward to hearing their thoughts on Kristy.

I took Friday off from work, and we headed down late in the morning. It was a three-hour ride from Toledo to Hebron, which is outside of Columbus. By late afternoon we cruised the lake while we enjoyed a few cocktails. Kristy and I sat near the front of the boat as my uncle maneuvered through the channels and into areas where beautiful million-dollar homes were nestled along the shore. Kristy and I marveled at the houses and pointed out the ones we pictured ourselves living in. Things felt perfect on the water, my arm around her shoulders, not a care in the world.

It was evident how much we enjoyed each other, especially to my aunt. As Jim turned the boat around in one of the inlets, Jo motioned to a beautiful home tucked away on a hill.

"That looks like it would be a nice place for your wedding," she smiled.

By "your" she meant both of us. I smiled back at her.

Everyone knew that what I felt toward Kristy was the real thing. My aunt had never made a comment like that until that moment, and she knew she could do so with complete confidence. After all, she was right.

Later that evening, Kristy and I sat alone on a canopy swing down by the dock. I held her in my arms and kissed her head softly as I looked out across the water. I threw caution to the wind, although it didn't seem like much of a risk, and told Kristy what was on my mind.

"I'm going to marry you."

Kristy focused her beautiful green eyes on me. She wasn't caught off guard, alarmed, or the least bit shocked by the words I had just spoken to her.

"I know," she softly replied.

We kissed and as I caressed her face, I reminded her that she had yet to tell me she loved me. Of course, I had yet to do the same, besides turning up the volume of a Coldplay song. She smiled again. And without hesitation told me the words I had longed to hear from the moment I first laid eyes on her.

"I love you."

In the warm, night air, as I held her in my arms along the water's edge, I told my future wife what I had already figured out that night at BW3s months earlier.

"I love you too."

# EIGHT
# PRIORITIES

The end of September arrived in a hurry.

Several months before I met Kristy, I had booked a vacation in Cabo San Lucas, Mexico through a timeshare I owned. I had invited my friend Kevin to join me for a week of surf, sand, and sun; however, by the time I would leave for Mexico, I was head over heels for Kristy and wanted nothing more than to spend the week in paradise with her by my side. As Kevin and I departed from the Detroit airport for Mexico, I was already thinking about getting back home to Toledo and to Kristy.

To say that my love of adventure and traveling had waned since I met Kristy would be an understatement. It wasn't so much that I no longer wanted to travel and discover new places; I didn't want to do it without her. I wanted the two of us to experience everything together.

My priorities had shifted entirely, and I wasn't willing to compromise them.

That revelation had been made quite apparent a few weeks earlier when Calphalon presented me with the job opportunity I had waited for my whole career. The company had set its eyes on international expansion and wanted me to investigate growth opportunities in the United Kingdom and China, two countries I knew well. Relocation would not be required, but the new role involved extensive travel, mainly to London and Hong Kong, for weeks at a time.

There was another reason to strongly consider the new position which had been presented to me. Calphalon's parent company, Newell Rubbermaid, was a strong proponent of succession and wanted a succession plan established for its key players within critical positions. As the Senior Product Manager who oversaw the entire cutlery and kitchen prep businesses, I held a very strategic role within the company. The executive team knew it was only a matter of time before I started to chomp at the bit for a new and more significant challenge, so they wanted to ensure something was lined up for me. They also needed a plan for the business segments I oversaw in the event I left the company.

Given my proven track record of growing new businesses, along with my international experience in England and China, and the fact that I spoke Mandarin Chinese, I was the ideal candidate for the position. It was the opportunity I had envisioned and worked toward since I embarked upon my international business career path all those years earlier. But this wasn't all those years earlier, and I now found myself involved in a serious relationship with Kristy. And Kristy wasn't just another girl.

The new job opportunity caught me as much off guard as Kristy had that night at BW3s. As I sat in my seat 33,000 feet above the ground, I did what I did best.

I made a list.

On a piece of paper, I listed the various pros and cons if I accepted the new job. I tried to be as objective as possible in my rationale, although I admit it was challenging to put aside my bias for not wanting to be away from Kristy. When we landed in Mexico, my brain was exhausted from the nonstop analysis I had subjected it to. Perhaps a week in beautiful Cabo San Lucas would recharge me.

Cabo certainly did not disappoint. The city is situated at the southernmost tip of the Baja California Peninsula, flanked on the West by the Pacific Ocean and the East by the Sea of Cortez. It was one of Mexico's top tourist destinations but was not as heavily trafficked as some of the other spots, which made it popular among the jet-setting Hollywood crowd. While mixing it up one night at Cabo Wabo Cantina, a favorite night spot owned by Van Halen front man Sammy Hagar, Kevin and I found ourselves at a table next to Christina Aguilera, who was celebrating her bachelorette party with a small group of friends. Another night, at the same club, we bumped into Simon Cowell.

The highlight of the week, though, was a charter fishing trip that consisted of a day on the Sea of Cortez with Pisces Sportfishing. During the weeks leading up to our trip, I had grown increasingly obsessed with catching a Marlin. However, even if I didn't snag a trophy fish, I figured it would still be a fun day in the area known as the Aquarium of the World, home to forty percent of the world's marine life. Kevin and I awoke bright and early, caught a cab down to the marina, and boarded, Andrea, the twenty-eight-foot Uniflite that would be our home for the next eight hours. In a proactive attempt to ward off any seasickness, I popped some Dramamine before we left the hotel.

I was ready to fish.

It took over an hour to head out to sea and find a fishing spot. It was finally time to get to work. We took our seats in the fighting chairs and cast our trolling rods into the deep, turquoise water. It wasn't long before my line snapped taut and I hooked my first fish of the day. Up until that moment, the largest fish I had ever caught was barely worthy of being served on a platter at Long John Silver's. However, as my reel hissed from the violent spinning, I knew that whatever was on the other end of my line was much bigger.

My first catch was a dazzling, blue-and-green Dorado, also known as mahi-mahi. One of the guides estimated it to be about twenty pounds, which easily usurped anything I had previously caught. Before the guide could finish filleting the fish, Kevin had a fish on his line. Another Dorado. Between the two of us, we caught over half a dozen Dorado throughout the day. Unfortunately, I also caught a bout of seasickness, and I think the Dramamine I had taken only served to exacerbate the issue.

I had spent a lot of time on the water and had never felt as bad as I did that day. I could no longer fish and had to sit down inside of the cabin with my eyes closed. I don't speak Spanish, but I am pretty sure I heard the captain and guide laugh and refer to me as, "gringo verde," or the green gringo.

As I rested in the cabin, I heard the familiar hissing whirl of the fishing reel. This time it wasn't a Dorado.

"Marlin! Marlin!" our guide yelled as he hopped down from the helm.

An instant surge of adrenaline took hold, and as horrible as I felt, I sprung to my feet, rushed to the fighting chair, and fastened myself in. This was what I had dreamed of, the chance to catch a Marlin, the most prized fish in deep-sea fishing!

I grabbed the pole and immediately felt the pull and strength of the magnificent fish. In my excitement, I started to reel as the fish swam out to sea. I had to consciously calm myself and remember to let it run before I tried to reel it in; otherwise, I would have an uphill battle against a powerful force.

I got my first glimpse of what was on my line after fifteen intense minutes, when the splendid Blue Marlin jumped from the water and sailed a few feet in the air before it disappeared back under the waves and into the sea. The fish, forty yards away, suddenly darted further from the boat. It seemed like my fishing line was endless and the reel would never stop spinning as the fish swam further and further away.

My body tightened and felt rock hard as blood furiously gushed through every single muscle fiber. I sweated profusely, not from the triple-degree weather, but from the contest I found myself locked in. I felt like one of the champion fishermen I had often seen on ESPN as I battled this brilliant fish.

The melee lasted an hour before I finally reeled the giant fish up against the side of the boat. I was spent and worn out. The guide slipped a steel glove on to his hand and leaned over the side of the boat and grabbed the fish by its razor-sharp bill. He held the fish in the water as its beautiful blue and gray metallic body sparkled in the afternoon sun. Kevin snapped a picture for me. Our guide estimated the fish to be about 160 pounds, relatively small for a species that can exceed 1,000 pounds. However, at that moment, it was the biggest fish in the world to me.

And I had caught it.

The Blue Marlin knew I had won the battle. I told the guide to release it back into the sea. Besides, the largest billfish tournament in the world, the Bisbee's Black and Blue Marlin Tournament, was a few weeks away and I didn't want to deplete the stock. Although, if the same fish were caught again it would inevitably be thrown back as no sportfishing professional would hang his hopes on a fish of that size. But for me, that 160-pounder allowed me to fulfill the dream I had set out to achieve.

I was done fishing. I barely had enough strength to crawl up the ladder to the boat's bridge, where I plopped down in the chair next to the captain. He told me the best thing for my seasickness was to perch myself up high, get some fresh air, and focus on the horizon. However, we were more than twenty-five miles off the coast of Mexico, and I could barely see any land in front of me.

By late afternoon, we were back in the harbor. We tipped our captain and guide with cash and some of the Dorado meat that had been cut up on the boat. Kevin and I had more than our fair share. We stopped at a restaurant along the pier and gave our catch to the maître d' with instructions on how we would like it prepared and what time we planned to return for dinner. That evening, after a shower and change of clothes, Kevin and I dined alfresco on the fresh Dorado we caught earlier in the day. It remains the best fish I've ever tasted in my life. We even invited a table of nearby girls to join us since we had so much fish. I proudly recanted my tale for them and sipped on tequila.

Eat your heart out, Ernest Hemingway.

Our entire time in Cabo was eventful. One afternoon we rented a car and drove up the Baja Peninsula to Todos Santos, a coastal town situated at the foothills of the Sierra de la Laguna Mountains, and visited the Hotel California, which inspired the Eagles hit song of the same name.

By day we soaked up the sun, and by night we smoked Cuban cigars and wandered the streets of Cabo, exploring its culture and cantinas. We both got quite a scare one night when our taxicab was pulled over by the Mexican police. They ordered the driver out of the car, and a shouting match soon ensued between the driver and the police. Kevin and I sat frozen in the backseat, both somewhat inebriated and unsure what to do. It didn't take long before there was rap against the back window.

One thought quickly filled my mind: Pablo Escobar.

The cartel member, posing as a policeman, was in search for the drugs the taxi driver had stolen from the cartel and the two Americans were accomplices in the matter. We would never see the inside of a jail. The cartel was notorious for dispensing a more permanent form of justice.

Fortunately, that wasn't the case. Instead, the cop told us to find another cab since our driver had been detained. We gladly obliged, hopped out of the car, and walked back into town. We never found out what the driver did.

Two days before we were to hop a flight back to the States, I broke down and called Kristy. We had agreed that we would not talk to each other that week due to the outrageously expensive cost of an international call. However, I couldn't help myself. It was pure bliss when I heard her voice for the first time in almost a week. Unfortunately, I would need to wait a little longer until I found myself back in her arms. In the meantime, I called her a few more times before we finally left Mexico. We had been right about the outrageously expensive international calling charges, and weeks later I received a $600 bill from the phone company. But it was worth every penny.

Kristy made the drive from Toledo to the Detroit airport to pick up Kevin and me. When I met her outside on the curb, I was overcome with the greatest feeling of sheer ecstasy I've ever had in my life. There was no doubt in my mind about how strong and how real my feelings for her were. As if I needed to be convinced. It was also evident I didn't need a list to make up my mind about the international assignment with Calphalon.

The following week, I turned down the amazing opportunity at Calphalon and resigned.

# NINE

# OH, THE PLACES YOU'LL GO

The decision to leave Calphalon was tough.

My time at the company was rewarding on both a professional and personal level, but good things sometimes come to an end.

I agreed to stay on with the company through the end of the year, finish up some key projects, and help orient another employee who would temporarily manage the business until a permanent replacement was hired.

I used the time off to write a screenplay about a story I had kicked around in my head for some time. I enrolled in a screenwriting class at the University of Toledo, a four-month course that motivated me to bang out a first draft. Hollywood has yet to call, but at least I'll have something to dangle in front of Tom Cruise if he ever does show me the ropes.

My break from work allowed me to spend more time with Kristy. On some days I would pick her up at work for lunch, other days I would bring lunch to her. Regardless, I took advantage of every minute to bask in her company.

As spring approached, so too did the need to resolve two major issues.

The first was to figure out my job situation. Several companies had approached me with offers of employment. One company, Douglas Quikut, called me every week in hopes of retaining my services. They manufactured several well-known products, their most famous being Ginsu knives, and given my background, they were extremely interested in me. The company was in Walnut Ridge, Arkansas, ninety miles northwest of Memphis, Tennessee, and it was a subsidiary of Scott Fetzer, which was owned by Berkshire Hathaway Inc.

They wanted me as their Vice President of Sales and Marketing, but I didn't want Arkansas. My feelings about Arkansas were reinforced after I visited the company. As rewarding as it might be to work for a Warren Buffett company, I couldn't see myself in Arkansas. And I didn't see Kristy there either.

And that mattered.

After all, the second pending issue was to propose to Kristy.

We had dated for a few months shy of a year, and neither of us had any intention of slowing things down. Together we had experienced a lot and we'd even picked out the names of our future children. Each moment we shared allowed us to get to know and understand each other on several different levels.

Even the tragic moments.

Several months after we started dating, we adopted a cat that had suffered a broken back and was left with nerve damage. We referred to him as the BBC, short for "Broken Back Cat," and aptly named him, Union Jack, after Great Britain's flag. It seemed appropriate given that BBC was the official television network of the United Kingdom. I even named a character in my screenplay after him. To us, though, he was affectionately known as Jack.

The morning after Christmas, while we were at my parent's home, Kristy hurried into my room and woke me up in a panic. She held Jack in her arms and cried hysterically.

"Something's wrong with Jack!"

Kristy told me she thought she startled him as he ate, which caused him to choke. We immediately hopped in my car and headed to the end of the street, where Saint Francis Animal Hospital was located. It was less than half a mile away. As soon as we ran into the building, one of the vet techs took Jack from us and rushed into the operating room. All Kristy and I could do was wait. A short time later, the head veterinarian and family friend told us that Jack was dead.

Kristy collapsed into my arms. We both cried.

The vet told us Jack had most likely suffered a small seizure that caused him to aspirate on a piece of cat food. The seizure was most likely due to his pre-existing condition, which, in her opinion, also included neurological damage. He had not choked from being startled. However, I don't think Kristy ever accepted that diagnosis, and always felt she was directly responsible for his death. She told me about the utter hopelessness and guilt she felt when Jack frantically scurried around the room after he had eaten the cat food, and finally looked at her with complete fear in his eyes as if begging her to save him.

A traumatic event such as the loss of a pet, can either drive two people apart or bring them closer together. It brought Kristy and me closer together. Months after we lost Jack, we drove to Paws & Whiskers cat shelter to adopt another cat. The ironic thing is that I was never much of a cat person; however, I had grown to love Jack, especially after seeing how happy he made Kristy. It made sense to get another one. I can't remember, but I might even have been the one who suggested it.

It didn't take long for us to come across a tiny kitten who shared a cage with its sibling. They had both been found in a dumpster. They even looked like Jack. We chose the female, stuck with the British theme, and named her Kingsly, short for Kings Lynn, the name of a London suburb. We both anticipated a future full of joy with Kingsly.

I also knew that a future full of joy was in store for Kristy and me. There was so much more that awaited the two of us, and I didn't want to waste another second delaying what I knew to be inevitable. It was time to marry her. Almost a year had passed since I first met Kristy, and our relationship had blossomed into a beautiful companionship full of deep love that brimmed with a genuine friendship neither of us had ever experienced.

"I love you," I would tell Kristy.

"I love you more," she'd reply.

Kristy was convinced that she would be the one to propose to me. On several occasions, she told me of her plans to one day ask me to marry her. And while it warmed my heart, I knew that I wanted to be the one to ask her to spend the rest of her life with me.

A few days before the first anniversary of when we met, I asked Kristy Costell to be my wife.

Initially, I planned to propose to her on our first night together in Winchester, Virginia, where I had accepted a job as a Senior Product Manager with Trex, a manufacturer of composite decking products. The position would be a great career move for me but required relocation to a new city more than 400 miles away. Kristy agreed to quit her job and move with me. We arranged for a farewell gathering with our friends at a bar in downtown Toledo. It would be the last time Kristy would see many of her friends for quite some time. I wanted her to be able to celebrate her engagement with her friends, so I decided to propose earlier than planned.

I visited her parents, stood in their kitchen, and asked her father for his permission. I promised them I would take care of Kristy and they could trust me with their daughter's heart. Although her parents had expected we would one day marry, they were relieved to know it was now on the immediate horizon, especially since she had decided to leave Toledo with me.

The day finally arrived when I would pop the question. After Kristy left for work that morning, I hurriedly set about to empty my apartment. It was a mess, with most of my possessions stuffed into boxes that were strewn everywhere in anticipation of moving a few days later. I could barely navigate through the place without bumping into something. By early evening, the place looked immaculate. Everything had been crammed into the garage except the couches and a coffee table. On the coffee table, I placed some candles, a bottle of wine, and two wine glasses.

And a book I had made for Kristy.

Her favorite book was, *Oh, the Places You'll Go!* by Dr. Seuss. I had rewritten the entire book to tell our story. How we had met, the things we had done together, the future we had talked about, were all part of the prose. I even held to the original anapestic tetrameter tone Dr. Seuss used.

The last line asked Kristy to marry me.

It moved later into the evening, and I called Kristy repeatedly to find out when she expected to come home. Little did I know how badly her day had gone. The realization of everything that had recently happened in her life had suddenly decided to hit her head on, and she was overwhelmed by all the events that took place.

She had quit her job, decided to leave her friends and say goodbye to her family, and move away from home for the first time. Furthermore, she had no guarantee what her future held with me. She was an emotional mess by the time she pulled into my driveway. She sat in her car a while, and I just figured she was on the phone with someone. I had no idea that as she lingered behind the wheel, she had prayed to God and implored him for a sign that she'd made the right choice to move to Virginia with me.

Her sign awaited her as she unlocked the door and stepped inside the barren candlelit apartment. I emerged from around the corner, dressed in a suit with Kingsly in my arms. I asked Kristy to sit down on the couch. In the CD player, I had queued up her favorite song, "Tiny Dancer" by Elton John. The song played and its melody filled the room.

I sat next to her on the couch and read aloud the book I had constructed. By the time I finished, she had tears in her eyes, still unsure of what exactly this all meant. That was until I got down on one knee and produced a diamond engagement ring.

I asked her to marry me.

She said yes.

The next song started to play. It was "My Best Friend" by Tim McGraw, which would end up being the song we had our first dance to at our wedding a year later. Days after I proposed, Kristy, Kingsly, and I journeyed south of the Mason-Dixon Line, where the next chapter of our lives waited to be written.

# TEN

# KEYS TO THE KINGDOM

Planning a wedding, purchasing a first home, starting a new job, and moving can be some of the most stressful things one will experience in life.

At least according to psychologists.

Granted, they may not be at the top of the list, like divorce or suffering a major illness or injury, but they can be daunting events. Always up for a challenge, Kristy and I took on all of them in 2006 when we made the move from Ohio to Virginia.

Well, technically West Virginia.

By the time Labor Day rolled around, we were the proud owners of a beautiful, new 3,500 square-foot house in the town of Inwood, West Virginia. Our delightful abode was situated eleven miles north of the Virginia border, located in the Shenandoah Valley, between the Blue Ridge and the Appalachian Mountains. The area was considered part of the metro Washington D.C. area, even though we were seventy miles away. However, several of our neighbors worked in the District.

The area was richly steeped in American history. The town of Harpers Ferry, where the Civil War arguably began, was less than a half-hour away. It didn't take long for it to become a favorite locale of ours, and we often took out-of-town visitors there to enjoy its beauty, culture, and boutique restaurants.

Another favorite pastime of ours was visits to the nearby wineries. My personal favorite was Hillsborough Vineyard, whose views were even more magnificent than its gourmet wines. The vineyard was tucked away in the Blue Ridge Mountains and endless miles of lush, rolling hills provided for a breathtaking backdrop. Its grounds made me feel as if I were thousands of miles away in the French countryside.

Unfortunately, the area we lived in also lent itself to several limitations. It wasn't exactly a booming metropolis, and a lot of creativity was needed on our part to find new and exciting things to do to entertain us. Kristy and I were both social individuals who had an appreciation for the bright lights of a city. We resided in a suburb of metro D.C., but at times felt like we lived smack dab in the middle of Wyoming.

Our second weekend in Winchester was spent in a grocery store parking lot in nearby Stephens City, Virginia, where we celebrated the Fourth of July with other onlookers. Looking for a fun way to partake in the annual Independence Day hoopla I had become accustomed to, we listened to the sounds of the Marshall Tucker Band and watched fireworks from Food Lion's parking lot. The band was too far away to see, and we could only listen to their southern rock ballads from the front seats of my Jimmy.

One of the bittersweet perks of my job at Trex was that I traveled quite a bit. The travel allowed me to escape the confines of Winchester, but it also took me away from Kristy. I hated being away from her. Many of the Trex events that required me to travel were exciting, and I wished I could have brought her along. I know she was less than thrilled when I told her that I would be gone for a week on a Caribbean cruise to entertain some of our valued deck-building contractors.

When the opportunity presented itself to bring Kristy to one of my business events, I did. One of the publications in which Trex advertised was *Forbes.* As a show of recognition and gratitude, I was invited by the publisher to attend an exclusive dinner cruise aboard the Forbes' family yacht, The Highlander. I brought Kristy along to enjoy the wonderful opportunity. No expense was spared as we enjoyed filet mignon, expensive wine, fine cigars, and single-malt scotch. We were given an all-access tour of the vessel, including its overwhelming engine room. We cruised the Potomac River aboard one of the most famous yachts in the world. Along the way we marveled at the multimillion-dollar homes adorning the river's bank, looking forward to the day when we would live in one of our own.

There weren't too many events I could share with Kristy, though. On one occasion, Trex rented out Dallas Cowboys Stadium and hosted a party that included NFL legends Emmett Smith, Randy White, and Drew Pearson. We even hired the famous Dallas Cowboys cheerleaders. The Trex customers certainly loved that!

On another occasion, we spent a week in New Orleans to build houses in the Lower Ninth Ward with Brad Pitt's Make It Right Foundation. It was 2007, two years after Hurricane Katrina, and we helped construct housing for many of the displaced residents. In the day we sweated in the hot sun framing houses, and by night we sweated in the Bourbon Street bars enjoying live music and sweet hurricanes.

As much fun as those experiences were, I would have given anything to have Kristy right there with me. The reality was that I never craved any alone time. Life tasted so much sweeter with her, regardless of what we found ourselves involved in.

In May of 2007, I experienced my first Kentucky Derby when I was invited as a guest of 84 Lumber Company. We spent the day in their hospitality suite, ate gourmet fare, and sipped on mint juleps, then watched the race trackside from club seats situated on the first turn. The Kentucky Derby was a magical moment for me. A daylong event full of horse racing, people watching, celebrity gawking, and pageantry. It was impossible not to get caught up in the excitement that took place at Churchill Downs on the first Saturday in May.

Had I not been an employee at Trex, I don't know if I would ever have attended a Kentucky Derby on my own. But I was hooked on everything about it. The following year I purchased tickets for Kristy and myself to attend. I wanted her to experience all the glitz and glamour the Derby had to offer. Not to mention, she looked breathtaking adorned in her heels, dress, and hat.

Kristy soon also found herself afflicted with Derby fever. On our flight back home to Dulles International Airport, we made plans to attend next year's Kentucky Derby. A tradition had been started, and we had an even more spectacular time than the year before.

Although Kristy's job as a Merck sales rep did not afford her the opportunity to travel out of the area, there was plenty to keep us distracted most of that first year. After all, we had a wedding to plan, which was scheduled to take place the following June in Toledo.

I will admit that I also enjoyed planning the wedding–although I'm sure Kristy would tell you that my fun could be classified more as a type of OCD. I got carried away when it came to the visuals, such as invitations, programs, and the seating chart. I even wrote to the Vatican and received a proclamation from Pope Benedict XVI in which he blessed our upcoming union.

I didn't see the wedding arrangements as work. I was ecstatic for the day I would stand next to her at the altar. Every day I reminded myself how lucky I was to share with her in this magical journey called life. Our future was full of so much promise.

Finally, June 9, 2007, our wedding day, arrived.

Our marriage ceremony took place at Little Flower Catholic Church, in Toledo, where Kristy attended grade school. It seemed fitting for her to celebrate another of the Seven Sacraments in the same place where she had experienced some of the others.

The day couldn't have been more perfect. God blessed our nuptials with beautiful weather, and our closest friends and family were there with us. Luckily, there were no significant snags that prevented anyone from being able to fully appreciate the day, as well as the previous night's rehearsal dinner which had been held in the aquarium section at the Toledo Zoo.

As I waited at the steps to the altar, my heart swelled with an unbelievable feeling of peace, love, hope, and joy. I don't know if I've ever been happier than when the music played, and Kristy's father walked her down the aisle toward me.

"She's all yours now, Scott. Take care of her," Gary said to me.

"I will," I promised.

A short time after that, Kristy and I made the same promise to each other as we exchanged vows. In the presence of God, we pledged to be there for one another through good times and bad times, in sickness and in health, and to love each other until death do us part.

That evening we laughed and danced into the night with 250 loved ones, and the following morning, we caught a flight from Detroit to Cancun, Mexico to celebrate our honeymoon on the Mexican Riviera. Our trip involved a connection at the Fort Myers airport, as our plane was scheduled to continue to Port-au-Prince, Haiti. I joked that our luggage was probably also on the way to Haiti. Later that afternoon our plane touched down in Cancun; our luggage didn't. Fortunately, the resort was like a small city equipped with just about everything, including a gift shop where we purchased the essentials: bathing suits, flip-flops, sunscreen, and a sarong.

Kristy and I couldn't have cared less about the luggage. We were on cloud nine and riding a wave of positive emotions that lost luggage couldn't damper. Neither of us stopped smiling the entire week, even when we toured the Mayan ruins at Chichen Itza on a one-hundred-degree day that caused Kristy to nearly suffer heat stroke.

If we could have stayed in Mexico forever, I think we might have. We both loved the tropical culture and decided to spend our first Thanksgiving as a married couple in Key West, Florida. It was just the two of us, once again in a tropical paradise, enjoying the sun, sand, and seafood. This time we had our luggage.

My career continued to plow forward at full speed. Things worked out well for me at Trex; I soon gained the respect of just about everyone within the company and became recognized as a leader with a promising future. That was also apparent to Ron Kaplan, who assumed the CEO position at the beginning of 2008. Ron was an outsider, brought in to help return the company to a profitable position. He was a no-nonsense guy with an intimidating presence and absolutely no patience for anyone who didn't work hard and buy into his vision.

He liked me from the start.

One evening he invited me to join him for dinner in downtown Winchester. Not one to beat around the bush, he quickly made his intentions known. Specifically, he wanted to know if I was committed to the company and in it for the long haul. It was no secret that Kristy and I weren't exactly thrilled with Winchester and Inwood. Although her job with Merck covered most of the Northern Virginia territory, she had quickly grown disenchanted with the area.

Ron wanted me to assume control of the entire Marketing department and help usher the company into a new era. He then laid a bombshell on me when he told me he had tapped me as his successor and envisioned me as the one to lead the company as its CEO in a few years. I'd barely be in my early forties. However, he wasn't going to invest in me unless I could guarantee him at least a few years before I made any decision about whether to leave Virginia.

"Stay with me, and you'll make a lot of money, and your wife will never have to work," was his direct and straightforward pitch to me.

Ron told me to discuss our conversation with Kristy and then give him my decision. I went home and did just that with my wife. Kristy had the reaction I expected. She didn't want to be in the Winchester area long-term. We wanted to start a family, and she was opposed to doing so where we lived. She sorely missed her family, especially her nieces and nephews. She missed the culture and vibe of a big city. Although we both had great jobs and lived extremely well, this wasn't where she wanted to be.

And frankly, I shared her sentiments.

I promised Kristy that I would continue to look for an opportunity that would allow us to move back to Cleveland, where we both wanted to be. However, it was mid-2008, and the economy wasn't exactly booming with an abundance of high-level leadership positions, especially in Cleveland. Unless there was something that made sense, I wasn't going to take it. It was my responsibility to do what was best for our future, even if it took some time. But we were both eager to settle into a lifestyle that would allow us to start a family.

I told Ron that he could count on me and I was excited about his vision and direction for the company. And I honestly was because I realized I could learn a lot from him. He quickly promoted me to Director of Marketing, the top position in the department, since he was serving as the interim Vice President of Marketing. He intended to promote me into that VP position soon, provided I didn't screw things up as Director.

As the Director of Marketing, not only did my responsibilities increase but so too did the weight of my opinion on strategic decisions that affected the company. I was expected to have an opinion and told to voice it. I was an active participant in the Board of Directors meetings and not afraid to offer my thoughts. I had tremendous respect for Ron. It was clear he planned to groom me to one day receive the "keys to the kingdom," as he had put it.

I had a great thing at Trex. I was in line to become an officer of a publicly traded company. I had a six-figure salary, stock options, a brand-new Lincoln MKX, and a beautiful home–and the company was poised for tremendous success. Not to mention, in a few months I would receive a hefty, six-figure bonus.

By some accounts, I had it all. But I didn't have peace of mind. I had grown obsessed with trying to find a way we could move to Cleveland.

A few weeks after Kristy and I returned from a vacation in the Dominican Republic, I called her while on my lunch break. I told her I felt as though the walls were closing in on me. As she had always done, she was able to calm me down. Kristy had a knack for putting my mind at ease and could always make me feel like it would be okay. One of the things I most admired about her was how calm and relaxed she always seemed in the face of adversity. She told me to put my worries in God's hands. I hung up and removed the Romans 8:18 verse from my wallet and read it a few times, along with a few others I had. I needed to remind myself that God was in control and would look out for the two of us.

The first thing I did when I got back to my office was to listen to my voice mail messages. The first message played. It was from the President of Halex. He had heard about me from his boss, a Group President at Scott Fetzer.

"Scott, I'd like to talk to you about our VP of Sales and Marketing position in Cleveland."

# ELEVEN
# INDEPENDENCE DAY

Waking up the morning of July 3, 2009, felt just as routine as waking up the day before.

It was Friday morning, the start of the Fourth of July holiday weekend. My favorite holiday. Kristy and I both had the day off and looked forward to celebrating our first official Independence Day as Ohio residents once again.

As Kristy awoke, I put the finishing touches on the egg, cheese, and avocado breakfast sandwiches I typically made for us every weekend morning. I poured a cup of coffee for each of us, opened the patio sliding door, and allowed the warm summer breeze to fill the apartment. It was still early in the day, but already beautiful outside.

In a few hours, we would be on the road, headed up to spend the weekend at her family's lake house on Coldwater Lake. We both loved spending time at the cottage. Some of our fondest memories had been spent together on the water at her parent's place.

Coldwater Lake was where I first met Kristy's family. And Coldwater Lake was where Kristy and I had told her family that we were finally moving back to Ohio. Our time at the lake had always provided us with magical moments and fond memories.

Nine months earlier I had accepted a job with a company called Halex, a manufacturer of electrical fittings, as the Vice President of Sales and Marketing. The company was part of Scott Fetzer, owned by Berkshire Hathaway and Warren Buffett. It was the same position as the Douglas Quikut opportunity in Arkansas that had been presented to me years earlier. The big difference, though, was that Halex was in Cleveland, along with a dozen other Scott Fetzer companies.

We had finally done it.

We resided in Cleveland, where we wanted to be, and we both held jobs with tremendous upside potential. Kristy worked as a pharmaceutical sales rep for a company called Merz that manufactured dermatology products.

I had accepted the position with Halex as a springboard to one day lead a company as its President. Scott Fetzer was a strong advocate of cultivating and keeping its leadership within its companies for the long haul. I would have the opportunity to move among several different organizations, all within the Cleveland area, and ultimately end up as a President in the not-too-distant future.

It was a perfect fit for the career that I had worked so hard for up to this point in my life. It was also an ideal fit for us since we talked about trying to have children once the summer was over. At last we knew we could start to build a family without the fear of being uprooted again. We were both happy with where our future was headed, and we both felt that great things were in store for us.

Being back in Cleveland with Kristy had been a wonderful experience for us thus far. I had reconnected with several of my friends from my Toledo days and now I had the opportunity to do things with them on a regular basis. It also gave us the chance to see our families much more frequently.

The years we spent in Virginia away from our families had been especially hard on Kristy. She was extremely close with everyone in her family, including much of her extended family. However, because of how far away we lived, there were several milestones, such as birthdays, first Communions, and other types of events, that Kristy was not able to witness. Being an active part of her nieces' and nephews' lives was extremely important to her.

Now she was doing just that, and it made her extremely happy, and her bliss delighted me as well. I was grateful to God for the way He had guided me. And it wasn't just the past few years.

I reflected on my life and felt a deep sense of gratitude and appreciation for all the opportunities I had encountered throughout my short time on this planet. Some were due to serendipity, but many more were because of hard work, a supportive and loving family, my faith in myself, and, especially, in the Lord.

I had been blessed with many gifts in my life, and the greatest was Kristy. Although we had just celebrated our second wedding anniversary, I reminded her that I was more in love with her now than ever. Three weeks earlier Kristy and I had enjoyed a Tuesday dinner at Pier W restaurant in Lakewood, Ohio. We were there to celebrate twenty-four months of marriage and had chosen the restaurant because of its exquisite views of Lake Erie and the Cleveland skyline. Plus, the food wasn't bad either.

My mom surprised us with a pre-ordered bottle of champagne. As she enjoyed the sweet bubbly, Kristy remarked that champagne was going to be her new drink. It was those simple and innocent comments that always struck a chord and warmed my heart.

I couldn't imagine my life without her in it.

A few nights before the Fourth of July we drove home late one night along Lake Road. As its name suggests, the street runs parallel to Lake Erie, blanketed on its north side by stellar million-dollar homes, with views that allow owners to gaze out across the magnificent body of water. I pulled my Lincoln into the Huntington Beach parking lot. A lot of memories had been formed at the beach, going back to my high school days, but I was about to make my best one yet.

Kristy and I both felt giddy from a few cocktails, ignored the park's "no visitors after dark policy," held hands, and bounced down the stone steps that led to the sandy beach below. I felt like I had entered a different world as I stepped off the last stone and onto the soft sand. Thoughts of vacations, God-painted sunsets, and Bob Marley melodies invaded my soul. Whenever I found myself near the water, I found freedom from the everyday stress of life that sometimes bound me like a pair of cheap handcuffs.

Massive, lake-washed stones formed an abutment that stretched out into the lake. Worry cast aside, Kristy and I walked out along the stone pier until we reached its end. We wrapped ourselves in each other's arms and beheld the glow of the city skyline that spread across the water.

*Thank you, God, for my life. Thank you for Kristy. Thank you for working things out.*

After several minutes we traced our steps back toward the beach, found a spot tucked under the trees and their nighttime shadows, heeded the spontaneous feeling of love and mischief that had drifted into our consciousness, and made love in the sand.

As we left the park, I noticed a cop car idled across the street.

"He's going to pull us over," I told Kristy.

Barely out of the parking lot, we saw red and blue flashers in the rearview mirror. I immediately pulled my vehicle to the side of the road and retrieved my West Virginia driver's license from my wallet. My inner salesman took over, and I struck up a friendly conversation with the cop. I explained that I was back in town visiting, hence my West Virginia license and plates. Although I had been living in Cleveland for nine months, I had yet to update my driver's license or plates. I apologized for being on the beach after hours. We just really wanted to see the city lit up at night.

He let us off, not even an obligatory warning.

We rolled the windows down, opened the moonroof, turned up the stereo, and drove back to the apartment. We were in a carefree mood, full of natural restlessness and wonderment, kids at heart who looked forward to the Independence Day fireworks in a few days.

The Fourth of July weekend presented a much-needed break for me. I had put in long hours at work and needed some downtime. A few days at the lake house would be the perfect elixir to help me decompress. Whenever I found myself stressed it always seemed like some time near the water was the perfect antidote. In a few months, Kristy and I would be in Destin, Florida. I had purchased airline tickets and booked a week for us at our timeshare so we could hang out with my friend, Rick, and his wife on the Panhandle's white sandy beaches. Until then, however, a couple of days on Coldwater Lake was just what the doctor ordered.

Before we left the apartment, I made sure to water the tomato plants on our balcony. The green tomatoes were starting to show a red hue, and I wasn't about to neglect them. I was proud of my tomatoes. The drive up to the cottage was another opportunity to roll down all the windows, slide back the moonroof, and turn up the radio so we could belt out songs together and enjoy the feeling of freedom the highway delivered. Kings of Leon, Bob Marley, and Jimmy Buffett sang to us from the dashboard speakers. And we sang back. Life was good.

Lately, though, Kristy needed to remind me of that. Although I was happy with where my life was, as was my nature, I found it nearly impossible to allow myself to relax and be content. I lived life at breakneck speed, filled with a need for adventure. Things were different since I'd matured and entered the professional arena. There were no planes to leap from, bulls to ride, or magnificent sport fish to haul in, and I missed that. Instead, I now measured my worth in terms of promotions, bonuses, and salary increases.

I had done remarkably well for myself, and admittedly, I knew most people my age weren't fortunate enough to be in a similar position. However, I still experienced a tinge of buyer's remorse when it came to my current employment situation. On several occasions, I questioned the decision I had made to leave Trex. I left a lot of money and career opportunity on the table when I chose to move us back to Cleveland. And although I was confident I made the right decision, thoughts of what might have been still crept into my head.

Kristy knew I struggled with that decision lately, but she was always able to help align my perspective, calm me down, and help me appreciate what we did have. On our way to the lake she did what she did best–reminded me to keep the proper perspective.

"You know, Scott, sometimes you're always in such a hurry to get to the next thing that you fail to appreciate the present. You need to just let yourself slow down and enjoy the moment. Sometimes it's okay to take a breather, be still. Life's too short."

Whenever I told myself the same thing, it never carried weight, but it was always loud and clear coming from her. I needed to learn to relax more and stop trying to plan everything out so much that I missed out on the beautiful present taking place before me. Slow down. Stop. Be still.

*God, thank you for this woman in my life. I don't know what I would do without her.*

By midafternoon we arrived at the outlet shops in Angola, Indiana. Our first stop was at the Gap outlet, where I was excited to find a navy blue, zip up, hooded sweatshirt. It reminded me of the hoodie that Matthew McConaughey wore in the movie *Fool's Gold*, about a young couple who search for buried treasure off the coast of Key West. It had played on TBS for the previous two weeks. Maybe it was the beautiful scenery, the idea of a career as a treasure seeker, or the feeling of adventure the water provided, but as I paid for the sweatshirt, I felt freedom course through my veins. I knew in a few hours I too would be in the water.

The final stop was to purchase a Mega Millions lottery ticket since somewhere deeply embedded in my crazy brain was the insane notion that I might win the thing and be able to build Kristy and myself the dream house we always wanted. Right on the water.

Perhaps that day was finally going to be our lucky day.

Coldwater Lake, located in Coldwater, Michigan, is about twenty miles north of the Indiana border. The body of water covers more than 1,600 acres and provides its visitors with a whole slew of recreational activities. Whether boating, swimming, bike riding or just hanging out, Kristy and I always had a fantastic time at the lake. I was genuinely excited as I pulled my MKX into her parent's driveway and shut off the engine.

It didn't take long to settle in and feel right at home. I always felt that way with the Costells. The whole family was up for the weekend, as well as the dogs, Gracie and Eddie. They knew how much I loved them. Gracie, a beautiful German shepherd, always greeted me with a tennis ball, and I was always happy to oblige her request for a game of fetch.

But I especially savored the time to hang out with my niece, Avery, and nephews, Colin and Ryan. Colin was the oldest and we immediately bonded when we first met. He looked up to me as an uncle, even before it was ever official. Ryan and I always had a special connection because we shared the same birthday. But lately, Avery, the youngest, and I had struck up a special relationship. She was always happy to see me, and it was impossible not to be in a great mood when she ran up, smiled, and called me, "Uncle Scott."

It didn't take long before Avery, Gracie and I were goofing around on the back lawn that overlooked the lake. I would've stayed out there the rest of the afternoon had it not been for dinner. Karen had made her world-famous Chili Mac, and I wasn't about to pass that up.

I filled my plate and sat outside with Kristy and her father. After we had finished, Kristy headed into the house. A few minutes later she came out and informed us of the discouraging news she just read on

The Weather Channel's website.

"You're never going to believe this," she said, "but they're saying it's supposed to rain later this evening and the rest of the weekend."

No way. There wasn't a hint of a storm in the sky. It was a gorgeous shade of blue with a few puffy, white clouds scattered in as though for artistic effect. I went inside the cottage and checked the forecast on the computer. The Weather Channel confirmed Kristy's comments: cloudy with thunderstorms. It was hard to believe, but I figured the weatherman knew more than I did so I went upstairs and changed into my bathing suit. I didn't want to miss a chance to get a swim in before the storms.

A few minutes later I made my way down the concrete stairs embedded in the hillside and strolled toward the end of the wooden pier where the boat was anchored. I took off my shirt and tossed it into the boat.

The hot summer sun felt terrific as it beat down on the back of my neck and shoulders. The intoxicating sounds of motorboats whirring across the water filled the air. The Independence Day holiday, the best time of year, was in full swing. And all my worries, even if just for a few days, were hundreds of miles away.

I took two strides toward the lake and stretched out my arms in front of me as I prepared to dive in, just like I had done ever since I first learned how to dive all those years earlier at the YWCA. My feet pushed off the weathered wooden planks, and with a smile on my face, I dove into the warm Michigan water and altered the course of my life.

Forever.

The sudden impact of the bottom of the lake left no doubt about how hard I smashed my head. Although soft underfoot, I careened into the sand with such intense force that it felt like I head-planted into solid pavement. The lake water did nothing to impede my body's momentum.

There was a loud crack, the kind of sound logs make in a

campfire. A warm twinge immediately followed the sudden crunch. Like the feeling one gets when twisting an ankle.

The horrific realization of what that "crack" signified instantly sent my brain into overdrive. I knew right away that I had broken my neck, and that in the blink of an eye I had incurred the most severe of injuries.

It was beyond surreal. Never in my life had reality hit me so hard.

My mind immediately tried to understand how this had happened. I had dived from this exact spot many times in the past but had never even come close to scraping the bottom.

*Did I not dive out far enough from the dock?*

*Was the water that much shallower than two weeks ago when I stood in the same spot, and it reached past my waist?*

*Had the lake dried up that drastically in two weeks?*

As much as I wanted to replay in my mind what just happened in the hopes that I could magically alter the inevitable outcome, there was no time to think about the past anymore. It was gone. There was no "do over".

And so too was the future. There was no denial or escape from the fact that I would be dead in moments.

The only thing I knew for sure was that now I was floating face down in the shallow water, and as hard as I tried to move something, anything, nothing worked. My body wouldn't listen to me.

I was paralyzed.

All I felt was the cool water on my face as I stared at the soggy bottom of the lake. It taunted me, invited me to reach out, touch it and push off from it. I could not turn over no matter how hard I tried. I was condemned to stare at the muddy sand and dirty rocks as the final images I would take with me from this world.

All I heard was the sound of my heart beating. At first, it was a rhythmic pulse, but as the gravity of the situation took hold my heart started to beat faster and louder. The loud pounding of my most important muscle filled the entire lake. Its beat was deafening. My heart was now beating so fast that a heart attack seemed imminent. I felt as though it would explode from the extreme overdose of adrenaline viciously pumping through my veins. There was no way my body could keep up with the frenetic pace of my heart.

Seconds earlier, the world had been my oyster and I'd had everything going for me. I had my life with Kristy all planned out. I thought I had control over my destiny. Now I was face down in a lake, unable to move or breathe, and no one was around to help me. My body floated on the water's surface and waited for death to take over.

It's amazing how quickly the world can change.

The realization of what happened to me was now as clear as the overhead sky I had looked at minutes earlier. I was so afraid, terrified that this was the end. I couldn't differentiate the tears streaming from my eyes from the lake water that blanketed my face. It was time to accept the cruel fate that had just been handed to me.

At some point during our lives, we might find ourselves wondering what death will entail. How will we die? When will we die? Will we feel anything? Regardless of the questions we may ask, or some vague notion of what we might comprehend, nothing can ever prepare someone for the incredible clarity that comes with knowing you are moments away from your death.

The clarity I was now experiencing was more horrific than anything I had ever encountered in all my time on earth. Although everything had happened in a nano-second, the excruciating thought of impending doom moved agonizingly slowly. Tremendous feelings of fright, panic, and regret immediately set in.

An overwhelming sense of guilt engulfed me as I realized what I had just done. Not only had I altered the entire course of my life in a millisecond, but I had also changed Kristy's fate as well. I felt selfish, like I had just torn apart all our dreams with no regard for what she might have had to say about the matter. I would never get the chance to raise a family and grow old with her. I would never be able to touch her face or hold her in my arms again. I felt so ashamed for having just shattered my neck. I would no longer be able to keep my promises to her.

And then came the sadness.

Of all the emotions I felt, the strongest sentiment I encountered was that of sadness. My mind processed what felt like thousands of thoughts per second, all of which led back to unbearable grief. There was no one to say goodbye to, no one to say I love you to one more time.

All I could do was die alone. Paralyzed. And wet.

Suddenly, an image of my four-year-old nephew, Ryan, popped into my head. He was sitting on the dock and would recognize that something was wrong and run for help. Surely, he would be able to find someone right away to help drag me out of this watery grave and get me on to dry land. I would be able to breathe again, and the precious oxygen I craved would fill my lungs once more.

But Ryan was not sitting on the dock and would not save me. He was up in the house with everyone else. I realize now that the image of him watching me float in the water was most likely the early stage of hypoxia that had begun to set in.

Who knows what the worst way to die is, but drowning is as ghastly as one might imagine. Usually, by the time most people drown they are exhausted from the inordinate amount of energy they exerted as they flailed and fought to stay afloat. I did not have that chance to fight, and instead succumbed to the exhaustion of the thoughts that raced around in my head. I was unable to move anything as my muscles refused to cooperate with my thoughts.

This was the end.

The sheer terror of knowing exactly how and when I was going to die was a horrific reality to face. And yet there I was, about to be swallowed up by death in less than three feet of water.

I had read accounts of near-death experiences where individuals claim their lives flashed before their eyes. Multitudes of thoughts flashed before my eyes. But it wasn't the life I had already lived. It was the life I would never live. The things I would never do. The people I would never say goodbye to, never say I love you to. The children I would never have.

And Kristy.

There would be no more butterfly kisses with my best friend.

As millions of unwritten tomorrows with Kristy teased my thoughts, the deafening sound and frenetic pace of my heart's final beats were impossible to ignore.

*I'm going to die of a heart attack.*

There was no way to avoid it. My heart beat too fast and too loud to sustain itself any longer.

It was a matter of moments before I would find out if I were destined for Paradise with Jesus Christ or eternal damnation with the devil. I had tried to live a good life, though it had been far from perfect. Nonetheless, I was terrified of what was happening. I had never felt more petrified, more dispirited, or more alone.

I prayed.

*Dear God, I'm sorry for my sins. Please watch over Kristy and keep her safe and protected since I will no longer be able to. Please watch over my family. Let everyone know that I love them. Please accept me into Heaven.*

And then there was nothing left to do. The culmination of thirty-three years of life was seconds away from being snuffed out like a candle in a storm. There would be no final words, no fanfare, and certainly no ceremonious ride off into the sunset.

There was only death. A terrifying, sad, and wet death.

I told myself there was only one thing left to do that would allow me to escape the suffering I was in–something from a scene I once saw in a movie.

I opened my mouth and swallowed as much water as I could. The water I once loved, I now loathed as it flooded into my lungs. It felt like a scalding hot poker had been shoved down my throat as it continued to flow into my body with no means to shut off the spigot. I have no recollection of how many horrifying breaths it took of me inhaling the water to stamp out my consciousness, but it felt like an eternity.

Everything went dark. I no longer heard my heart beating.

My eyes closed for what I thought was the last time.

I had drowned myself.

# PART TWO

# TWELVE

# THERE'S BEEN AN ACCIDENT

It was late Friday afternoon when the telephone rang at my parents' house in Strongsville, Ohio.

My mom, who was busy vacuuming the foyer rug, would later tell me she had just finished saying a quiet prayer to God minutes earlier, in which she reflected on how blessed our family was to be safe and in such good health.

She answered the phone. It was Kristy's sister, Angie, on the other end.

"Bobbi, there's been an accident."

After hearing what had transpired, my mom began to hyperventilate. She made Kristy's sister remain on the phone as she ran from the house, hopped in the car, and frantically drove down the street and found my dad who had taken the dog for a walk. Immediately, she handed him the phone.

Over the next several hours, my parents scrambled to get things in order. They packed some clothes and boarded Rusty, the family dog. At 2 a.m. they got in the car and drove the more than 250 miles to the hospital in Kalamazoo, Michigan.

Kristy had been the one who found me floating face down in the water. She was up in the house and heard a splash as I dove in. She glanced out the window when she heard one of the dogs, Eddie, bark at something. Unbeknownst to me, Eddie had followed me down to the dock. She noticed me motionless in the water. At first she thought I was fooling around, but moments later her intuition warned her that something was wrong.

She darted from the house down to the edge of the dock. She stood there for a second, tried to get a handle on what happened, and came to the immediate conclusion that I needed help. Without hesitation, she plunged into the water, fully clothed in jeans and a T-shirt, and swam to where I was afloat. When she reached my body, she lifted my head from the water and turned me over. She heard water gurgle from my mouth and watched in horror as my eyes rolled back in my head and the color disappeared from my face.

Kristy screamed for her nephew at the top of the hill to call 911. She continued to yell for help, pleading for anyone within earshot to rush to my aid. A nearby neighbor heard her terrified shouts pierce the late afternoon calm. He swam over to her as she dragged my body across the surface of the water toward the boat landing. Once he reached her, he helped her lift me onto the wooden planks of the dock.

It didn't take long for pandemonium to break out. Several folks had assembled on the dock to assist in whatever way they could. Kristy pleaded over my lifeless body for me to wake up. Her sister, Angie, an intensive care nurse, quickly joined the chaos. She dropped to my side and began life-saving measures.

No one had any idea what had happened. For all they knew, I could've suffered a heart attack, a stroke, or a myriad of other things. A broken neck was the last thing anyone suspected. However, it was clear I was in dire need of medical attention. The most pressing issue was that I had no pulse and was not breathing. Angie started to perform CPR and was soon assisted by another neighbor, also a registered nurse. Over a dozen people had gathered on the dock to help in whatever way they could.

Although multiple calls were made to emergency services, it took longer than it should have for them to arrive. Through a cruel twist of fate, the paramedics headed to the wrong side of the lake due to the poorly designated GPS mapping of the rural area. Fortunately, those who were present worked to keep me alive. I will forever be grateful and indebted to Kristy, Angie, and everyone else who assisted their efforts. And of course Eddie, the dog.

By the time the EMS technicians did reach me, Kristy was in the throes of a nervous breakdown, physically and emotionally distraught. She repeatedly became sick to her stomach as she tried to comprehend what had transpired. As the rescue workers relieved Angie and continued to administer CPR, one of them noticed I had an erection, a condition known as priapism, which often results from injury to the spine. It was at that point he concluded I had suffered some neck and spine trauma and was in critical need of advanced care.

The paramedic team worked quickly to keep me breathing, maintain a pulse, and stabilize my body. They placed me onto a stretcher, carried me up the embankment, and loaded me into the back of the ambulance. Once en route to ProMedica Coldwater Regional Hospital, the local emergency facility, the paramedics radioed ahead for a life flight transport to a Level I trauma center.

A short time later I was flown via helicopter by the West Michigan Air Care medical transport team to Bronson Methodist Hospital in Kalamazoo, in hopes that they could properly address the severity of my injury. While in the air I needed to be intubated to breathe since I could no longer perform the once-simple task on my own.

Upon touching down on the hospital's helipad, I was wheeled into the emergency room and prepped for surgery. Once in the ER the endotracheal tube inserted into my windpipe during transport was confirmed for proper placement, and I was connected to a ventilator. A nasogastric tube, known as an NG tube, was inserted through my nose, down my throat, and into my stomach to allow medicine to be administered. A urinary catheter was inserted through my penis into my bladder so I could go to the bathroom. Finally, a small catheter was inserted into my artery to monitor blood pressure and arterial blood gases. After the "prep work" was completed, the necessary x-rays and CT scans of the head, spine, chest, abdomen, and pelvis were conducted.

The human spine is one of the most oft-studied and fascinating subjects on the entire planet. It is comprised of thirty-three vertebrae with a series of nerves intertwined throughout. The spinal cord itself is divided into thirty-one nerve segments, each specific and deliberate in the function they provide. There are eight cervical nerves, twelve thoracic nerves, five lumbar nerves, five sacral nerves, and the coccyx area. In general, the higher the level of injury, the more function a person will lose, with cervical injuries resulting in the most devastation.

The findings of my x-rays and CT scans were startling and cause for grave concern. The radiographic studies revealed that I had suffered an atlanto-occipital dislocation (AOD), cervical fractures of the C2, C3, and C4 vertebrae, as well as fracture dislocations at the C3, C4, and C5 vertebrae.

AOD is also known as an internal decapitation, or orthopedic decapitation. It is an extremely rare medical condition in which the skull separates from the spinal column during severe head injury. In most cases it is fatal.

My head had careened into the lakebed with such force, and at such an angle, that my neck had snapped apart, bending itself into a grotesque forty-five-degree displacement. Honestly, I should have died on impact. This obscene deformation of my upper spinal column resulted in the fracture dislocations that damaged the spinal cord nerves and caused my cervical vertebrae to abnormally separate from one another.

The odd thing was that there weren't even any cuts or scratches to be found anywhere on my head.

Not only was I going to require a highly complicated and intense procedure to reattach my head to my neck, but I was also going to need an exceptionally skilled surgeon to perform the operation. To make matters worse, it was the middle of the night during a holiday weekend, a time when many doctors were away with their families. The physician on call that night was Dr. Bratislav Velimirovic, MD, a board-certified neurosurgeon formerly from Belgrade, Serbia with over twenty years of experience.

In the waning hours of July third, I was wheeled into the operating room, and my fate was placed in the trusted hands of Dr. V. The impossible task he was faced with would test his complete repertoire of faculties, education, and experience to the extreme. Over the next several hours a series of complex procedures was performed.

An anterior cervical discectomy and fusion was performed at the C4 and C5 levels to relieve pressure on my spinal cord and the nerve roots, as well as stabilize my spine. The doctor cut into my throat, moved aside the neck muscles, trachea, and esophagus, and removed the damaged disc. He then inserted a bone graft where the disc had been and secured it in place with a metal plate and some screws.

A cervical laminectomy that stretched from the C1 to the C5 level was also performed. The operation was done from the back of my neck to remove the bony roof of the spinal canal and soft-tissue that were compressed. It also relieved pressure on my spinal cord and nerves.

After he completed the proper steps to alleviate the pressure on my cervical nerves, the crucial element of reattaching my head and neck needed to happen. A posterior spinal fusion from the base of my skull, or occiput, all the way down to the C6 vertebra was required. Bone grafts were placed along the sides of the cervical vertebrae to fuse.

The real coup de grace was the two titanium rods that were embedded inside my neck to provide further stability. Six small holes were bored into my skull, and the rods were rooted in place, each one anchored by three screws drilled into a flattened piece of metal affixed to the end of each rod. The rods extended from the occiput bone at the base of my skull down along the six uppermost cervical vertebrae and were fastened to the bones of my vertebrae on each side with more screws. In total, two titanium rods, a metal plate, fourteen screws, and several bone grafts were used to reconstruct my neck.

Talk about a headache.

The marathon surgery took more than ten hours to complete. Afterward, my neck was wrapped in a hard, plastic neck brace known as a Miami collar. This collar would later prove to be the bane of my existence.

Once the surgery was over, Dr. V. met with Kristy. The good news, he proceeded to tell her, was that I survived the taxing surgery. Unfortunately, there wasn't more good news. He informed her of the extent of my injuries and asked if she knew of any pre-existing conditions I might have had, due to the severity of the damage. She knew of none. He tried his best to communicate to her just how destructive the damage to my neck had been.

"In all my years, this is in the top three of the worst injuries I have ever seen," he told Kristy.

He told her he had done everything he could to ensure I had the best fighting chance. He proceeded to state that he was a man of faith and believed God had worked through his hands during the operation. I think those words helped Kristy find some solace in the face of an extremely daunting situation.

A lot of things went wrong for me that day, but fortunately, having Dr. V. on call was something that went right.

After the surgery, I was moved to the intensive care unit, where I could be closely monitored, as the next several days would be critical to my survival. My parents arrived at the hospital later that morning and were greeted by the unsettling appearance of their battered son hooked up to a myriad of machines, tubes, and wires.

I wasn't much to look at.

I lay on a hospital bed, naked, save for the pale blue gown that loosely covered my midsection. A damp washcloth stretched across my forehead as a futile attempt to help keep me comfortable. Small pieces of white tape held the NG tube jammed in my nose in place, and a large, plastic breathing tube shoved down my throat provided my body the oxygen it needed. My neck was firmly encased in the hard collar, while some plastic inflatable thing that looked like a pool flotation device was draped around my shoulders. My tanned skin was punctuated with pieces of tape, numerous electrical leads, and several needles. Inserted into my torso was a PEG tube for feeding, as well as a chest tube to drain excess fluid. There was a blood pressure cuff wrapped around my bicep, intertwined with a PICC line, IV lines, and more needles, which all vied for their piece of precious real estate on my arm. My finger was adorned with a pulse oximeter to gauge my blood oxygen levels. The catheter that extended from my penis was attached to a plastic bag that hung on the bed rail to collect urine. Finally, inflatable compression pumps were tightly wrapped around my lower legs to guard against edema, phlebitis, and blood clots.

My body was a tangled mess, stuffed full of tubes, hoses, and wires, plugged into high-tech beeping machines and computers, each doing its part to provide some critical function my body could no longer do on its own. Unfortunately, it's an image still lodged somewhere in my parents' minds today. I can't imagine what it must be like for a parent to see their child lying in bed looking the way I did.

A few hours later my sister, Lindsey, arrived at the hospital. My parents met her outside the room and wouldn't let her come in because she was so upset. They didn't want her crying in front of me, for fear that it might upset me. However, at that point, I was so sedated and oblivious to everything that I don't think I would have noticed. Ironically, once my sister entered the room, she felt a calmness.

Something about seeing me asleep with my eyes closed soothed her.

Later, my family went to the hospital's chapel to pray. Over the next couple of weeks my family would wear out a path from my ICU room to the chapel to the Ronald McDonald House they stayed in across the street. Occasionally, small respites for food were sprinkled in to break up the wearisome routine. However, all anyone could do was wait and pray. Wait and pray.

I would need a lot of prayers going forward.

Although I had survived the surgery, I was nowhere near out of the woods, and it didn't take long for the onslaught of complications to pile up. During the marathon surgery, I had developed a pressure sore on my coccyx due to lying on the operating table in the same position for so long. The sore presented concern since it could lead to sepsis. Every two hours nurses repositioned my body to alleviate the pressure my body weight placed on it.

And then there was the risk of pneumonia.

Because I was no longer able to cough, breathe, or even speak on my own, I had no way to dislodge any of the mucus, secretions, and other irritants that accumulated in my airway. Not to mention, I had swallowed an excessive amount of filthy lake water, which had deposited a host of bacteria and other nasty stuff in my lungs.

Almost immediately, atelectasis began to occur on a repetitive basis, in which my lungs collapsed and were unable to fully inflate to deliver enough oxygen to the blood. It wasn't just one lung that was affected; it was both lungs–all five lobes. The entire mechanism for distributing oxygen throughout my body was in disarray. My respiratory system ceased working correctly and was no longer able to process and exchange the deadly carbon dioxide gas that amassed inside of me. Pseudomonas pneumonia developed from the atelectasis, which further compounded my breathing issues and my ability to get my body the essential oxygen it craved.

In addition to pneumonia, I developed a pleural effusion and an unusual amount of fluid pooled inside one of my lungs. Multiple bronchoscopies needed to be performed because my lungs were so collapsed. During one of the procedures, the flexible tube that was pushed down into my throat removed a piece of seaweed stuck in my lungs, which was why the doctors felt it necessary to insert a tube into my chest wall to help drain the fluid from my lungs. It was next to the feeding tube that had been implanted through my abdomen and allowed my body to receive nutrition, which consisted of a beige-colored sludge paste injected through a syringe and provided all my meals for the next couple of months.

A tracheostomy was performed shortly after my surgery, and an incision was made in my neck, which allowed a surgical airway to be created in my trachea. A white plastic cannula was then inserted through the hole in my throat to which the ventilator was attached. I was now connected to a cumbersome machine at my bedside that injected intermittent bursts of air into my lungs and permitted me to breathe. Provided the machine went wherever I went, I would continue to be able to breathe.

Even though I had been outfitted with a chest tube to help rid the excess fluid that continued to accumulate, I could no longer generate a cough to clear any debris or phlegm that accumulated in my lungs, so it needed to be suctioned out.

The suctioning process involved removing the ventilator from my trach and inserting a thin plastic tube down my windpipe. The tube was attached to a machine that, when turned on, acted like a vacuum and sucked out the mucus. I hated being suctioned. It felt like I couldn't breathe, and the piece of plastic jammed down my airway just lead to more anxiety. Unfortunately, I needed to be suctioned quite a bit. No pun intended, but it sucked. Besides these measures and medication, I slept on a bed that vibrated at ridiculous levels in an attempt to loosen up the mucus plugs that would develop and jam my airways.

At one point, a doctor commented to Kristy that I was lucky to have been in such great physical shape and cardio health, otherwise I most likely would not have survived the constant barrage of sickness and numerous lung collapses. Interestingly, I had never been a big fan of running, and it wasn't until about six months before my injury that I incorporated it into my exercise regimen. Funny how something that I despised helped save my life.

By the time Kristy had reached me in the water, my heart had stopped beating. Luckily, it started to pump again after I was resuscitated through the lifesaving efforts performed on the dock that day.

However, I had no idea that wasn't the last time I would be brought back to life.

And it never did rain that day.

# THIRTEEN
# HELL DOLL

The initial days that followed my surgery were a blur, blended into one convoluted sequence that left me unable to discern the difference between the minutes, hours, and days.

My sense of time was nonlinear, as if all the events that transpired were tossed into a pillowcase, shaken up, and then randomly removed one at a time and placed on a table in a jumbled order. The main factor that contributed to my inability to make sense of any natural progression was, quite simply, drugs.

It was critical that my body get as much rest as possible to allow itself to begin the healing process. A tremendous amount of swelling had occurred around my spinal cord and this needed to subside before doctors could make a more accurate assessment of my situation. They knew the initial prognosis appeared bleak, but just how bleak was yet to be determined.

To help keep me calm and minimize anxiety, I was heavily medicated with Haldol, an antipsychotic medication typically used to treat schizophrenia and drug-induced psychosis. Unfortunately, the Haldol resulted in more harm than good and launched me into a psychotic state of hallucinations, bizarre happenings, and severe cardiac events.

If there was such a thing as an alternative reality, then I had found it. The strange new world I inhabited was full of constant pain, discomfort, depression, uncertainty, anguish, and every kind of despair one's mind could construct. I had relinquished control of my body, and for all intents and purposes had also ceded control of my thoughts and actions. I was a prisoner trapped in a place I did not know. A passenger on a journey I did not want. The worst part was I didn't know when, or if, it would ever end.

But it was not an alternate reality. It was my reality, my new existence, and there was no "happy place" I could escape to for some slight reprieve. My reality transcended into the torture I was forced to endure, regardless of how hard I tried to ignore it or block it out.

Welcome to hell.

The hell I found myself in was different than what my Catholic upbringing would've led me to envision. My surroundings were off-white painted walls, linoleum floors, and particleboard ceilings infused with plastic-encased florescent lighting that highlighted the banks of beeping machines, monitors, and other devices neatly arranged to keep me alive.

My hell was E-130, a hospital room situated in the East Pavilion of Bronson Methodist Hospital.

Although it was the safest place I could be, my mind was convinced I was in utter peril. There was no sense of time to illuminate how long I had been there, the time of day, or even what day it was. All I knew was that I was scared to death.

On random occasions, without warning, a group of bizarre-looking individuals would enter my room, always in the same order, each donned in the guise of clown makeup. In unison, they approached my bed and leaned in so close I could feel their hot, wretched breath on my face. I watched in sheer terror as their happy faces melted away, their skin dripping off to reveal a much more demonic presence.

They communicated terrible and evil things to me and showed me images of my family and closest friends being murdered. Their rants drove my anxiety through the roof, leaving me to feel even more hopeless and despondent than I already did. They made it apparent that I would never be able to escape the hellhole I believed I was stuck in. I was there for eternity, their little hell doll to torment and do with as they pleased.

After they had their fun with me, I watched as they laughed maniacally and slipped through the walls, back to the netherworld from which they came. Unable to move or speak, I was left to lie in bed in sheer terror awaiting their next visit. Even if I wanted to sleep, there was no escape from the constant dread. I was trapped in an unending nightmare.

My hallucinations also included a group of orderlies, dressed in their hospital whites, who would visit me as they made their rounds. But they weren't there to help. Instead, they too would toy with me like sinister guards in some third-world prison, also telling me they would never let me leave the hospital to reunite with my family. They had devised an elaborate system where they would push a button that silenced my voice and prevented me from communicating my misery and suffering to others.

Perhaps the worst hallucination of all was the twenty-foot-long anaconda, coiled and perched inside the light fixture directly over my bed. The dark snake was so massive that its weight slowly caused the light fixture to begin to crack. A flimsy piece of plastic was the only thing between the snake and my paralyzed body below. Sheer terror flooded through me as I helplessly awaited the inevitable.

*Dear God, please help me.*

The vivid hallucinations and confusion were not just limited to figments of my imagination. At times, my state of puzzlement crossed over from the ether and infiltrated the actual physical presence around me. On one occasion in which I was able to muster enough of a whisper to call for Kristy, I watched as a figure, which I thought was her, approach my bed. She leaned in and asked what I needed. I stared at the face that had responded to my request and had no idea who it was.

"I need, Kristy, my wife," I told her.

"Scott, I am Kristy."

It was Kristy, but I didn't recognize her. It was as if I'd never seen her before in my life.

Unfortunately, I was so weak and my ability to speak was so severely impaired, that I was powerless to let others know what was going on. I had no idea, nor did anyone else, that it was the Haldol that caused my mind to drift back and forth between altered states. I only knew something wasn't right.

I remember a specific experience that seemed like some metaphysical event. As Kristy and a nurse bathed me, my body floated off the bed and hovered several feet above them. I watched as they cleaned me and discussed my situation. The nurse asked Kristy if I had ever given her any indication of what to do should I find myself in this very predicament. Kristy couldn't recall a time in which we had talked about it. Of course, we hadn't. It wasn't exactly the kind of subject matter two people planning a life together think to discuss over dinner. Nonetheless, it was a surreal experience in which I felt even more disconnected from my surroundings, yet at the same time, strangely in tune with what was happening.

During those initial days, my ability to speak was impaired due to the extent of my injury. I moved my lips to say words, but no sound would emit from my mouth. This was incredibly frustrating, as it was difficult to communicate my needs to others. A "blink board" was created to help me express myself. Rows of letters and numbers, written on a board, would be held in front of me. I blinked my eyes until I got to the corresponding letter or number I wanted. For someone such as myself, in which patience was never a strong suit, communicating like that was torture. However, it was the only way.

Kristy spent most nights at my bedside, not wanting to leave in case something happened. One evening, she overheard nurses whisper in the hallway that my room was known as the "miracle room" since the last two patients who stayed in it had miraculously overcome their injuries. She prayed to God to make me the third.

Kristy did whatever she could to involve herself with my care. She assisted with my bed baths, brushed my teeth, combed my hair, and tried her best to help keep me comfortable. She also started to provide updates on my situation through a website called CaringBridge. Each day she chronicled the good, the bad, and the ugly that took place, so friends and loved ones could be kept in the loop. The website also allowed others to post messages of encouragement and leave comments offering their support and prayers.

As word of my accident spread, messages poured in from friends, former and current co-workers, fraternity brothers, grade school classmates, teachers, even people I had never met.

"Keep fighting Scott, the world isn't ready to be without you yet."

"You are the guy who will do more in a year than most of us will do in a lifetime."

"If anyone can come out of this, it's Scott, a guy who's determined and tackles any obstacle that lies in his way. Someone who knows no limits and lives life to the fullest."

Their words of encouragement were also meant for Kristy.

"I'm just about a month away from my wedding and I'm so inspired by the love you two share."

"Kristy, with your and Scott's combined strength, faith, and love you will recover and the two of you will be embarking on a new and exciting adventure together."

My wife read every message to me in hopes they would help lift my spirits. Of course, she was struggling to keep her own hopes up too, so sharing them aloud was a way that we might both remain somewhat positive.

It was tough for Kristy and my family to witness the difficulties I encountered each day. They prayed, hoped, and wanted to believe things would improve despite the impossible odds and gloomy statistics that confronted me.

Six days after my injury the doctor handed my family more devastating news. The MRI results indicated that my spinal cord was severed. The cervical area of my spinal cord where the damage occurred resembled a rope that had been cut leaving two loose and frayed ends. My brain and body could no longer communicate. The highway of nerves that ran throughout my body and controlled such vital functions as breathing, blood pressure, temperature, bowels, bladder, movement, and sensation was destroyed. I had suffered irreversible damage at the C3 level of my spine. He then proceeded to inform them that according to Michigan law, patients on a ventilator who received artificial life support had the right to decide whether they wanted to continue to live.

In a few days, I would be faced with that question.

***

During the brief periods of respite in which I wasn't imprisoned in a zombielike state, I still couldn't escape the comatose feeling that constantly kept me in its grip.

More tests were run that showed my hemoglobin levels to be critically low. I had lost a tremendous amount of blood during surgery and was in dire need of transfusions. Luckily, some of my blood had been saved and was infused back into me, avoiding the need for another foreign substance to invade my body.

My state of haziness was most often interrupted while I was being shuttled back and forth between x-rays, MRIs, and other tests. I'd often awake to find myself strapped to a gurney, being whisked down the hall, watching a steady stream of ceiling lights pass by overhead. Gradually, I became more aware of my surroundings. I knew I was hurt but hadn't yet grasped the magnitude of just how beat up I was. At some point, I asked Kristy if we could go back to the lake because I didn't want to be at the hospital anymore. She explained I was injured, and we would have to wait and see. I was confused and full of sadness, unable to make sense of what was happening. That led to more anxiety, which in turn led to increased levels of anger and frustration.

Ultimately, it all just led to more Haldol.

As I grew more alert, the doctors ordered more things for me to try. One of the exercises was attempting to breathe with just the use of the CPAP settings on the ventilator. The CPAP provided my lungs with extra pressure but forced me to generate my own breaths. The first time I tried, I only lasted fifteen minutes; however, I had produced my own breaths. I got upset, felt as if I could not breathe, and mouthed the words "Put the damn ventilator back on," to my friend Bryan, who had flown in from Boston. The respiratory therapist assured everyone it was a normal reaction since my mind didn't believe I could do it. It would take a lot more practice. Later that evening I tried again. This time it was a completely different story, and I lasted several days on just the CPAP setting.

I began to grow increasingly uncomfortable, not due to the CPAP, but because my body was unable to get any meaningful rest. The hallucinations grew more severe and led doctors to surmise I suffered from "ICU psychosis syndrome." I developed something known as tardive dyskinesia, a side effect of antipsychotic medications, which caused me to contort my face, stick out my tongue, and scrunch my eyes. It looked like I was trying to scratch an itch by wiggling my face, while simultaneously trying to clean my teeth with my tongue. Unfortunately, if not treated, the condition could become permanent. It was difficult for my family to watch the way my body responded to the medications I was taking.

Things also grew increasingly difficult for Kristy. She made daily calls to my cell phone to listen to my voicemail greeting just to hear my voice. She vented in the regular updates she posted on CaringBridge:

"I've been really having a tough time the last few days. I've been mourning so many things. There are no words to express the pain I feel for Scott and for the loss of the life that we once knew. I find myself waking up every day wishing that I could wake up and this nightmare would be over ... I miss my old life SO much. I miss my best friend. I miss his laugh, his smile, his energy, his spontaneous ideas, the way it felt to have his hand squeeze mine, I miss his everything. I feel so angry that he had so much taken from him. I know that I need to stop looking back at all the good I once had in my life and start looking forward at the good to come. I also know that Scott has made remarkable strides so far and I am SO grateful to God for them but I just wish I could take this from Scott somehow. I don't want him to feel any physical or emotional pain. He is such an amazing person. He doesn't deserve this. No one deserves this. Please continue the prayers ... I'm sure God will bless us all with a better day tomorrow."

The following day was not what anyone had hoped for.

# FOURTEEN
# DO YOU WANT TO LIVE?

For the first time in three nights, Kristy stayed in a sleeper room at the hospital. She had not been getting the rest she needed, and the lack of sleep made her even more emotional. Before she left for the evening, she told the nurse to call if I asked for her.

Her getaway was short-lived.

In the middle of the night, Kristy received a call that something was wrong, and it was urgent she immediately get to my room. My heart had stopped at two different times during the night, and each time I had ceased to breathe. The doctors were unsure if it would happen again or if I'd even survive if it did.

Without saying it, the nurses told Kristy to come say goodbye to me.

In a panic, she sprinted to my room. She called my family in hysterics to inform them what had happened. It wasn't long before everyone had congregated in a vigil at my bedside, where a priest administered Last Rites.

The doctors had resuscitated me and stabilized my heartbeat. However, I was incoherent. I needed to be placed back on the ventilator, the CPAP turned off, and I needed to be monitored very closely until they could determine what was wrong. My white blood cell count was extremely elevated, and my eyes were glassy and bloodshot. The doctors feared I had suffered a pulmonary embolism. An electroencephalography, or EEG, was ordered to measure my brain activity since I was unresponsive.

As the doctors and nurses scurried about to get things prepped, Kristy slid a chair next to my bedside, pulled out her iPod, and stuck one of the earbuds in my ear and the other in her ear. She pressed "Play" on the tiny device and the song "I Can Only Imagine" by the Christian group MercyMe played on repeat. It was a song we both loved and had listened to on numerous occasions, but never like this.

Kristy held my hand and gently stroked my head as tears rolled down her cheeks. She prayed to God and asked Him to take care of me as He saw fit. The doctors feared that if my heart stopped again, it would be for the final time. One's heart could only take so much stress over such a short timeframe, and it was unknown how strong my heart was given the current condition I was in. My sister was adamant the doctors continue to revive me if needed.

As the music played, Kristy whispered that I no longer had to fight if I was tired. She understood if God was calling and told me it was okay to let go and join Him in Paradise. Of course, she didn't want to lose me, but she also didn't want me to continue to suffer.

During my stay at Bronson Hospital, I had a vivid dream in which I sat outside in a garden with Kristy. The warm sun fell across our faces as we relaxed in the lush, green space and listened to music. I remember how peaceful I felt as I took in the beauty that surrounded me. I don't remember how I arrived in the garden, nor how long I was there, only that a sense of tranquility existed that I had never experienced before. Although I may never know, I believe it was during that moment with Kristy at my bedside and MercyMe singing in my ears, that the dream occurred. Today, the thought of that dream fills my mind whenever I hear the song.

Eventually, my body stabilized itself, and the natural color returned to my face. Fortunately, the EEG results were normal and showed no signs of brain damage. The doctors concluded I had a severe reaction to the Haldol medication they had been pumping me full of. The drug had caused bradycardia, an abnormally slow heart rate, which led to asystole, the absence of ventricular contractions. In other words, I "flat-lined" and went into cardiac arrest. Asystole is the most severe form of cardiac arrest and is often irreversible due to the total cessation of electrical activity and lack of tissue contractions from the heart muscle, and therefore no blood flow to the rest of the body. Most people who experience it never leave the hospital alive.

The Lord looked out for me that night.

Although they stopped the Haldol, I continued to experience irregular heart rhythms, which prompted more EKG tests. The doctors felt my brain was trying to relearn how to send messages to my heart. The right upper lobe of my lung once again collapsed and an Ambu bag was needed to inflate it.

The effects of the Haldol soon dissipated. Without it, I felt and acted more alert. One of the first things I noticed was how uncomfortable I felt. Although I only had sensation from my neck up, I was in an incredible amount of pain. My head felt like it was being squeezed inside of a vice grip that showed no signs of loosening anytime soon. The plastic Miami collar strapped around my neck irritated the hell out of me, its hard edges dug into the base of my skull with no way to alleviate its awful discomfort. Not to mention, my neck itched constantly, and I had no way to scratch it.

An overwhelming sense of anxiety and depression permeated my mind as I began to comprehend the state of my body. My brain was in overdrive, bombarding itself with sad thoughts of how miserable things would be for me now. Perhaps it was due to the physical pain and anxiety, but I allowed myself to be consumed and swallowed up by my depression. There wasn't one positive thing I could focus on. I was convinced life was over for me, and I wanted to die. I did not want to live like this.

I obsessed over the different ways I could end my life. Since I was unable to move, I needed to convince Kristy to help me. I dreamt up an elaborate scheme that involved injecting rat poison into my IV line so it would course through my veins and snuff out my existence. Surely, I would be able to convince her. I mean, she didn't want to see me in this state either.

Somehow, I had to find a way to kill myself.

When I tried to communicate with others, I quickly became incensed. Not only was it frustrating to blink my words to them, but I also hated the answers they gave me in return. No one could tell me how long I would be like this. Why things were not getting better. When I could go home. For the first time in my life, I felt completely helpless.

Even the cherry tomato plants I had planted earlier that summer at the apartment were no longer mine. I kept going on and on about them. During a trip back to Cleveland, my sister swung by my place and picked several tomatoes off the plant. She brought them back even though she knew I couldn't eat them. She just wanted to do something to try to help me. I don't think it was the tomatoes, but at one point I heard her eating something and snapped at her. It wasn't fair. I also wanted to eat something. Everyone agreed they would not eat within earshot of me anymore.

***

I had been in a hospital bed for twelve days. I was extremely uncomfortable, unable to breathe or move on my own, and full of a depression unlike anything I had ever experienced, when Kristy told me that the doctor needed to speak with me. He had some significant things to discuss and I could either speak with him alone or have people in the room. I requested that just Kristy stay with me. I had never liked being away from her, and now was no different.

An imposing man with thick biceps and a buzzcut entered my room. My mind was still foggy, but clear enough to discern that he was not another hallucination. There was a seriousness about the man who stood at my bedside. Kristy was on the other side, holding my hand that I couldn't feel.

He spoke with a matter-of-fact tone, all business and to the point. He coolly explained what had happened and laid out the facts. The doctor seemed to go out of his way to really drive home the point of just how dire my situation was. He wanted to make certain I fully comprehended its solemnity.

"You will never walk again."

"You will never move anything again."

"You will never breathe on your own again."

"You may never be able to eat or swallow again."

"You will never spend long periods out of bed again."

He didn't even give me a proverbial "one percent chance" of ever moving anything again. Nothing. Never.

I lay there and listened to this stranger tell me my life as I knew it was over. For the rest of my life every day going forward would be a challenge greater than anything I had ever faced.

After listening to him deliver my death sentence, it was now my turn to talk. He asked me if I had any questions.

"Will I be able to hug my wife again?" I asked him.

"No."

"Will I be able to have sex?"

"It's possible. But it will be different from what you're used to."

There was nothing else I wanted to ask. There was nothing left that needed to be asked.

He knew I fully grasped the circumstances. What followed was a question I never anticipated I'd have to answer in my life. However, because I was on a ventilator, being kept alive with artificial means, Michigan law compelled him to ask a question I will never forget.

"Scott, do you want to live?"

What I didn't know, was that earlier that day the gentleman in the room next to me had been asked the same question. He had also suffered an accident that left him paralyzed. With his family and children at his side, he chose to end his life. My family watched as his body was wheeled out of the room, covered in a sheet, while his loved ones cried in each other's embrace. And now a few hours later, my family, save Kristy, huddled together outside my room, helpless, as they awaited my response.

The answer should have been easy. I knew how shitty my situation was. After all, I had orchestrated ways to kill myself over the past few days. I had prayed for this very solution. Yet at that moment something different happened. I thought of how great a life I had lived up until that point. I thought of my family. And I thought of Kristy. I thought of the life I still wanted to have with her. I didn't want to leave her or my family. I loved them too much and wasn't ready to say goodbye.

"Yes. I want to live."

And with that, the doctor left the room.

Although it was my voice, I am convinced that it was the Holy Spirit that gave me the strength to speak those words. God had been with me my whole life and He was there with me that day as well. If I needed a reminder, I only needed to look up on the wall of that hospital room.

Shortly after my accident, Kristy had told her aunt about the Scripture verse I carried in my wallet. The verse I first became aware of when I read of Dennis Byrd's spinal cord injury all those years earlier. Her aunt transcribed the words onto a poster in beautiful calligraphy. The same Bible passage that hung above Dennis Byrd's hospital bed after he broke his neck now hovered over my bed:

"For I reckon that the sufferings of this present time are not worthy to be compared with the glory that shall be revealed in us. – Romans 8:18."

I needed to look no further to know God would be with me on the journey I now faced. The room I was in, affectionately referred to as the miracle room by some of the nurses, had once again lived up to its name.

Kristy was ecstatic with my decision. She kissed my head, told me she loved me, and ran into the hallway to tell my family I had decided to push on and fight. I was exhausted and I passed out.

Shortly after I decided to carry on, I had to give thought to the immediate next steps. This meant choosing a specialized facility I could be transferred to in order to begin my rehabilitation process. Fortunately, Cleveland's MetroHealth Hospital was designated as one of only fourteen Spinal Cord Injury Model Care Centers throughout the country. The choice was easy. Even better, there was availability, and I would most likely be transferred within the next few days.

Unfortunately, I developed another bout of pneumonia. It seemed like whenever I gained even the smallest positive step forward, it was quickly marred with another cruel reminder of the reality I now faced. This revelation pushed me further into a depressive state. I told Kristy we would get through the challenges and things would be great again, as I tried to lift her spirits. However, it was apparent to her that I didn't even believe it myself.

Nonetheless, there was no other choice but to push on. Almost two weeks after I broke my neck, I was loaded onto another medical helicopter for transport. This time, though, the helicopter ride was a bit longer and took me back to Cleveland to begin the next chapter of my life.

## FIFTEEN

# STREETS OF WORRYVILLE

It was late in the evening when we touched down on the helipad at MetroHealth Hospital in Cleveland and I was admitted to the Surgical Intensive Care Unit (SICU).

I was in a relatively good mood, even though it would be the first evening I'd spend alone in the hospital. Kristy and my family were on the road, making their way back from Kalamazoo. However, Kristy called to check in, and I made sure the nurse told Kristy I loved her.

The positive vibes were short-lived. Early the following morning I was assessed by an on-call physician who told me that my injury was at the C2 level instead of the C3 level. This meant it was unlikely I would ever breathe on my own again. The news rocked me. By the time Kristy arrived, I had spiked another fever. My temperature was 103 degrees and I was covered in ice packs.

I immediately told Kristy about my conversation with the doctor. Always one to calm me, Kristy softly explained it was still too early for anyone to determine what kind of long-term recovery or prognosis I would have. She further stated that it was my mind that made me who I was. Even if I never regained the slightest bit of movement or sensation,

I still had more than most people in this world. She made it a point to reiterate that even though my body wasn't what it had once been, it was my mind that she fell in love with. I was her best friend, and she couldn't imagine a life without me. Her words soothed me more than any medication could.

A few hours later I was visited by a team of physicians who would serve as my primary doctors once I was transferred to the spinal cord unit for rehab. They introduced themselves and explained their roles in my recovery. They also did an initial assessment to determine my level of injury. Their assessment was more encouraging as they believed my injury to be C4 Complete. One of the doctors explained that most individuals who experience a spinal cord injury (SCI) would eventually regain at least one level of function. In her opinion, this meant that at some point in the future I would regain the use of my biceps. Kristy and I were both filled with a sudden air of optimism!

As Kristy liked to say, we had now embarked upon "Chapter Two," and it was off to a promising start. For the first time in several weeks when I smiled, she could tell it was genuine and not just me putting on a good face. My voice was still weak, but I sang to her, lip-synching the words of love songs that played on the radio in the room. It warmed her heart to see this side of me again.

The effects of the Haldol were out of my system, and my mind was back to analyzing and operating at warp speed. I wanted to know everything about my injury–what I could expect, how long it would take before I would regain any movement, other people who had experienced a similar injury, and how they had progressed. I mentioned the story of Dennis Byrd and asked Kristy to track down a copy of his autobiography.

A day later, while Kristy was at the apartment getting some things in order, she received a call from one of the doctors. Four of the five lobes in my lungs had collapsed, and my heart rate and blood pressure plummeted into dangerous territories. They had stabilized my heart rate but needed her permission to perform a procedure that would help remove some of the thick mucus plugs that were stuck in my lungs.

Unfortunately, my confidence also plummeted. My body was losing more battles than it was winning. It had only been a couple of weeks, but it already felt like a lifetime. I struggled to find that positive attitude that had been instilled in me from the time I was in diapers.

Once again, I relied on Kristy to help me maintain some sense of calmness. She usually achieved that by reading to me. Her soft, gentle voice quieted my mind and afforded me a little bit of peace, even if only for a short time. She often read the comments posted on CaringBridge. The outpouring of support was incredible, as well as humbling. Somehow even strangers had discovered my story and felt compelled to share personal anecdotes. Many of Kristy's updates were just as much for herself and served as a type of therapy. However, as we discovered, they also had a powerful impact on others who read them.

People wrote about how inspired they were by the love Kristy and I shared. They related stories of how our love helped them rediscover their faith, find the courage to do something that terrified them, and reunited them with loved ones. Kristy said it gave her goosebumps to know that God had worked through us to help others fix the broken things in their lives that needed to be repaired. But I'd be remiss to think that it didn't go both ways. All their prayers and support certainly resonated with me and helped move me through those difficult days. I told Kristy to make sure each time she posted a new update that she expressed my gratitude and told everyone to keep the prayers coming.

The incision sites on my neck itched incessantly as they healed, and I relied on Kristy to constantly scratch them for me. I got snippy if it took her too long to find the exact spot. Everything, even the littlest things, frustrated me. I was always quick to apologize and felt horrible by how frustrated I got but I couldn't find any relief from the multitude of annoyances that piled up around me.

Upon my transfer to the spinal cord rehab floor, Dr. Gregory Nemunaitis, M.D., was the lead physician in charge of my case. He was a physiatrist with over twenty years of experience, most of it with spinal cord injuries. Dr. Nemo, as I liked to call him, visited me daily in the SICU. During one of his rounds, he explained that because I had full sensation at the C3 level and partial sensation at the C4 level there was a good chance my diaphragm might still be intact. He believed I would probably be able to breathe without the assistance of the ventilator but was concerned with the susceptibility of my lungs to pneumonia. Only my upper lobes operated; the bottom nodes were full of fluid. He told me that if I had been a smoker, I wouldn't have survived the injury. I needed to get my lungs healthy, but besides rest, there was nothing I could do to expedite the process.

Despite the rough shape my lungs were in, the doctors wanted me to continue trying to breathe with just the use of CPAP. Kristy arrived one morning to find me amid a CPAP session. She was proud to see me working hard but could also tell how scared I was. Because I had no sensation in my chest, I was unable to feel the rise and fall of my rib cage with each breath I took. It freaked me out since it reminded me how little control I had over my body. She plugged her iPod into my ears and hoped the music would help me relax. The hospital chaplain, Father Art, frequently visited and told me to imagine God was breathing for me, pushing each healing breath into my chest. I just needed to close my eyes and let Him work.

One CPAP session lasted over seven hours and probably would have gone longer, but my family was getting ready to leave due to the strictly enforced visiting hours. I got anxious and needed to go back on the ventilator. Subconsciously, I didn't feel I could continue without them there, even though the doctors would still be with me. I struggled to find my confidence. As I was breathing, though, the doctor said that he could see my stomach move in and out and was encouraged by this since it meant that more of my diaphragm worked. Despite the fluid in my lungs, they were getting better, and I would soon move to the rehab floor. Kristy and my family left feeling more optimistic that evening.

The following morning, I had another surgery. This time an IVC filter was placed into my femoral artery. Since I was immobile, I was at high risk for blood clots. The purpose of the filter was to catch any clots before they traveled to my lungs and killed me. I was apprehensive about another surgery but agreed since it reduced the risk of a pulmonary embolism. Although the filter was beneficial in the short term, it could become detrimental and cause clots if left in the body for too long. Thus, it would need to be removed in a few months.

While I had agreed to the IVC filter, I was adamantly against another procedure the doctor suggested. Because my heart rate would drop unexpectedly, the doctor wanted to implant a pacemaker. For some reason, the idea of a pacemaker made me feel more decrepit and seemed more permanent than being paralyzed. We agreed to hold off but monitor the situation. Ultimately, I never had a pacemaker implanted.

As I became more stable, I would be able to leave SICU and transfer to the rehab floor. Kristy was excited to hear this news as it meant she would be allowed to spend nights with me in the room's extra bed. It also meant she could bring our cat, Kingsly, to visit me. I missed playing with her and lit up when I watched videos Kristy recorded of her.

One evening before Kristy left for the night, I mentioned that I was afraid and insecure about what people would think when they saw me. I fixated on the fact that I would be in a wheelchair for the rest of my life and people would probably stare. My looks and physique had always been important to me, and I probably placed too much of an emphasis on them throughout my life. But now here I was, a man in his early thirties, stuck in a wheelchair. Kristy told me that people would stare, but only because I was incredibly handsome. She pulled her compact from her purse and held it in front of my face.

"I am still good-looking!" I joked.

At times I allowed myself small, jovial moments like that, but mostly found my spirits to be down. The fiery drive I always had within me had taken a monumental blow and was reduced to an ember. Kristy felt confident the inner athlete in me would resurface once I began rehab and physical therapy. She knew how stubborn and determined I could be once I set my mind to something. The problem was, I didn't share that feeling.

Although a hospital bed was the best place for me at that moment, it was the worst place for me to find my positive attitude. The constant influx of doctors and nurses with all their poking, prodding, and fancy medical jargon did nothing to put my mind at ease. My anxiety continued to overwhelm me, and I confided in Kristy how scared I felt that I no longer knew how to stay positive. All the tools I needed to recalibrate my attitude existed within me and were at my disposal; however, I refused to access them, and instead allowed myself to succumb to the angst I felt.

My body needed rest, but my anxiety made resting difficult. My mind raced through the Streets of Worryville with no signs of slowing down. I tried to combat it by distracting myself with other stimuli, but it was to no avail. I wanted the TV on, and then I wanted it off. I wanted music on, and then I wanted that off. I wanted my itches scratched. I wanted Chapstick on my lips. I wanted the TV back on. Hell, one would have thought I'd wear myself out with all the back and forth, but I couldn't be still, figuratively speaking. Others hoped when I got to the rehab floor, I'd harness my nervous energy and focus it toward my rehabilitation.

As a teenager, my father shared with me a maxim from Earl Nightingale's *The Essence of Success*:

"According to the Bureau of Standards, a dense fog covering seven city blocks, to a depth of one hundred feet, is composed of something less than one glass of water. So, if all the fog covering seven city blocks, one hundred feet deep, were collected and held in a single drinking glass, it would not even fill it. And this could be compared to our worries. If we can see into the future and if we could see our problems in their true light, they wouldn't tend to blind us to the world, to living itself, but instead could be relegated to their true size and place. And if all the things most people worry about were reduced to their true size, you could probably put them all into a drinking glass, too. It's a well-established fact that as we get older, we worry less. With the passing of the years and the problems each of them yields, we learn that most of our worries are not worth bothering ourselves about too much and that we can manage to solve the important ones. But to younger people, they often find their lives obscured by the fog of worry. Yet, here's an authoritative estimate of what most people worry about. Things that never happen: forty percent. That is, forty percent of the things you worry about will never occur anyway. Things over and past that can't be changed by all the worry in the world: thirty percent. Needless worries about our health: twelve percent. Petty, miscellaneous worries: ten percent. Real, legitimate worries: eight percent. Only eight percent of your worries are worth concerning yourself about. Ninety-two percent are pure fog with no substance at all."

Throughout my youth and into my adulthood, my father reminded me of this axiom–and he still does today. He continued to remind me of it after my accident in those moments of despair when I let myself slip into the vortex of worry. As difficult as it might be, I needed to force myself to remember Mr. Nightingale's wisdom.

However, I couldn't shake the negativity I felt about my situation. Each morning when I awoke, the first thought that popped into my mind was that I was still paralyzed. I still couldn't move. I still wasn't where I wanted to be. I hated my new situation. I began to question whether I made the right choice by wanting to live.

*What if things never got any better? Did I think I could live a fruitful life like this?*

Although Kristy tried her best to be positive around me, it was apparent the whole situation also took a toll on her. She expressed her thoughts in one of her CaringBridge updates:

"Please pray that Scott's fear subsides and it is replaced with confidence and determination. We all know his outlook will determine his success. I told him that God wouldn't bring us to this if he wasn't going to bring us through it. I appreciate all the prayers. I am finding that the last several days have been emotionally tough on me as well. I'm trying to take care of all our personal affairs, maintain a positive outlook for Scott, and sort of just survive but lately my mood has been down too. This is an emotional roller coaster that I pray that no one else ever has to ride. I know, deep down, we'll get through this but sometimes I can't see how. Pray that I can just leave it to God."

Even though we both had our low moments, a hope lingered in the air that once I moved to the rehab floor, my outlook would improve. Perhaps having new goals to work toward would allow my mind to focus on overcoming the challenges in front of me and not dwell on the negative. I had gotten proficient at conjuring up rotten scenarios and was in desperate need of putting my thoughts and energy toward accomplishing my therapy goals.

The night before I transferred to the rehab floor Kristy prepped me for my big transition. She bathed me, shaved my face, trimmed my nails, and even applied a cleansing strip to clean the pores on my nose. She tucked me in, kissed me–always my favorite part of the routine–and wished me a good night of rest.

Tomorrow would be a new day, the beginning of "Chapter Three" as Kristy called it. After diving into a lake and breaking my neck twenty-five days earlier, I was finally headed to Floor 7A, Spinal Cord Rehab, to begin the long and arduous road back to where I wanted to be.

# SIXTEEN

# WHY ME?

When it comes to SCI rehabilitation, it's a multifaceted approach.

Rehab isn't just about trying to move muscles and body parts that no longer want to listen to the brain. It's an extensive and comprehensive education process about how to live with an SCI. There's the physical aspect of it, but most people don't realize how much of an emotional and mental adjustment needs to occur to live as productive a life as possible. That adjustment isn't something that came quickly to me. It would take me several months to come to grips with my injury, and several years to eventually accept my situation.

The first phase I contended with was the grueling rehabilitation the next few months had in store for me. Each day on 7A had a very specific structure to it, designed to maximize what activity the individual was capable of while seeking to educate him or her and their family on proper care once they are discharged from the hospital.

I was awakened every morning at 7 a.m. by the doctors who made their rounds and told me what my latest batch of tests revealed. Most of the time, I listened with my eyes closed, secretly hoping I could fall back asleep for a few more precious moments. It didn't take long before I could predict what they were going to say. They would inevitably comment about the state of my lungs; some days they were in great shape, other days not so much and in need of a new medication. Then came talk of my bloodwork, blood gas levels, and liver enzymes. I quickly grew weary of the liver enzymes conversation because it meant I would not be allowed any pain meds, not even an aspirin or ibuprofen to help alleviate the unbearable pain in my neck. Dr. Nemo was adamant about no pain medication. I don't think he allowed more than four aspirin during my entire hospitalization at MetroHealth.

On the heels of the doctors was the wound nurse, who examined and recorded the measurements of the wound on my coccyx. If untreated, a pressure sore could lead to significant complications including sepsis and ultimately death. Unfortunately, it was a pressure sore that tragically took down the Man of Steel and contributed to the death of Christopher Reeve. Thus, it was crucial for my sore to be monitored and properly treated.

Shortly after rounds, the nurses prepared me for the day. The first item of business was to administer my medications, which consisted of a dozen pills chopped up into a fine powder, mixed with water, and injected through a syringe into my feeding tube. I wasn't allowed anything to eat or drink for several weeks, and the plastic syringe inserted into the tube every morning served as the closest thing to an eating utensil I would get. The next order of business was to dress me in shorts and a clean gown. I had no desire to put on any regular clothes, so I spent most of the next several months in shorts and a hospital gown. Other patients donned appropriate workout attire for therapy. I just chose to remain draped in a gown even though I was repeatedly hassled by my therapists to put on a T-shirt. Too depressed, I didn't feel like getting dressed. In addition to my "outfit," pressure stockings, were pulled up my legs and wrapped with ACE bandages from the toes to the groin. The purpose of the wraps was to do what my muscles couldn't and regulate my blood pressure so as not to pass out once transferred to a somewhat upright position in my wheelchair.

After I was dressed, I was usually left alone for thirty minutes until my first session of therapy began. I cherished that time and tried to get more rest since every previous night proved to be an exercise in futility as far as sleep was concerned.

My therapy was divided into hourly increments and kicked off with occupational therapy (OT). The purpose of OT was to reacquaint me with simple tasks like making a fist, gripping something, or learning to brush my teeth. However, I couldn't move or feel anything below my shoulders, and the hour was spent stretching my upper body and trying to knock out a couple of shoulder shrugs. Sometimes I fell asleep while the therapist worked on me. However, most of the time I watched the other patients work their upper bodies and wondered when I would move my muscles again as they did.

After OT I was shuttled back to my room, transferred into bed or left in my wheelchair, which I hated. It was extremely difficult for me to sit upright, let alone even sit in a wheelchair, due to the constant fluctuations in my blood pressure. Each time someone tried to sit me up, I started to grow nauseous and began to pass out, and thus needed to be laid back down. I dreaded the time spent in a wheelchair. All I wanted to do was sleep. I just wanted to close my eyes and escape the hell I found myself in. I hoped that when I awoke everything would be back to normal.

But that was never the case.

My second session of the day was speech therapy. My voice slowly started to return, but because of the ventilator, I could only muster short gasps of breath, barely enough to utter a few syllables. I had to learn to time my speech pattern with the rise and fall of the ventilator pump. Reciting a single sentence left me exhausted. My speech therapist also worked on my mental stimulation. She gave me puzzles, riddles, and other problems to solve. To her surprise, I aced every test she threw my way. Fortunately, my brain had not suffered any damage, but she had to be sure. Besides, I liked demonstrating how smart I was and enjoyed the time since it was the one therapy session where I felt progress was being made.

The first afternoon session was computer therapy, which was basically me in front of the computer, watching one of the aides navigate the keyboard as we played Bookworm, a game that reminded me of a combination of Connect Four and Scrabble. Ideally, this session was for others who had mobility in their hands, whether on their own or through some adaptable products. Since I didn't have any motor function, my hour was spent playing a child's computer game. I usually aced it, though.

The final session of the day, and the toughest, was physical therapy (PT). I was transferred back into the wheelchair and pushed down the hallway into the gym, where a therapist stretched my legs and tried to elicit any movement, voluntary or involuntary. I nearly passed out in several of the sessions due to the onslaught of stimuli and various positionings of my body. I just wasn't strong enough to do anything other than lie in bed. Having spent the previous month flat on my back, trying to sit upright without getting dizzy or nauseous seemed like an impossible task. As the weeks wore on it became easier to tolerate my legs being moved around and stretched, but I still couldn't do anything on my own. Again, I found myself subjected to watching others around me make what seemed like significant progress. Most of the time I left my final therapy session of the day feeling dejected and saw myself as the only patient on the entire floor who appeared to be moving in the wrong direction.

There were over a dozen patients on the spinal cord rehabilitation floor during my stay. Of all the different spinal cord injuries, mine was the most significant. I was one of the only patients who required a ventilator to breathe. I was the only patient who could not move any part of my body other than a weak shoulder shrug. Whenever I saw another patient, the first thing I did was compare myself to their situation. This led me to quickly conclude that I absolutely had it far worse than anyone else and further propelled me into an emotional and mental downward spiral.

After therapy was over, it was back to bed, where I would drift in and out of consciousness while Kristy or my family kept me company. My focus was merely on trying to fall asleep and escape the constant physical pain. When the background noise of some random TNT rerun on the television wasn't being used as a sleep aid, either Kristy or my father would read to me. Most often I asked them to read stories about others who suffered an SCI and overcame the odds to achieve some variant of an extraordinary comeback. I desperately wanted and needed to convince myself that I too would one day join the ranks of the miraculous.

My room was adorned with a litany of pictures and letters of support, and of course a bevy of motivational messages, all with the single aim to lift my spirits and keep me positive. At times it worked. But most of the time I studied the minutiae of every picture and wondered if I would ever re-create the adventure and jovial atmosphere of the former version of myself who stared back at me from the glossy photos.

As I listened to Kristy, or my father, recite some astonishing account of recovery detailed on the pages they read, I wished for those precious hours to last forever. The thought of what the night had in store for me always filled me with an intense sense of dread. It was in those periods of isolation, after my family left, surrounded by machines, medical professionals, and other staff designed to care for me, that I felt the most vulnerable and alone. The fact that I found it nearly impossible to sleep certainly contributed to my sense of isolation.

Every two hours a nurse repositioned my body onto its other side to alleviate pressure and ward off any additional sores. Unless you're passed-out drunk, there's no way to sleep through someone manhandling your body, especially when the slightest touch triggered a spasm.

Because my brain lost its ability to communicate with the nerves below my level of injury, a spasm occurred when my spinal cord generated a response to certain stimuli. The spinal cord isn't as efficient as the brain, so it prompted an exaggerated reaction in the form of uncontrollable "jerking" movements of the muscles. It appeared as if I was having a seizure, even though I found the spasms to be beneficial at times.

Every four hours a respiratory therapist performed a series of procedures. The first was always the unpleasant process of suctioning my airway, followed by something more tolerable, which in some cases relaxed me. A handheld device that vibrated was moved back and forth across my chest to break up any mucus plugs in my lungs. There were also breathing treatments applied by a mask to inhale a fine mist of albuterol–Mucinex on steroids–to further break up the persistent plugs. Finally, another round of suctioning completed the process.

Throughout my hospital stay, I developed friendships with the different respiratory technicians. In the still of the night, we shared our thoughts about God, the universe, and the power to heal. I found it very cathartic at times. But at other times, I looked at the multitude of letters of support and motivational messages that decorated my hospital room and contemplated the stark reality of my new life.

My mind replayed the events of that July day and analyzed all the "would haves," "should haves," and "could haves," that if properly executed would have rendered a different outcome. However, no matter how many times I replayed the situation and willed an alternative result, there was no way whatsoever to change what had happened.

Although I thought about dying, something deep within me knew death wasn't the right solution. I still trusted in God's plan though I wanted to curse Him, and at times question His will and pleaded for some miracle to restore movement to my lifeless limbs.

My childhood home was a half hour away. The love of my life, Kristy, was also thirty minutes away. Yet I felt trapped in some distant and foreign universe. I didn't have my wife, my parents, my sister, or anyone to cling to. I had no one other than myself. Some nights it seemed like an entire week just dragged on with no semblance of daybreak to be realized. The monotony of night was its own form of torture and turned seconds into minutes, minutes into hours.

I did whatever I could, counting ceiling tiles, memorizing the intricacy of the walls, reciting song lyrics in my head, sometimes performing an entire concert, to speed up each second, minute, and hour, knowing that tomorrow I would see Kristy again. Each day when she walked into my room or surprised me in a therapy session, it was the greatest moment of the day. Just seeing her instilled in me a sense that anything was possible, and I had everything I needed to overcome the adversity I now faced.

There was no blueprint for success or guidebook to help me navigate the treacherous waters. Yet I had something much more powerful, although I might not have fully appreciated its strength at times.

I had prayer. I had God.

God would get me through this. He had to, right? My Catholic upbringing didn't preach of a vindictive God who sought to purposely hurt me. What happened was an accident, although, for the longest time I struggled with how God could allow this "accident" to happen. *Why didn't He intercede in some fashion to stop me from diving into that lake?*

There were a million questions I had for God. Sometimes I'd spend the whole night asking Him nothing but questions. Would I get better? When? And the question I asked Him ad nauseam, *Why me?* I'll be the first to admit that I wasn't one of those individuals who encountered some horrific type of adversity or disability and just accepted it and started to move on. Not me. I demanded answers from the man upstairs. I told myself that He owed me that much.

Every morning one thought immediately filled my consciousness.

*I'm still paralyzed.*

Try as I might to move an arm, or lift my leg, it always yielded the same fruitless result. God still felt the need for me to be paralyzed.

*Why?*

Every night before my family left, we made it a point to pray. We prayed the Lord's Prayer, followed by a Hail Mary and then recited a list of saints, asking each one to pray for us. It wasn't just my family that I prayed with, either. Several of the doctors and nurses also stopped by to pray. On several occasions, a group of doctors huddled around my bed and sang psalms of worship in what felt like some type of church revival. For everything society told me about the great debate between science and religion, I found it comforting and reassuring that these great men and women of science were also among the most religious people I have ever encountered.

In addition to my regular therapies and activities, the doctors thought it beneficial I speak with a counselor. They hoped it might relieve some of the constant anxiety that consumed me. During our first visit, I shared several positive things with the counselor, which surprised Kristy, who was also in the room, since a lot of what I shared with her had been so negative. Who knows, maybe I just tried to put on a brave face.

One of the more amusing things I shared was the obsession I had developed for blue Kool-Aid. Although I was hooked to an IV that administered a saline drip to keep me hydrated, I'd had nothing to drink in over a month. Although hydrated, I often felt I was in a perpetual state of thirst. I had dreams in which I walked down a supermarket juice aisle and tossed every type of liquid into my cart–water, Gatorade, Capri-Sun, pop, and of course an inordinate amount of blue Kool-Aid! When Kristy and I had frequented Bob Evans, I always ordered blue Kool-Aid with my meal. Perhaps because it was the only place I knew that served it, or maybe for the childhood nostalgia factor, but whatever the reason, every visit involved a glass or two of the delicious, sugary, blue stuff.

Later that day, after my counseling session, Dr. Nemo came in and told me that everything was progressing well. I was happy to hear this and even made a few jokes with him. He had lectured me days earlier that I needed to develop a better attitude, so I'm not sure if the jokes were genuine or me trying to convince him that my attitude had improved. Nonetheless, I made it a point to interact with him and the other doctors more when they were there to give me my test results, rather than close my eyes or stare at the wall.

The importance of a positive attitude wasn't lost on me, though. More than anything, I wanted Kristy, my parents, Lindsey, and those who came to visit me to see that mindset on display. I told myself it was just as important for their healing process as it was for mine. Somewhere inside of me, that positive mindset remained; it had just gone dormant and decided to take some time off. I knew it was time to make the conscious effort to bring it back to the forefront.

To do so, I needed to string together some victories, some tangible achievements that I could point to and recognize as progress.

# SEVENTEEN
# HIM AGAIN

As a child, there was hardly a night I went to sleep that wasn't preceded by a bedtime story from my father, a natural when it came to storytelling.

Perhaps he perfected his art during his years as a salesman, forced to take over the family insurance agency after the death of my grandfather, whom I never met. Whatever the case, I loved when my dad told my sister and me one of his world-famous bedtime yarns. I even interrupted him whenever he skipped over the smallest of details and made him tell it again.

If he ever put them down into a book, it would be titled *Stories Off the Top of My Head*, which is what they were. He told several different tales: *The Sandman*, *The Little White Cloud*, and *The Boy Who Didn't Like Milk*, to name a few. Although the plots varied, the themes were consistent. Each story centered around the importance of positivity and persistence despite the odds.

This message was especially on display in his version of *The Little Engine That Could*, my all-time favorite. It was a simple tale of a boy and his dad on the way to the kid's first Major League Baseball game.

However, all the trains to the ballpark were full, except for an old, dilapidated engine that didn't have what it took to make it up and over the steep hill that stood between them and the ballpark. Nonetheless, they hopped on that little engine and chanted along, "I think I can, I think I can," as it chugged with all its might, made it over the hill, and delivered the father and son to the stadium gates on time.

Now it was my turn to play the role of the little engine and make it over the hills that confronted me. As an eighth-grader at Incarnate Word Academy, I won a contest for an inspirational speech I wrote about Wilma Rudolph, a girl born with polio who went on to win several gold medals for track in the 1960 Olympics. I had first heard her story on one of those Earl Nightingale cassette tapes my dad always played. Twenty years later its message resonated more than ever:

"What you believe, you can achieve."

It was time to practice what I used to preach.

The first challenge that confronted me was to pass the swallow test so I could finally eat and drink real food for the first time in a month. The doctors needed to ensure my esophagus could safely handle anything I ingested. They were concerned that if I tried to eat or drink something, I might experience a pulmonary aspiration and fill my lungs with what was supposed to fill my stomach.

I was given a liquid substance to swallow that contained, barium, an earthy, alkaline metal that could be tracked through an x-ray once swallowed. Most found it disgusting, as it tasted like a metallic, chalky version of Pepto-Bismol. I didn't care. I was so ecstatic to have real liquid run down my throat that I even asked for more. The technicians were shocked and told me no one had ever made such a request! I was also given a small piece of a cookie to eat, but for some reason found the barium more delectable.

I passed the test.

That night my first meal was chicken Parmesan, not exactly light fare. I nearly devoured the entire plate of food. Oddly enough, I passed on the blue Kool-Aid and opted for the more traditional beverages such as water, milk, and Gatorade. I even wanted to drink Ensure.

The fact that I passed the swallow test meant more than just being able to eat and drink solid food. It was a milestone I desperately needed to allow my mind to finally focus on something positive.

Another colossal milestone that lay in front of me would be breathing without the use of the ventilator. My lungs were getting a bit stronger each day, although there were still a few setbacks here and there. Getting off the ventilator would allow me more independence and freedom. However, my confidence was still low, and I wasn't sure that I could accomplish it. I knew it would require a substantial effort.

However, it wasn't just me that needed more victories. Kristy also continued to suffer even though she tried to hide it from me. One month after the accident, she posted a journal entry on CaringBridge, part of which read:

"So today has been one month since the injury. I feel that this has been the longest, most trying month of my life. I really can't believe it's only been a month since this nightmare started. I look at my life before the injury and everything looks so bright in my memory. Post accident [sic] everything seems so dark. I know that we have had a lot of great, positive steps forward and we are progressing but it's still hard to really wrap my mind around this. I'm so grateful for our daily miracles but another part of me wishes we didn't have to even be here. I loved our life and I know that we'll be happy again but with a new norm. Part of me wishes that we could go back to our old norm."

I longed to hug my wife again, softly stroke her face, wipe away her tears, and gently kiss her forehead. I wanted to tell her everything would be like it once was, yet I knew nothing could be further from the truth.

A few days after the swallow test, I awoke to find I had gotten several hours of sleep. For the first time in weeks, I didn't feel anxious. I was rested and felt optimistic that a good day was in store for me.

The day started with a strong OT session in which I found myself focused and talkative. Kristy fed me a quick lunch of mashed potatoes and applesauce before I was transferred into the wheelchair and rolled down to the gym for my PT session. Afterward, I headed to my room and remained in the wheelchair for my speech therapy. Midway through I endured a nasty coughing fit that persisted for over an hour. By coughing, I mean trying to cough and go through the motions without exerting any force. The paralysis rendered my muscles useless as a means of clearing my throat. I was transferred to the bed so the respiratory therapist could administer a breathing treatment, and of course, a suctioning procedure. What usually took a few seconds lasted several minutes. The mucous plug in my lung was so thick and sticky that the therapist needed several attempts to extract it from my airway. It left me tired and uncomfortable.

I rested until that evening when Kristy's parents came to visit. It was the first time I had seen them since Bronson Hospital, not because they didn't want to visit, but rather because, I didn't want any visitors, aside from my parents, sister, and Kristy. As I had done every day with Kristy and my family, I asked Gary and Karen if they thought I had made any progress. Since I saw my family every day, I refused to believe them when they told me I had made progress. However, for some reason, hearing Kristy's parents tell me I looked better reassured me.

I asked them to call Angie, Kristy's sister who had performed CPR on me on the dock, so I could thank her for saving my life. It was an emotional conversation for everyone in the room, as I told her how happy I was to be alive and determined to fight this battle. Everyone was thrilled to hear me say those words, including myself.

Late in the evening, the respiratory therapist returned for another treatment. She performed the chest percussion procedure and administered some medicine. However, the moment she mentioned that it was time to suction, anxiety set in, my heart rate soared to 130 beats a minute, and I grew agitated. I was still worn out from the suctioning earlier and told her and the doctor I felt fine. They both listened to my lungs and agreed to hold off until I settled down. I eventually calmed down and fell into a peaceful sleep.

Then all hell broke loose.

Several hours later the respiratory therapist returned to suction my airway and encountered another large mucous plug. As she tried to remove it, the plug occluded my airway and deprived my body of any oxygen. My heart rate began to slow and eventually stopped.

It was another code.

Quickly, others rushed to my aid with the crash cart and began the lifesaving steps to resuscitate me. I was injected with a medication to jumpstart my heart and CPR needed to be administered. At one point, I regained consciousness as the doctor performed chest compressions on me, and I blurted out, "I'm going to die!"

Eventually, they stabilized me, and I was transferred to the ICU. However, my blood pressure remained extremely low, and I had to be closely monitored while doctors tried to figure out what had happened.

I was stable for a few hours, and then it happened again.

My heart crashed and then stopped for the fifth time in as many weeks. Once again, a code was called. Medical staff scrambled to my aid from every direction. Another intracardiac injection of Epinephrine was administered, and more CPR performed. This time, Kristy witnessed the entire terrifying ordeal.

Once stable, it was discovered that both the bottom lobes of my lungs had collapsed again. Another bronchoscopy was performed, and they removed an incredible amount of thick "goo" from my lungs. The two bottom lobes of my lungs were obstructed with thick, superglue-type mucous plugs. I was outfitted with a larger size trach, just days after having been downsized to a smaller size. I was stripped of all eating and drinking privileges.

So much for that sense of optimism and the great day I thought was in store for me.

I remained in the ICU for the next week, most of the time in an extremely sedated state, and I barely uttered more than a few sentences each day. My blood pressure stabilized but remained very low. My spirits were even lower. Kristy summed it up as follows:

"This has been one sharp downward turn on this roller coaster we are riding. Scott and the rest of us need your prayers. It is terribly exhausting and frightening to go through an ordeal like this. It strains every fiber of the body. I think we are all shaking our fists in frustration. I knew we would take steps backwards, but I feel like we've had everything taken from us from the trach reduction, eating/drinking, and even talking! Please pray. I know Scott will bounce back but I'm fearful of his confidence level. Pray that he gets stronger both physically and mentally."

The doctors theorized that when I ate or drank something, in addition to saliva and digestive secretions, I produced lung secretions, which led to increased mucous plugs. My bottom lobes were still collapsed, so I was given a few days of noninvasive treatments to inflate my lungs. They inflated my trach cuff, which silenced my ability to speak. It was back to lip reading, although it didn't matter to me. I had nothing to say and pretty much slept for several days. Even though I had no sensation, my body was exhausted, my chest was sore from all the CPR compressions.

Dr. Nemo revisited the idea of the pacemaker. He explained that because my brain was unable to balance the sympathetic and parasympathetic nervous systems, the parasympathetic wanted to take over, which caused my heart to run slow. He felt confident that a pacemaker would help regulate my heartbeat and prevent any further cardiac arrests. He encouraged me to strongly consider it. Not the type of decision I thought I'd have to contemplate at thirty-three years of age. Fortunately, the cardiology doctors concluded a few days later that I did not need the device.

There was one decision, though, that didn't require a tremendous amount of thought on my part. While in the ICU, a test was performed to determine how much function my phrenic nerves still had. These are two nerves that originate at the C3 level and extend past the lungs and heart and connect to the diaphragm. Their primary purpose is to aid in breathing. Simply put, if they are not fully intact, an individual is unable to breathe on his or her own. If I ever hoped to shed the ventilator, I would need my phrenic nerves to function. Because my injury was at the C3 level, there was concern that my phrenic nerves might be damaged. Two doctors performed a procedure that stimulated the nerves and recorded the corresponding response.

One doctor firmly placed a Taser device against the side of my neck, pressed a button, and administered an electrical jolt that was anything but pleasant. I felt like a bull getting stung with a cattle prod. Four shocks were dispensed on the left side and another three on the right side. Kristy thought it looked like a form of torture and had to look away. The other doctor used ultrasound to measure the level of nerve stimulation triggered by the shocks. The results indicated my phrenic nerves were intact. The potential existed for life without the use of a ventilator one day!

Even more encouraging was the fact that a device existed that could help me learn to breathe without a ventilator. This is what Dr. Nemo had asked me to consider in the event I was a potential candidate. The decision was a no-brainer.

The Diaphragm Pacing System (DPS) was designed to do what the body no longer could and stimulate the diaphragm to allow an individual to breathe once again. It is an artificial breathing muscle which consists of external and internal components. The external device is a 3" x 7" battery pack attached to five electrical leads. The tips of four of the wires are implanted on the diaphragm, and the fifth is implanted under the skin in the chest cavity. All five of the leads protrude from a small area in the skin and are grouped by a plastic connector which can then be attached to the battery pack. Once a button is pushed and the machine turns on, it stimulates the ribbonlike muscle of the diaphragm. Voilà, breathing occurs.

Dr. Raymond Onders, a pioneer in the field of diaphragm pacing, was a surgeon based out of University Hospitals in Cleveland. He was the guy who gained notoriety when he implanted Christopher Reeve with the device in 2003. And he would be the guy who I hoped would also implant me. I made an appointment to speak with him.

A few days after I was transferred back to 7A, I resumed my rigorous therapy routine. My room once again became a revolving door with the constant rotation of doctors, nurses, respiratory therapists, counselors, physical therapists, occupational therapists, and speech therapists. Additionally, I received frequent visits from various case managers. Kristy and I would soon need to plan for the next phase of my life once I was discharged.

Although still restricted from eating and drinking, and for the most part talking due to the inflated trach cuff, I found myself on somewhat of a sleep schedule. I listened to relaxing music at night as I slept, and the consistent nights of rest helped my anxiety. The upside to the inflated cuff was that my lung capacity gradually increased. Each morning a test measured the strength of my lungs, as I tried to exhale with as much force as possible. Every day I tried to better the previous day's results and soon began to demonstrate steady progress.

Although I had yet to regain use of my body, I was optimistic about the improvement my lungs showed. They had been a problem since day one of the accident. I had swallowed an inordinate amount of lake water, aspirated vomit while being resuscitated, battled several bouts of pneumonia, dealt with collapsed lungs, mucous plugs, and multiple codes, and come to find out that my body produced more secretions than most people. There was also the obvious fact that the muscles used for coughing were paralyzed. Despite all this, by some act of God, my lungs had improved. And I believe it was an act of God.

Kristy would tell me, "God is healing you from the inside first before he gets to the outside."

I think she was on to something.

It wasn't all good news, though. The time spent in the ICU had worsened my pressure sore. The doctors also had serious concerns with the elevated liver enzyme levels my blood tests indicated. They were stumped by what led to the increase and made the decision to cease with any pain medication. Even though I had not received much, every bit afforded to me was needed to alleviate the constant pain in my neck. I was also fed up with the Miami collar I wore. In addition to its hard edge digging into the back of my skull, and constant itchy skin that could not be scratched, it had also shifted my bottom teeth out of alignment due to the jaw being fixed in a constant position. So much for all the money my parents had spent on my orthodontic devices throughout my adolescence.

But most of all, the neck brace just plain hurt. I told Dr. Nemo I was willing to risk the liver damage from the pain meds if they'd help relieve some of the intense discomfort in my neck. I lost that argument.

There was one thing, though, that no amount of medication or therapy helped with no matter what I tried.

My emotions.

There are five stages of grief: denial, anger, bargaining, depression, and acceptance. However, my grief included one more stage.

Love.

I loved Kristy with a love unlike any other love I had ever experienced in my life. After I dove in the lake, I was immediately overcome with an unbearable sense of guilt and concluded I had just robbed us both of our happiness.

I desperately wanted us to both be filled with an extraordinary sense of happiness again. Every day I broke down with emotion and told the nurse or therapist just how much I wanted to hold Kristy again. There was not a single person on the floor who didn't know how much

I lived for her arrival each morning. It was the best part of my day, and they all knew it.

It was also apparent to the resident doctors how much I loved her and what type of relationship we had. They frequently told Kristy and I that they could see how special our relationship was, and if there were ever two people who could overcome this challenge, it was us.

I wanted to move my arms and hands more for Kristy than for myself. She so needed to feel my touch again and experience my arms wrapped around her. On one occasion, a resident attached the wires of an electrical stimulation machine to my forearm muscles. She turned the knobs on the device, and its electrical current caused my wrist to flex upward.

It was the first type of real movement I had seen from my body in several weeks, even if it was unnatural. Kristy and I cried tears of joy and sorrow. I could see my hand move but didn't feel a thing. There was no sensation, just a mechanical reflex to a stimulus.

Kristy also dealt with her own emotions. She vented about how bitter she was that on top of the fact that I was paralyzed, nothing else seemed to go smoothly. She expressed the heartache she felt when she saw me sob from the pain I was in, not having the voice even to have a proper cry. She said it was worse than any sad, heart-wrenching scene from any movie. This was real. This was our life.

It was equally heartbreaking to learn she had arranged my clothes on the bed next to her in our apartment to give the illusion I was still with her. Finally, after more than a month, she got up the courage to remove our travel bags from the trunk of the car.

On CaringBridge, she wrote, "I remembered, like it was yesterday, packing that trunk with excitement and anticipation for the weekend ahead of us. I pulled the bags out and made my way back into the apartment. I sorted through the bags with a heavy heart and I was doing fine until I came upon the shorts Scott had worn the day of the accident prior to changing into his swim trunks. The belt was still on and his boxers were still inside and I lost it. I sobbed as memories of that tragic day resurfaced. I remembered the fun we had driving up to the cottage. We had hooked my iPod up to his car so we had the windows down and we were singing at the top of our lungs laughing at our own terrible voices. It was a perfect day until, in one moment, our lives shattered with Scott's vertebrae. I know it may sound like I've lost it, but I laid those shorts and the T-shirt he wore that fateful day on our bed where Scott used to lay. It makes me feel closer to him in some way as though he's sleeping again, where he should be. Now I only pray for the day that he will be there again."

Every night as I lay in bed, I prayed for the same thing. I wanted the old Scott back too. I wanted to be "him" again.

# EIGHTEEN
# THANKSGIVING

During my stay on 7A, there was never a shortage of people wanting to visit. Whether friends or strangers, there was a barrage of requests for a visit.

For a while, I didn't want to see anyone other than my immediate family. I didn't want people to see me in the state I was in. I was accustomed to having a strong and confident persona throughout my life and hadn't yet come to grips with what I believed to be a weaker version of me.

However, people still came. Several of the people I met were former patients who stopped in to say hello to the doctors or visit with current patients. Almost all of them were in wheelchairs and hardly looked any different than the patients I saw in the therapy room every day. At times it made me feel more depressed. I didn't want visits from people who were still injured.

I wanted to meet and speak with the people who had defied all the odds and recovered–the ones who looked normal, like nothing had happened. I didn't want to confront the fact that my future might resemble what I saw when I looked at those around me, those who were still forced to succumb to life in a wheelchair.

Although confined to a wheelchair, most told me how fulfilled their lives were and how they had learned to enjoy life again. They offered encouragement, served as a sounding board, listened to the questions I asked, and prayed with me. I didn't realize it at the time, but their visits filled my reserves with strength that I would be able to draw from down the road.

My high school football and baseball coaches, former teachers, coworkers, and friends all came to visit. I wore a brave face and tried my best to be positive, not wanting to admit how dejected I felt on the inside. I was grateful for those who took the time to visit, even if I told myself I didn't want any visitors.

On one occasion, my friend Kevin stopped in with our mutual friend, Mike, both with their guitars in tow. They were soon joined by a grade school friend of mine, Damian Ference, now a Catholic priest. Damian, also an avid musician, brought his guitar as well. For the next several hours they sat at my bedside and put on one hell of a jam session. They played a lot of Bruce Springsteen, my favorite artist, and I sang along at the top of my lungs. Although I didn't have much of a voice, the effort I exerted was enough to set off the alarm on the ventilator machine. After the second time the nurses came to see why my oxygen levels were so sporadic, they decided it was better to turn off the alarm and just let me sing away.

One afternoon a gentleman by the name of Ryan Housholder stopped in with his mother to introduce himself. Ryan had an injury similar to mine. He was also injured in a July diving accident, only three years earlier. We immediately connected.

Ryan demonstrated a spinal cough assist system that had been implanted. Kristy and I watched in amazement as his mom pressed a button on a small device that triggered a cough and allowed him to clear secretions in his throat. He said the device made his life more comfortable and allowed him to venture out with friends without having to lug around a suction machine.

Between the diaphragm pacing system and the cough assist system, I envisioned a life free of the ventilator. The doctors had told me I would potentially have a longer life if I didn't require a ventilator to assist with breathing. I would also be able to taste and smell again.

More importantly, living sans ventilator might significantly decrease my anxiety. I had become obsessed with the tubes attached to the ventilator. Whenever someone turned me in bed or tried to reposition me, I exclaimed, "Watch my tubes!" My biggest fear was the hose would accidentally disconnect from my trach and I would be unable to breathe. I was told not to worry about it.

And then one night it happened.

It was the middle of the night, as I lay in bed and prayed for sleep, suddenly, without any warning, the ventilator hose popped itself free and detached from the connecting cannula that protruded from my throat. Immediately, warning alarms blasted from the ventilator machine and pierced the quiet room.

Panic set in as I tried to gather some breath. I couldn't breathe. My mind raced with thoughts of dread and impending doom. The shrill alarm grew louder, and I prayed one of the nurses would quickly get to me. More angst set in alongside the panic as I was convinced my final moments were at hand. I'm not sure how long the alarm sounded before one of the nurses entered my room. Instead of rushing to the machine to investigate what might be wrong, he just stood in the darkened doorway, arms crossed, and told me to calm down.

I couldn't believe it! I was fighting for oxygen, thrashing my head side to side on the pillow, and mouthing for him to help, and all he did was stare at me. And then even worse, he started to lecture me.

"Scott, you really need to calm down."

*Did this idiot just say that?* Could he not tell that something had me extremely worked up and agitated? I suddenly felt more terrified. I was going to die from asphyxiation while a "medical professional" idly stood by and watched. After what seemed like minutes, it dawned on him that something wasn't right. He finally approached the side of my bed, peered around, and noticed the ventilator tubes weren't connected. He plugged them back in.

As soon as the precious oxygen returned, I lashed out at him with complete disdain.

"What is your problem! I can't breathe, and you're just standing there telling me to calm down! Get out and don't come near me again!"

I was beyond pissed with him and the lack of urgency with which he responded. I called for another nurse, told her what had just happened, and demanded he no longer be responsible for any of my care. In hindsight, I might have overreacted; however, given the situation I had found myself in and my inability to breathe on my own, I understand why I responded the way I did.

One thing was abundantly clear. It was imperative that I find a way to shed the ventilator and learn to breathe on my own again. I did not want to live a life dependent on the proper and secure placement of plastic hoses to keep me alive.

In early September I was approved for the DPS surgery, underwent the laparoscopic procedure, and was implanted with the device by Dr. Onders. The surgery turned out to be trickier than envisioned because my diaphragm was moving on its own. The possibility existed that not only would I be able to breathe without the ventilator, but I might also eventually breathe without the pacer.

Around the same time, the muscle spasms I experienced began to intensify, and the doctors prescribed more baclofen to help treat them. They did not want to eliminate the spasms since they helped keep my blood pressure regulated and aided in blood circulation and muscle tone. However, at times the muscle tone was so severe that even the slightest touch would send my body into a full-on shake, legs and arms flailing so much that it became challenging to stretch me. The worst, though, was the havoc the spasms inflicted on my neck, causing me to feel more pain than I already did.

I continued to work hard in therapy and tried to put aside the frustration I felt from not seeing any progress in my muscle function. My shoulder shrug had gotten stronger, but that was about it. One afternoon after I was done with my sessions and transferred back to my room, I had a conversation with my father about the progress I desired to make. He took out a pen and paper and wrote down the following goals and plans to achieve each one:

Get off the vent by pacing. Continue each day with stronger paces.

Get out of hard collar. Faith, prayer in God's healing.

Get back arms and hands–hug my family. Visualize and do the exercises.

I now had my marching orders and knew what needed to be done to achieve what I desperately wanted. It was time to get to work.

One of my goals was realized a few days later when I was cleared to have my neck brace removed. Hallelujah! I hated that damn thing. I prayed I would never have to wear it again. Although I was restricted from pain medications, the doctors applied a patch to my neck that slowly released a muscle relaxant. I started to feel some relief.

Kristy was permitted to crawl in bed with me. It was a bit awkward for her to maneuver her body next to mine as I lay flat on my back in the small hospital bed but well worth it. Although I could only feel her body against my neck and face, I was at peace with her next to me. We both closed our eyes and pretended things were "normal" again.

We imagined it was July 2nd again.

Having her body once again next to mine, instilled a renewed sense of purpose and fight and further reinforced that my place was at Kristy's side. I was determined to beat this, not so much for me, but more for her.

And Kristy needed me to beat this.

The nurses had started to teach her my care routine. In her eyes, this was the beginning of a shift from her role as wife to that of a caregiver. Another grim and unrelenting reminder of how much our reality had changed. She expressed her frustration with this new role:

"I have completed most of my training of Scotts [sic] care and I have to tell you that it is NOT easy. I hate the fact that I have to do things to my husband that are so private and personal. It is hard to be a caregiver and a wife and sometimes those lines can feel real [sic] foggy. I have learned to build a massive wall around my heart because that is the only way I can protect myself and to get me [to] do some of the tasks that I have to do for him. I want to take care of Scott but I hate that I even have to. I hate that no one asks me if I'm okay doing these responsibilities and that it is just expected. I know that if anyone took the time to ask me if I'm okay doing it that I would for Scott but it bothers me that so many things are just expected of me.

"I wonder if anyone ever takes the time to consider what it would be like to have to catheter their husband or to do his bowel routine. It's painful and oftentimes I feel that it's just thrown at me with no regard to my feelings. I know I'm supposed to be strong for Scott and just bravely do these things that make me uncomfortable and I will but it doesn't mean it doesn't hurt me to do them. I always put on a smile for Scott and make jokes to make him more comfortable and he does the same for me but I see the pain in his eyes and I know he sees it [in] mine despite my best efforts. I also know that in time this will get easier but at this point our past is still so tangible making me desperately miss the way we were before."

I couldn't escape the feeling that everything was my fault.

There was a lot that required Kristy's attention. Insurance gave me a late October discharge date, but Medicaid wouldn't assist with any at-home nursing until I had been hospitalized for at least six months. This meant Kristy needed to find me an assisted living facility until early December.

In the meantime, she solicited the help of her family to move everything from our third-floor apartment to a first-floor unit. Finally, there was the matter of our house back in West Virginia, which still had not sold.

Heading back to pack up the home proved to be more emotional for Kristy than she planned. She told me that while in the house she could see me everywhere. She saw me chasing Kingsly, working in my office, opening the refrigerator to complain about how hungry I was, cutting the grass, and lying in bed. It broke my heart.

On top of everything else, the bills began to pile up. The first hospitalization bill she received was for $161,000–after insurance. And more were on the way–they would eventually top two million dollars. An uneasy feeling set in as she started to stress about future bills, cost of equipment, and everything else that would be needed going forward. I told her we would find a way to get through it, but I don't think she believed me. Hell, I don't think I believed myself.

Fortunately, friends and family stepped up and put together fundraisers to assist toward the bills. My former Calphalon colleagues hosted a golf fundraiser in Toledo and my sister, Lindsey, organized a massive event at Camp Cheerful in a short amount of time. Bryan organized a tailgate with my Delta Tau Delta fraternity brothers at the Lehigh vs. Yale football game in South Bethlehem, which became an annual event for a few years. In addition, monetary gifts flowed in from Calphalon, Trex, and Halex. The fundraisers proved successful, especially the Camp Cheerful affair, which ultimately allowed for the purchase of a brand-new accessible van.

To help combat some of her anxiety and stress, Kristy began running, often down by Lake Erie. She found comfort in the gentle sound of the lapping waves through which she communicated with God. Every day she prayed for a miracle to make me whole again, or at least give me the use of my arms. Regardless, she thanked Him for not taking me and allowing me to remain on this earth with her.

One afternoon while in my computer therapy session I received an email from Kristy. The therapist opened it for me, and upon seeing the attached photo, I was overcome with emotion. It was a picture of her at Huntington Beach, the words "I Love You Scott" scrawled in the sand.

By mid-October, I had been on the ventilator for more than fourteen weeks and had battled several bouts of pneumonia and a slew of other breathing complications. A few weeks prior, the DPS had been installed, and it was time to put it to use. I was transferred to Regency Hospital, a long-term acute care facility, where I would be weaned off the ventilator. After a week I no longer needed the ventilator and I was breathing with the DPS full-time. I also got in some practice time learning how to operate the sip-and-puff wheelchair I had been outfitted with a week earlier.

While at Regency, Cleveland's newspaper, *The Plain Dealer*, interviewed me for a short documentary film that was ultimately submitted for consideration to several film festivals. The film was intended to complement an eight-part series chronicling my story and would soon be published in the newspaper.

I arrived back at MetroHealth, sans ventilator, on a late October afternoon. Less than twenty-four hours later I was back in the ICU with a severe case of bronchitis, which caused more breathing problems. I couldn't seem to catch a break when it came to my lungs and breathing. The bronchitis was caught early, and I was back on 7A after only one night in the ICU. However, more medication was administered, which left me exhausted and barely able to participate in my therapy sessions for a couple of days.

Fortunately, my lungs quickly cleared and my vital capacity, or lung strength, was the strongest it had been since the accident. I was almost back to breathing as I used to, apart from needing the DPS. However, as I used the DPS, my diaphragm grew stronger on its own, and breathing without the ventilator not only improved my lungs but also had a significant effect on my attitude.

I became more engaged in my therapy sessions and worked harder than ever before. I also made it a point to encourage the other patients around me. No longer detached and reserved, I became a cheerleader and supporter for the others. It didn't take long for everyone to see me as quite the comedian. My knack for making others laugh was on full display, and there were quite a few days I found myself in tears from laughing and cracking jokes with my hospital mates.

One day I got the crazy idea to wear a sign around my neck that read: IF FOUND PLEASE RETURN TO FLOOR 7A. I planned to ride one of the elevators up and down as I drooled on myself and acted as if I was in a vegetative state. Fortunately, for the sake of others, I was prevented from doing so before I ever made it to the elevator.

There were still moments of despair, though.

To help with my feelings, I developed a routine where I'd try to move each body part before I went to bed and after I woke up each morning. I tried to move my biceps, then my wrists, then my fingers, systematically working all the way down each major muscle group until I finished at my feet by trying to wiggle my toes. By the time I had worked all the way down, I was exhausted and dejected. Although nothing moved, I wore myself out trying to elicit a reflex.

Even the not-so-significant things, like having an itch I could not scratch, weighed me down. I hated that I had to call for assistance with everything and anything. I developed a routine to alleviate my itches in which I closed my eyes and envisioned God's fingers scratching my face. Sometimes this worked, other times I had no choice but to call a nurse for relief.

I wondered why my situation had to be different than others I read about, including Dennis Byrd, whose autobiography I had recently finished. It seemed as if his story had always been with me, like a traveling companion, since I first read about it all those years ago in high school.

Kristy returned to work full-time, so she couldn't be at the hospital with me throughout the day as much as she used to be. It was difficult not to have her around. She was my rock, the one I most wanted to get better for. Upon her return to work, her job required her to travel more than usual. I repeatedly promised that each time she returned home, I'd be able to move my arms and hug her.

The insurance company continued to apply pressure and push for my discharge. Kristy and my family had yet to find a skilled nursing facility where I could live while we figured out the next steps. The doctors agreed to do their part to talk with the insurance company to see what could be done to ensure I was not discharged until a plan was in place.

However, one day I was unexpectedly moved from 7A to another facility operated by MetroHealth. The entire move was an absolute nightmare. I was taken by stretcher to the facility and upon arrival discovered it was not adequately suited to meet the needs of someone in my situation. After several hours, I was shuttled back to the hospital and admitted onto floor 6A, MetroHealth's skilled nursing floor.

I was completely demoralized.

I was powerless over my situation, subjected to the cruel reality that my well-being was out of my control and in the hands of insurance companies. It was a sickening and helpless feeling.

A few days later I celebrated my first Thanksgiving with a broken neck. Kristy and my family set up a makeshift feast, complete with all the fixings, in the common area of the skilled nursing floor. It felt great to dine on something other than hospital food, and I made sure to eat my full share. At the time of my injury, I was in great shape and weighed 175 pounds. However, between the muscle atrophy and food restrictions, I eventually lost fifty pounds and weighed an unhealthy 125 pounds at my lowest. Thus, I tried to eat as many calories as possible whenever I could.

The irony of the holiday was not lost on me.

Surrounded by Kristy and my family, I was extremely appreciative to be alive and loved by so many people; grateful God brought me through the hell that had been my life just a few months earlier.

However, it still required effort to block out the acrimony of my situation, and although I remained intent on keeping the flicker of hope for a miraculous recovery aglow in my heart, there was no escape from the sad feelings of loss and rancor that rooted themselves deep in the cracks of doubt.

Less than two weeks later, a monumental day I had looked forward to for some time was finally upon me: my Day Pass. The chance to venture from the hospital, free of nurses and doctors, and engage in some semblance of normalcy. Its true intent was to measure how I would do on my own and experience what type of adjustments awaited in the "real world."

It was Saturday, December 5 when I left the hospital alone with Kristy for the first time in five months. My best man Bryan had flown in from Boston once again, to spend this important day with me as well. Accessible transportation was arranged and dropped us off at the apartment in the late morning. It was the first time I had seen the new digs. A small, portable ramp was needed to get into the place.

The three of us ordered pizza and watched the SEC Football Championship. I also finally had the chance to spend some time with Kingsly, who was happy to see me, but confused by the whole situation, as she tried to make sense of why I sat in a chair and refused to pet her like she was accustomed to. For several hours we laughed and enjoyed our time and did our best to put aside any awkwardness we might have felt.

The plan was to spend the entire day at the apartment; however, toward the late afternoon, I began to feel uncomfortable. My whole face felt clammy, and an excruciating headache took hold. My heart beat slow and hard. Although I didn't know it, my blood pressure had rapidly risen to an unsafe level.

I was in the throes of an autonomic dysreflexia attack.

Autonomic dysreflexia (AD) is a life-threatening condition that affects individuals with a damaged spinal cord. It causes the blood pressure to skyrocket to unsafe conditions and coupled with very low heartbeats, can lead to a stroke, seizure, or cardiac arrest. AD occurs when the autonomic nervous system, which controls internal body processes such as blood pressure, heart rate, body temperature, bowel, bladder, and sexual function, overreacts to a noxious stimulus below the level of injury. Nerve signals are sent along the spinal cord until they are blocked at the damaged level and unable to reach the brain. Thus, the body responds by increasing activity of the sympathetic portion of the autonomic nervous system, resulting in a narrowing of the blood vessels and a rise in blood pressure. Receptors in the heart and blood vessels detect the increase and send a message to the brain that causes the heart to slow and the blood vessels above the level of injury to dilate. Since the brain is unable to send messages below the injury level, the blood pressure cannot be regulated.

My headache escalated from excruciating to intolerable. It was apparent something was very wrong. A similar thing had happened days earlier in the hospital due to my Foley catheter being blocked and not allowing urine to drain from my bladder. Now it had happened again. It felt like pure hell. Kristy tried to irrigate the Foley as she had been taught, but it didn't alleviate the issue. I'm not sure we even knew the proper way to irrigate it. What I did know was that I needed to get to the hospital. And fast.

Kristy called for transportation to pick me up. After what seemed like an eternity, the transport finally arrived and I was loaded back into the vehicle. I was in so much pain I barely mustered the energy to say goodbye to Bryan.

Throughout the ride back I tried to contain the agony I was in, but my wife wasn't blind to how bad I hurt. My distress caused her to grow more desolate, and she tried her best to hide it but felt utterly helpless. It was at that instant I realized how much of a toll my injury had taken on Kristy. She had broken. I didn't want to admit it, but somewhere deep inside my soul, I knew our relationship was no longer strong enough to handle the reality of our circumstances.

The tears that filled my eyes were no longer from the pain of autonomic dysreflexia, but from the unsettling revelation that had just been made apparent. Each tear only seemed to widen the gulf that had formed between us.

# NINETEEN
# NEW NEIGHBORS

Two weeks before Christmas I was discharged from MetroHealth.

After nearly five months in the hospital, I was finally cleared to go home–and somewhat forced out by the insurance company. However, until insurance approved at-home nursing services, I needed to go to a skilled nursing facility, so I became a resident of Rae Ann Suburban Nursing Home, situated less than a mile from our apartment.

Although the nursing home was a change of scenery, it certainly was not ideal. I was thirty-three years old and wanted to live at home with my wife, not in a place meant to house the sick and the dying. Nonetheless, I told myself I would make the best of it, as it would only be for a short time. Little did I know that I would end up at Rae Ann for the next fourteen months.

When I arrived at Rae Ann, I was still not anywhere near the shape I wanted to be in. My body experienced constant discomfort, coupled with nausea and lightheadedness, as well as all the other complications that accompany a broken neck. I spent more time in bed than in my wheelchair. It was a loaner that wasn't correctly outfitted for me, so when I was in the wheelchair, my body grew sore from the way it was positioned. I wouldn't get my own chair until I left the nursing home, so in the meantime, I had to deal with the discomfort of the loaner chair.

It didn't take long for me to benefit from one of the advantages Rae Ann had to offer: the physical therapy. Like Metro, I had physical therapy every day. But unlike Metro, Lauren, the therapist I worked with, was willing to take an aggressive approach and try new things, not afraid to challenge me with unconventional exercises. I found myself invigorated and upbeat after every workout. Each time Lauren worked my arms she felt twitches in my biceps as if they tried to fire back up. I also felt progress was being made and my body would soon respond as I continued to work it.

Unfortunately, shortly after my arrival, I experienced respiratory issues, and hospital visits bookended Christmas. I spent Christmas Eve in the ER and needed a CAT scan for suspected blood clots in my lungs. When it came to my health, I didn't have much luck the day before a holiday. Fortunately, no clots were found, and I was back at the nursing home in time for Christmas.

Kristy and I spent our third Christmas together as husband and wife in the nursing home. We exchanged gifts and had a lovely meal with my parents and sister. Father Damian stopped by to celebrate Christmas mass with us in the small chapel that was on site. Not the way I ever envisioned spending a Christmas holiday, but I did my best to make the most of it.

The following day I found myself back in the hospital with pneumonia.

My anxiety also returned with the trip back to the hospital and the realization that this might be my new "normal," complete with frequent hospital stays, constant pain, and a steady dose of fretfulness. Not the Christmas gifts I had hoped for.

A week later I was back at the nursing home and back in the therapy groove. Physical therapy soon became the highlight of each day as Lauren continued to push me further. I looked forward to the hard work that left me exhausted yet renewed after every session. Able to appreciate the benefits of aggressive therapy, I researched the resources needed to travel to one of the handful of spinal cord injury rehab centers across the United States that provided intense therapy.

I read a story in *The Plain Dealer* about a resident named Chris Wynn, who planned to open a rehab facility in Cleveland explicitly geared toward individuals with SCIs. Chris was an Air Force veteran who broke his neck when he dove into the ocean while stationed in Hawaii. In 2006, thirteen years after his injury, he participated in an aggressive therapy program at Project Walk in California.

Recognized as the pioneer in activity-based therapy, Project Walk developed programs designed to retrain the central nervous system through assisted and repetitive exercise. Chris was able to move his legs on his own and improve his abdominal strength after just a few sessions with the Project Walk staff. He returned to Cleveland determined to find a way to bring this same philosophy to his hometown and help others living with SCIs. He received a grant from the Veterans Affairs Department that allowed him to open his facility, Buckeye Wellness Center. I reached out to Chris, and he came to visit me at Rae Ann to introduce himself and tell me about his gym. Unbeknownst to either of us, a year and a half later I would become Buckeye Wellness Center's first client. In the meantime, while at Rae Ann, I was determined to continue my daily workouts with Lauren and make further progress.

The progress my body had already shown from the aggressive therapy was rewarding and reassuring. In addition to the physical benefit, my emotional and mental well-being had improved, and I allowed myself to entertain the slight notion that recovery was on the horizon. I hadn't yet comprehended that recovery would come to mean so much more than just the physical.

At the end of every therapy session, I worked in the standing frame for a few minutes. It soon got to the point where my blood pressure was no longer the limiting factor; instead, it was the intense cramps that developed in my shoulders and neck muscles. At times it felt like my neck was encased in concrete and it required all the effort in the world to raise my head a few inches while upright.

I was soon introduced to someone who arranged for me to receive a weekly massage. Just thirty minutes of a shoulder and neck rub went a long way to alleviate some of the discomfort I lived with in those areas.

As I started to feel better, I spent more time in the wheelchair each day, which in turn led me to be more productive. I familiarized myself with voice software that allowed me to use a computer independent of others' assistance. I started to post my own updates on the CaringBridge website, as well as send emails to friends. A former business contact from my Calphalon days generously donated their services to create a personal website where I could provide updates on myself, as well as receive donations to my discretionary trust. Several people offered some financial assistance. Even strangers were eager to help. As I watched my wealth dissipate through Medicaid, the benevolence I received from others was much appreciated.

There were other forms of assistance I benefited from like homemade dinners, audiobooks, technology devices, and other such items given to me by friends, fraternity brothers, former coworkers, new acquaintances, and others that made my time at Rae Ann much more tolerable.

Additionally, my friend Eric and his wife's family purchased an EasyStand for me, a piece of equipment that cost thousands of dollars. It's basically a chair that is cranked to a standing position. A fantastic machine that could help ward off osteoporosis, improve circulation, and decrease spasms. The best way I figured I could thank them was to use the machine as much as possible. I started standing for thirty to sixty minutes every day during my therapy sessions.

There were countless other gifts that would require a whole chapter to recognize. I hope that everyone who has assisted me over the years knows how much I appreciated and benefited from their acts of kindness.

To this day, I am humbled and grateful for the generosity bestowed upon me. I didn't feel like I did anything different than anyone else would have if they had been forced into a similar situation. The human spirit is resilient, and I believe people are more capable of weathering the storm than they realize. Unfortunately, one often needs to be put into a specific predicament before he or she can truly appreciate that fact.

***

Life at a nursing home can be an adjustment for anyone, but when that someone is a Type A thirty-three-year-old, the contrast is glaring. I was a go-getter in the prime of my life. I lived with a mindset of "Go, Go, Go," but now I was surrounded by timeworn individuals whose common mentality was "No, No, No." The juxtaposition of personalities was both cruel and bizarre at the same time.

And there were undoubtedly some personalities at Rae Ann.

A favorite of mine was Katherine, the frail and feeble woman who sat in her wheelchair and recited the Hail Mary throughout the day. I often prayed with her, drawn in by her always present and magnetic smile. When she passed away, her family asked that any donations be made to my discretionary trust fund instead of anything made to her family.

Another favorite was, Betty, a surly woman who I'm pretty sure never took shit from anybody in her life. When she wasn't yelling at the staff, she would wander the halls in what could only be described as a portable safety cage. On a few occasions, I witnessed her argue with the Coke machine that refused to get out of her way.

There was a lovely old woman, Dal, who took a liking to me. She was always worried about my well-being, and although legally blind, always quick to tell me how good-looking I was. She was also practically deaf, and our conversations might have been misconstrued as loud arguments to a passerby who didn't know better. We spent numerous afternoons together in the courtyard soaking in the warmth of the sun.

And then there was Al, a perpetually disgruntled man who had lived a life beyond his actual years. Burdened by a stroke at a young age, most of his life had been spent in nursing homes. At Rae Ann, he cruised the hallways in his motorized wheelchair and criticized everything that crossed his path. However, we had a very cordial relationship. I always chuckled when I asked how he was, and he responded in his typical demeanor, "Barely adequate."

The weary, destitute and ornery personalities of the residents at Rae Ann Suburban could have provided any Hollywood writer with enough fodder for an Emmy award-winning sitcom. But they weren't just characters meant to provide some off-beat hijinks for others' entertainment. They were genuine individuals, who each had his or her own story to tell, but now found themselves much closer to an end than a middle. These delicate and disoriented seniors, along with the constant presence of death, were now my new neighbors.

Rae Ann was not meant to be the final stop for me, but before I could move back in with Kristy much work needed to be done. In addition to any physical modifications, at-home nursing care also needed to be set up. I applied for the Medicaid Waiver program, which had a waiting period that could take years. To help expedite the application process, I hired a leading disability lawyer in the area who was skilled at navigating the tricky waters that accompanied the government healthcare program.

Stringent income limits applied to an individual seeking Waiver services, and I was thus forced to "spend down," basically liquidate the assets I worked so hard throughout my career to attain. All my savings, including retirement, had to be assigned to an irrevocable Medicaid trust that made the government the primary beneficiary of my assets. Provided my cumulative assets never exceeded a paltry total of $1,500, I remained eligible to receive Medicaid Waiver services. Additionally, the company I worked for, Halex, and I came to a mutual agreement that I would resign my position. At the time it seemed inevitable; however, it was difficult to accept the fact that my professional career might be over, with me being forced to retire thirty years too soon.

It was disheartening, to say the least, to watch everything I worked years for be taken from me in a matter of weeks. Acquiring a disability was a costly proposition. Getting hurt was expensive and getting severely hurt was extremely expensive. My family set up a discretionary assistance trust in my name, that others could contribute to. Contributions were not subject to Medicaid ownership provided they were used for my well-being, and I did not personally contribute to the trust.

The money I had left to spend went toward a private room at Rae Ann–a cold, stale, linoleum room. It was a far cry from the dream home I envisioned living in with Kristy one day.

# TWENTY
# REVELATION

Kristy began to spend more time away.

During the week she often traveled for work, more frequently than she had before my accident. While I had been hospitalized with my most recent bout of pneumonia, her parents and sister visited me, but Kristy did not. She spent her weekends visiting friends back in the D.C. metro area or on other out-of-town jaunts. I wanted her to take time for herself, and even encouraged some of her excursions; however, I also knew something was amiss under the surface. I sensed her loneliness in my presence, and I could tell our relationship had changed in her mind. To me, it seemed like it became easier for her to be away, and although I didn't want to admit it, I think she preferred it that way.

Most noticeably, she had stopped wearing her wedding ring. I was bothered by this and asked her why, but she never really gave me an answer, always changing the subject.

Exactly seven months after my injury, on her thirtieth birthday, she wrote:

"I lost my able-bodied husband that day. I have been mourning that loss and I cannot say that I have handled it with half the courage or gracethat [sic] Scott has. I have resorted to feeling angry and resentful at the situation at times. I would be lying if I said that I do not lament over the past. I miss my old Scott with all of my heart. I have ached in places I did not even realize I had inside me. I miss having him hold me. I miss lying on the couch with my legs on his legs and making barking noises while wiggling my feet in his face to "hint" that I wanted a foot rub while he watched basketball. I miss all the spontaneity that we once had. I miss having Scott open jars that I could not open. I miss not having to do the bills. I miss the way Scott made me coffee and fried egg sandwiches on Saturday mornings. I miss having him kill the spiders and other insects that creep into the apartment. I hate that I did not cherish all of the moments I just mentioned as much as I should have. I still lie in bed at night going over all of the little details of my "old" life and remember all the fun we used to have. Sometimes after a glass or two of wine, I allow my mind to wonder about where we would be today if that day never happened. Would we have bought a house by now? Would I be pregnant? Would we be booking this years [sic] vacation? The happy possibilities seem endless.

"I know it is human to just assume you will always have another opportunity to hug your loved ones but I wish I would not have. Sure, I can still hug Scott but many times that triggers a painful spasm and after seven months, frankly, I miss being on the receiving end of the hugs. It is difficult to not feel like we were robbed of so much ... I recognize that it probably sounds like it is all sadness and blues on my end and I want to clarify that it is not. Pieces of my soul are coming back to me. It still hurts to think of that fateful day but the edges are getting less jagged and I do not think of that day as much as I did. I laugh now. I actually laugh a lot. I feel hopeful at the simple prospects in life and I have many moments of peace ... I feel thankful that Scott is still here. Despite the pain, we do still laugh and we are still making memories. They certainly are not the memories we wish we were making but they are pleasant moments nonetheless.

"This accident has changed our relationship and our love but although it feels different, I love Scott more today than I did seven months ago. It is a very overwhelming, unconditional, absolute love. I have learned a lot from the accident. I have learned a lot about life and love. I am also learning to accept a past that I regret ... I am sorry for the silence on my end but I've been struggling and mourning this loss and unfortunately I don't always know how to deal. I've lived a relatively charmed life up until this point so grief and loss this great are new emotions for me."

At times it felt like there was nothing I could say to Kristy to convince her in the slightest that things would get better. The space that continued to widen between us scared me more than a broken neck or my paralysis did. I could not begin to, nor did I want to, imagine a life without her at my side. She was my soulmate, my best friend, the one person I loved and needed more than anyone else in my life. The only solution to set her at ease was to get my body back to some semblance of what it used to be.

I continued to work hard to do that.

As soon as I rebounded from pneumonia, I began to spend more time with the DPS turned off. I was determined to breathe on my own again. Completely on my own. And then one early February evening I asked my mom to stay the night in my room so I could turn the system off and attempt to sleep without it.

I turned it off. I made it through the night. And I never turned it back on. Several months later I had the system removed from my body. I was the $250^{th}$ person ever to be implanted with the DPS and one of only a handful to ever have it removed.

I worked hard to string together consecutive good days. I garnered significant strides in physical therapy. I made a conscious effort to spend more time among the other residents and bestow as much enthusiasm and positivity on them as I could. Despite the perils my relationship with Kristy faced, I persevered and believed that the tide would soon turn.

Things had progressed well enough that I allowed myself to believe that a fruitful and exciting life might one day be attainable. However, there was never complete escape from the fact that each day was a battle to stay the course and remain positive. Without warning, those dark, old moments when I found myself trapped within my mind, bombarded with negativity, unable to flee, would come back. It was at those times I found myself stuck in the past, unaccepting of the present, and scared of the future.

*Why me?*

I had read about individuals who endured horrible predicaments and chose not to question their situations, and instead just powered through what came their way. At least that's what they said. I wondered how they were able to do that.

I found it tough not to ask "why me" when it seemed like I lost everything for no other reason than a freak accident that wasn't supposed to happen to me.

It was tough to not feel like a burden to those who loved and cared for me. Although I was thankful for all the support I had received, I wished there was some way to give back and not always take, take, take. I questioned if I had the strength to continue to pick myself up.

As horrible as it sounds, I wished I had something like cancer instead. I told God I would give up twenty-five years of my life for just a few more years of the way it used to be. Enough years to have children; to celebrate a tenth wedding anniversary with Kristy; to throw her surprise birthday parties; to travel; to build my dream home. Sure, people told me I could still do some of those things–but it wasn't the same.

And I found it very difficult to accept the fact that it might never be the same again.

I told myself "might never" because a part of me wanted to believe there would be a miracle, a breakthrough in medicine and science, a way to get back to the way I was eight months ago. I was conscious of the fact that all the negative thoughts brought me down and rendered me depressed, but they were natural feelings and emotions too powerful to keep suppressed in the annals of my mind. I found it best to let them out, deal with them, and then try to move on again.

My dad reminded me that I began to have more good days than bad days. He told me to stay focused on all the progress I had made. Although it was true, I still hadn't reached the point where the good days felt great and the bad days felt not so bad.

I needed to find that point.

On March third, I celebrated my thirty-fourth birthday in the nursing home. The week was filled with some of my best therapy workouts. First, I no longer needed to wrap my legs in Ace bandages since my blood pressure would remain stable during workouts, even when I sat up. That was a small victory. Second, many workouts were now geared toward arm and hand motion. One such exercise involved strapping my hands to a hand cycle and using my shoulders to help pedal. In another activity, beanbags were aligned near the edge of the table, and I used my shoulder to generate enough strength and force to slide my entire arm forward and push the bags off the table. At times the workouts felt more grueling than what I used to do in the weight room. But I found those simple events to be rewarding achievements.

I also took my first shower in over eight months, which was a wonderful gift to receive. However, the best gift I received was from my mother who hired a personal chef to prepare dinner for Kristy and me. We feasted on filet mignon, potatoes, brussels sprouts, Caprese salad, and bread pudding with hard sauce. And, of course, a bottle of Cabernet. Kristy hooked up her iPod, and we listened to our favorite music while we dined.

Things felt normal, at least for a few hours.

On my way back to the room that night, I ran my wheelchair into the wall. It was quite humorous, and several of the aides accused me of having too much wine.

"Nonsense," I told them, "you can never have too much wine!"

Soon after, Kristy left for another work-related trip to North Carolina that would keep her away for two weeks.

During her hiatus I celebrated St. Patrick's Day with my sister, Lindsey, who surprised me with an insulated thermos of freshly poured Guinness. She wasn't about to let the day slip away without me enjoying a pint.

A few days later, Kristy returned.

It had gotten harder to be away from her, but I knew it was vital she get some time off as well. I could tell she was burned out and I held out hope that each time she went away, she would return energized.

She arrived at the nursing home one afternoon to review some forms she had received from the Medicaid attorney with me. Kristy, my mother, and I convened in a room and did our best to dissect the information. At one point, Kristy reached into her folder to retrieve a form, and a picture accidentally slid out. It happened fast, and she quickly pushed it back into the folder, but it was too late. I had already noticed it.

It was a photograph taken while she was in North Carolina of her standing next to a guy with his arm wrapped around her. My heart sank in my chest. It took me a moment to wrap my head around what I had just seen. I didn't want to believe it was a picture of what I thought it was.

"What was that a picture of?" I asked. "Let me see it."

"It's nothing."

I didn't need her red face to give her away. I knew what I had seen. Several minutes passed as we argued about the picture. She refused to show it to me. Instead, she continued to try her best to convince me that it was nothing. My mom remained silent as Kristy and I went back and forth.

Eventually, Kristy relented and showed it to me.

Sure enough, it was a picture of her with some guy I had never seen before.

"My friend thought he was cute and said I should get a picture with him," is how she explained the whole situation.

Of course, I knew better. I wanted to believe it was as innocent as she described it to be but couldn't help but feel skeptical. Mostly, I felt betrayed and hurt. It didn't take an advanced degree to know she wasn't happy anymore. In her mind, this wasn't what she had signed up for when she said "I do" almost three years earlier. Hell, it wasn't what I signed up for either. But together we had made our wedding vows to each other.

"For better, for worse. In sickness and health. Until death do us part."

Those were now just words that we had once said to each other.

It was Kristy who told me after my accident that the injury might have affected me physically, but it didn't take away the parts of me that she loved the most: my mind, my personality, and who I was. I wondered if that had changed. It sure felt like it had. I spent the next few days in a depressed state and didn't want to do much of anything. I didn't even care to be around those closest to me.

And then one afternoon it happened. Everything I had feared.

Kristy told me she wanted a divorce.

Hearing those words come out of her mouth caused my world to once again crash down upon me. Her revelation devastated me more than breaking my neck had. She was my entire world, and it scared the shit out of me to imagine a world without her.

Kristy said she still loved me, but not in the way that a wife should love a husband.

*What the hell did that mean?*

I had no idea what to do. I was still very much in love with Kristy and wanted to believe she would somehow change her mind and come to accept a future with me. However, it was apparent her mind had been made up. Still, I held out hope I could have my best friend back again.

In the meantime, I enjoyed as good a relationship with her as I could.

However, her desire for a divorce meant I would not be heading home to live with her. Although my Medicaid application still awaited approval, I needed to determine where I would go once discharged.

It was back to the drawing board to start all over again.

## TWENTY-ONE

# PLATEAUED

Although I had tried to prepare myself that Kristy would one day no longer want to be married to me, I was still extremely saddened and rocked by her request. Especially the timing of it.

It hadn't even been a year since my injury, and my prognosis for recovery was still very much unknown. Her urgency to dissolve our marriage left me in a dispirited state. I didn't want to do much of anything, but I continued with my therapy as I knew how important it was.

I received a well-needed break one weekend when several of my old Trex colleagues, most of whom I hadn't seen in a year and a half, journeyed from Virginia to visit me. A dozen of us dined on pizza and beer as we watched the NCAA March Madness games in the nursing home's common area, which we had commandeered. A few of the residents were brave enough to enjoy the games with us, including Helen, an ailing woman with dementia, who told me she loved me every time she saw me. I think a few of my buddies might have been jealous.

By the time Easter rolled around, the weather had cooperated enough that I would spend hours outside in the courtyard at Rae Ann. The sun developed into a wonderful source of energy for me, much more than it had ever been in the past.

This injury has taught me a plethora of lessons over the years. One of the first I learned was to calibrate expectations. In the past, on sunny days, I would be happy to go for a run or walk with Kristy and then pop into a local watering hole for a cold adult beverage. We would often talk for hours, and many a time those afternoons turned into nights. Afterward, we'd head home to watch a movie and enjoy some wine.

Since my accident, I was happy to simply be outside.

Although I'd rather still do those things with my wife, I had become so appreciative to feel the sun on my face, smell the aroma of the air, listen to my music, and occasionally sip a beer. Those events became more of a treasure to me than any precious metal. In the courtyard, I closed my eyes and visualized sensation and movement in my limbs. Additionally, I put myself through a long neck and shoulder stretching routine as I sat alone.

All these years later I have not taken these treasures for granted. I can still be found outside whenever the opportunity affords it. By mid-summer every year my skin boasts a wonderful golden hue that would earn the envy of George Hamilton.

However, just like anything with an SCI, there are always trade-offs. Since I can only feel the sun's warmth on my face, neck, and upper shoulders, I need to be very conscious of the heat's effect on my body. If I'm not careful, autonomic dysreflexia can strike, and the life-threatening condition might rip away any future sundrenched afternoons I ever hoped to enjoy again.

Easter Sunday was celebrated with another mass by Fr. Damian. At the beginning of the year, I had dubbed 2010 as the "year of the miracle" and asked those who prayed for me to pray to Pope John Paul II and ask him to intercede with God on my behalf. I had prayed to several saints since my injury and hoped that perhaps a miracle would find its way to me.

I firmly believed that some miracles had already happened, though.

By medical standards, I should have been dead, or at the very minimum, in much worse condition. My heart had stopped on five separate occasions and I believed it was God who had worked through the doctors each time to resuscitate me. A ventilator, something I was initially told I would always need, was no longer required to breathe. I could eat whatever I wanted and had grown accustomed to spending more time in my wheelchair. Not to mention I could stand with assistance. I had accomplished more than I had been told I would ever do.

Everything was relative, but I felt blessed to be where I was. Although movement still eluded me, I remained confident that amazing happenings were on the way. I knew that prayer was a big part of that process. But as much as I believed in the power of prayer, I still became dejected with each setback.

Shortly after Easter, I was forced to spend two nights back in the hospital. My bladder had been nicked when one of the nurses changed my catheter. I immediately started to bleed profusely from my penis. There was a lot of blood, and they were unable to stop it, so I needed to be transported to the ER. While there my blood pressure climbed dangerously high. The nurses were unfamiliar with how to treat spinal cord injuries and uninformed with autonomic dysreflexia. I pleaded with them to administer Nitro paste, a last-ditch effort to bring down the blood pressure, which they finally relented to do.

After five minutes I told the nurse she needed to take it off because it was dangerous to leave it on my skin any longer. My blood pressure was still slightly elevated, however, so she left it on a bit longer. Moments later, I told my dad I felt very weird and needed the nurse. An uncomfortable weakness came over my body, and I felt like I was floating above the bed, struggling to find the energy to keep my eyes open. My blood pressure had plummeted to 40/28.

Months later, to avoid such "nicks," I had surgery for a suprapubic catheter, which is inserted directly into the bladder, a few inches below the belly button. Plus, I liked the idea of not having anything permanently attached to my manhood.

As I lay in the hospital bed, I reverted to asking that litany of familiar questions that had plagued me since my injury:

*Why me?*

*How much can one person endure?*

*Why haven't I gotten any movement or sensation back yet?*

*Do I want to live my life feeling this way?*

*Is something special in store for me? If so, when will I realize it?*

I once heard it said that the doubt and fear of living with paralysis the rest of your life was like a monster under the bed. Was it real? Could I deal with it? It became challenging to block out the negative thoughts and remain positive when I found myself in those dire situations, as I imagine it would be for a lot of people. However, the positive upbringing that was with me throughout my childhood into adulthood evaporated in those moments of despair.

My Dad reminded me, "Everything passes. Every day's a good day, but some days are better days."

And he was right. But I was tired of feeling helpless, working so hard and not getting the results I had been used to achieving throughout my life. It just plain sucked. Being trapped in the hospital also kept me away from my physical therapy. Often in the morning when I awoke and felt despondent, I told myself to at least get up and go to therapy. I knew the way the workouts made me feel afterward. That's when I felt my best.

I was still learning how to define myself. It was hard not to focus on the physical aspect. A part of me accepted the fact that I should not let the physical define me. My mind was sharp, my personality was still intact, and I had not forgotten how to dream big. However, another part of me couldn't help but stare at my arms and legs the way a kid gawks at a puppy through the pet store window. They are right there in front of me, and I can imagine what they feel like but can't seem to make them mine. They just won't listen to me. I believed that would change one day and continued to work toward that. I just wished I knew when that day would arrive.

Several years after my accident, I watched a TED talk by a married couple, Mark Pollock and Simone George. Although blind, Mark lived a high-octane life before suffering an SCI. When Simone asked what led to all the adventure he sought, he quoted Friedrich Nietzsche: "He, who has a Why to live, can bear with almost any How."

Mark recounted a story about Admiral James Stockdale, a POW in the Vietnam War, incarcerated and tortured for more than seven years. His circumstances were bleak, yet he survived. As he recalled his experience, he stated that the ones who didn't survive were the optimists. According to Stockdale, they told themselves they would be freed by Christmas. Christmas came and went, and soon came again. They hadn't gotten out. They grew disappointed and demoralized, and most died in their cells. However, Stockdale, a realist, confronted the brutal facts of his circumstances while he maintained faith that he would prevail in the end.

Although I might not have realized it at the time, I had begun to evolve into a realist. Despite the challenges that awaited me each day, I discovered a strength inside myself that allowed me to persevere and push through the adversity I faced. Although I missed my life before the injury and all that it entailed, I was not done with my life, nor had I accomplished the goals I set out to achieve. However, my future was unclear, with no way to know if those goals would be realized. What I did know was there were new objectives that would prove much more meaningful.

One afternoon, I was visited by a customer I met while I worked at

Halex. He had also been in a severe accident the previous year and had faced a long recovery. One of the last calls I had made while at Halex was to his hospital room in Atlanta to wish him well. Now here he was to repay the gesture. As we talked, I asked him what helped him persevere through the tough times he faced during recovery. He shared something that a friend had told him while in the hospital:

"Celebrate every victory no matter how small."

I thought about those words long after he left and continue to put them to use in my life today.

I found small victories by setting goals related to personal independence that I worked to achieve every day. My aim involved everything from mastering my speech recognition software, to spending more time in the chair, to getting stronger in therapy. I made the conscious effort to push on and cultivated the spirit necessary to do so. Although my body was paralyzed, I got to decide whether my will would also be paralyzed.

That will was tested one morning when the director of physical therapy came to my room to deliver the news that my insurance company had terminated my therapy. According to them, I had "plateaued" in my workouts and no foreseeable progress was on the horizon to warrant additional therapy.

In my eyes, as well as others, I had come so far in such a short time, and there were still gains to be made. Statistics showed that after an SCI any sensation or function that might return was likely to do so within the first twenty-four months. Not even a year removed from my injury, and the insurance company pulled the plug on any potential for further recovery through physical therapy. Well, of course, there might not be any more progress without the therapy!

"All of the goals that were set for you have been achieved," the director told me.

"What do you mean? I'm not walking yet, that's a goal."

"Well, that's not exactly realistic," he said.

Immediately, I grew irate.

"What did you say! I dare you to tell me that again!"

It didn't matter. Even if the guy wanted to believe in me, he couldn't do so without the proper evidence. Physical therapy was vital at that stage in the game, and my doctors submitted for allowances to the insurance company, which unfortunately fell on deaf ears. I researched other rehab facilities across the United States, but logistics and financials proved to be hurdles too significant to overcome.

The frustration pendulum continually swings back and forth with an SCI. It's an injury with a recovery process where you never get out what you put in. It's especially frustrating for results-oriented individuals like me who often measure success by tangible results. However, I continued to remind myself that these injuries take time, extraordinary amounts of time, before results are sometimes seen.

In 1995, Will Steger set up the International Arctic Project that allowed people to follow a dogsled expedition he led to the North Pole via an online journal the famous explorer kept. I made my own trek to the library each day on the campus of Lehigh to read the daily update transmitted from the frozen, barren landscape. One of those passages has remained with me.

"The question of the meaning of life stares me in the face and begs me to try to answer the unanswerable. What is it about, what is death, what is life? Life out here is like living on the needlepoint of the present. It is easy to go in any direction, back to past, or forward to future, but to make a movement off the point is not reality. But the needle is so tenuous to be on. My memory is so sharp here. The past or dreams of the future are the escapes, but there is only so much thinking I can do about the past or future before I become weary of it. This leads me again to here–getting caught up in the progress made each day or not made each day, deadlines and imaginary pressures that become as real as the snow and the wind. I let go and bob up into the present. I can tick off our daily progress on my tent wall with a magic marker and, when I look up a month later, indeed, we have made progress. There is a hope. But the snail's pace is our daily life and that is the reality. Accepting the present is becoming peaceful. Actually, this is my life. It is life in a capsule, little pleasure, hard work, a mischievous mind that always wants to be elsewhere. Why worry, why mourn or smile at the past, why give weight to the future instead of just being here and letting it happen?"

Steger's insights on progress struck a chord with me then and were more relevant than ever all these years later. At times I found myself frustrated with the molasses-like measure in which my body seemed to repair itself. However, when I looked at pictures or thought about instances over the past year that served as my measure of progress, it reinforced the reality of how far I had come.

Sometimes, it's all about the inches.

# TWENTY-TWO
# WHAT IF?

As Kristy and I moved forward with the necessary steps for a divorce, we still spent a tremendous amount of time together attempting to forge a different type of relationship.

Although she was adamant about the divorce, I clung to the belief that our marriage could survive, however unlikely that might be. Regardless, I loved her deeply and wanted to spend as much time as possible with her, cherishing every minute of it.

I had been introduced to a gentleman, Will Voegele, through a family acquaintance. We immediately hit it off and formed an incredible friendship that has continued to this day. His daughter, Kate, an accomplished musician, was in town for a concert and Will arranged for Kristy and me to attend the show.

Days later Kristy and I spent the afternoon at an outdoor shopping complex not far from the nursing home. While out, we picked up a bottle of wine and some food and then ventured over to the grounds of our apartment complex. Kristy brought Kingsly outside to join us. Everything added up to a feeling of happiness I gladly welcomed.

On June ninth, we celebrated our third anniversary, albeit in a different fashion. Together we had shared an exciting and deeply enjoyable marriage. We experienced a lot together, from the trips we took, places we lived, people we met, things we did, pets we lost, new pets we gained, to all the in-betweens. However, neither of us had ever hoped for the experiences of the past year. It was only twelve months earlier that we celebrated with dinner at Pier W, drank champagne, and talked about the future. We were happy to finally be back in Cleveland close to our families, excited about the new chapters of our lives we were about to write. Less than a month later, I was injured, and those unwritten chapters took on a different meaning of their own.

The past year had been full of ups and downs for both of us. Although I sat immobile in a chair, we were both paralyzed that July day and we had both had our dreams ripped away. Our lives were thrust down a path different than what we discussed a year ago. The only difference was that Kristy could move. I couldn't.

Unless someone has experienced a catastrophic injury, it's hard to appreciate its effect on those closest to the person. In Kristy's case, a different type of love had replaced the previous love we shared. She told me it was deeper and more profound, but it was impossible to ignore the dramatic effect it had on our relationship. I was deeply hurt and scarred by the distance she had put between us.

There was no one to blame for my accident, so we just blamed the situation. It was all we could do. The night of our anniversary we drank champagne and watched a movie, probably what we would have done anyway had my injury never happened. Only it wasn't so much as husband and wife, but more as best friends.

And it hurt.

***

The one-year anniversary of my accident arrived on the third day of July. Prior to that day, I had wondered what I might feel. Although I figured there would be moments of sadness and despair, I planned to celebrate a year of life that doctors told me would never happen. What a difference a year made. The journey thus far had been tough, and at times, extremely tough, yet I was confident each subsequent year would be better than the one before. God would determine most of it, but I knew I would also have a role to play.

It wasn't just an emotional day for me. My mom wrote:

"It was exactly one year ago today that our lives and the lives of many around us were drastically altered ... I remember that all I prayed for was that God would save his life and let him continue to be a part of ours. God granted my wish ... I have had a very difficult time dealing with Scott's injury–it is now a year and I am not sure I have yet come to terms with it. I know it was a tragic accident and there must be a reason it happened, but I haven't figured that one out yet and probably never will. I still have a great deal of emotional difficulty talking about the accident and accepting the fact that things are different for Scott right now. As a parent, you never think that something so devastating will happen to one of your children; they always seem so resilient and fearless. Parents are the ones who should suffer before their children–I always thought that was the master plan ... I have spent as much time as possible with Scott over the past year–maybe even too much time. But suppose he needs his head scratched, his eyebrows scratched, his shoulders rubbed, his arms or legs straightened after a spasm–who will do it? What if all the care staff are at lunch with the other residents?"

She went on to talk about the guilt she struggled with:

"I don't think I have cooked but three meals for Felix in all that time, and I have not been there for Lindsey when she has needed me. Both of them were greatly impacted by Scott's injury and have each dealt with it in their own way. I often feel very guilty for not being there for them; however, at this point in time, I believe I am where I should be. I have tried to do whatever I can for Scott, but I know it is not enough. I haven't been able to provide all the necessary people or equipment he needs to recover. I realize I can't do it all myself and I have started to reach out to others. I need to be able to save some emotional support for Felix and Lindsey who have both suffered deeply over this accident ... There are so many wonderful people that we would have never met under 'ordinary circumstances.' All of us, but especially Scott, have truly benefitted by the Angels that God has sent our way."

She concluded with what I hoped would become prophetic:

"I know I may sound naïve, but I still believe that Scott will accomplish all he intends to and then some. I don't believe that he should give up on ANY of his dreams no matter how impossible they may seem right now. I think that he can still have whatever he wants–it might take some extra adjusting and will probably be expensive, but IT CAN AND WILL HAPPEN! ... So on this SPECIAL day we will CELEBRATE LIFE–Scott's life as well as everyone else's ... Let us all be thankful to God for what we have no matter what difficulties we might face as a result. I know the Fedor family is!!!"

I haven't hugged my mom in over a decade. She gives me plenty of hugs, which I relish, but it's not the same. A bit of effort is needed to hoodwink myself into believing it's not so one-sided. If I could hug her, it would be a long time before I'd let go. She has been at my side since my injury. Of course, she was there before my accident, but in a different way. I often joke that a mother and son aren't supposed to spend as much time together as we do. Inevitably, the more time spent with someone, the more time exists to get on each other's nerves. But when someone can take you at your worst and still see the best in you, it's a relationship more valuable than anything on earth. If I'm not at my best, my mom still lets me know it.

When I think back to that Witness I gave in high school about my relationship with God and my mother, it seems so much more profound after everything I have since experienced. My mother has been a constant source of strength for me and one of the greatest gifts

God has given me.

I'm not a parent and thus cannot begin to appreciate what it must be like to see a child go through what I have gone through. I know my mom's faith has been tested to the extreme and at times I fear her relationship with God has weakened. I hope that is not the case and want her to realize how far I've come and the life I enjoy today. I want that image to give her strength, peace, and most of all restored faith in our Lord.

On July third, I also journaled my thoughts, which were slightly different:

"I wasn't quite sure a few months ago how I would feel when today finally came around. Would I be happy? Sad? Scared? Excited? Thankful? Regretful? ... Today didn't feel any different. I didn't wake up with some weird tingling feeling, or some heightened sense of being. Nope–I felt the same as I did yesterday, and I will probably feel the same way tomorrow ... But maybe that's a good thing. Maybe I am better equipped at dealing with my situation than I thought I would have been had you asked me several months ago. Today is a celebration."

That afternoon and into the evening, my parents, Kristy, and Diane, a reporter from *The Plain Dealer* who was planning to write an in-depth story about my accident, sat outside, drank champagne, told stories about the past year, and laughed and cried as we recalled all that we had been through. My in-laws, who I was still close to despite Kristy and me deciding to part ways, sent me a beautiful picture of everyone gathered together at the lake as they toasted me at 5:45 p.m. (the time I dove in the water). Throughout the day I focused on everything I had accomplished in the past year. I was reminded every day about what I could no longer do but didn't always give myself enough credit for what I could do. That night I asked my mom to make a list for me of what I had been able to do over the past year. It wasn't a glamorous list, but one I was very proud of. Probably one of the best lists ever for the simple fact of how hard I worked to accomplish each item.

I was not done by any means and planned to add a lot more to the list. I stuck it out when a lot of others may have chosen to give up. I would never fault anyone if they decided not to stick it out, for a high-level SCI is a catastrophic injury, impossible to comprehend its totality unless you've been through it. Many unpleasant idiosyncrasies accompany an SCI, and to adequately explain them would be like trying to describe the color "red" to a blind person. However, knowing the road that was ahead of me, I still chose to go on. And for that, I was grateful and proud.

That summer, a favorite artist of Kristy's, Carole King, came through town on tour with James Taylor. Music had always been a common bond between Kristy and me, and throughout our years together, we enjoyed several concerts together. I arranged for us to attend the show at Quicken Loans Arena in downtown Cleveland. The final song of the night was a duet between King and Taylor as they sang, "You Can Close Your Eyes" with its haunting lyrics:

"You can close your eyes, it's all right; I don't know no love songs; And I can't sing the blues anymore; But I can sing this song; And you can sing this song; When I'm gone."

As we listened to the song, Kristy held my hand and cried.

Seeing the tears in her eyes left me with a weird feeling of confusion. I knew how much she loved me and wanted to be with me, but I also knew she felt that for her, her only option was to move on. The moment was beautiful, yet sad; hurtful, yet appropriate.

And it made me miss her even more.

***

Early one August evening, Diane stopped by the nursing home to talk with Kristy and me. It had been almost a year since she first walked into my hospital room at MetroHealth and said she wanted to write a piece about my injury and subsequent journey toward recovery. The three of us sat in the lobby of Rae Ann where Kristy and I updated her as to where things stood between us and Kristy's desire to divorce.

"It's hard to accept a life without intimacy, and I'm not talking about just sexual intimacy," Kristy said. "I just mean the touch, the human touch. I don't have family here. I don't have anybody who hugs me, or touches my hair, or scratches my back or just holds my hand."

"You have my family," I told her. "But in all fairness, you pushed them away."

"In all fairness," she interrupted, "they're not the most ..." Kristy stopped herself and then continued, "Your family and my family are just very different. Very, very different."

My family loved Kristy and had always been very supportive of her. However, Kristy had retreated into a very private place in the months after my accident and at times closed herself off to others, including my family. I felt like Kristy was selfish. Although she had suffered greatly, she wasn't the only one who was affected by my accident. My parents had lost their able-bodied son, someone who was supposed to take care of them as they grew old, not the other way around. My sister had been engaged and broke it off with her fiancé because she felt she needed to be there for me, although she would never admit that to me.

Kristy continued, "And then there's a lot of things with the relationship too. Things that make it difficult, like who I am, I'm very spontaneous, a free spirit."

One of the many things I loved about Kristy was her wonderment and giant curiosity about life, something we shared until I felt like it was stolen from me.

"My wings have been clipped. And it's difficult. It's hard not to fly when you know you can," she said.

It hurt to hear her say this. I appreciated what she meant yet struggled to accept how unfair the whole situation seemed.

"All of this," I told Diane, "is probably worse than the accident. I feel like if I work hard, I could get my body back."

However, I'm not sure I entirely believed my own words. I had worked incredibly hard but felt I had nothing of substance to show for it. At least nothing strong enough to convince Kristy to stay. I wanted her to be happy; I just wished it could be with me. However, I wasn't going to prevent her from finding her happiness. I told her numerous times from the onset of my injury that I wanted her to be happy and able to go on with her life. I guess, deep inside of me, I just hoped she could find that happiness with me at her side.

"This isn't the decision I want," I said, as tears rolled down my cheeks, "but I recognize it's what needs to happen. Either way, one person loses."

It had started to rain outside, which seemed apropos for the moment.

"If you truly love someone, if they need to go, you let them leave so they can be happy," I said with no anger or fight, only resignation, "so, Kristy, be happy."

Kristy responded, "I know what I'm doing is probably the wrong thing to do, but I feel like it's my only choice if I want to live a happy life. You know, the romantic feelings are gone, but I have very strong feelings toward Scott. I still feel a connection with him that I don't feel with any other friend. I want to stay in touch. I hope that he can."

There was nothing left to say, at least not that night. A few minutes later Diane left, and then shortly afterward, it was time for Kristy to go. We said goodnight the way we usually did, with an 'I love you' and an innocent kiss.

As I lay in bed that night, I reminisced about the times Kristy and I used to lay in bed next to each other and play the "What if" game. We asked one another questions we never expected to confront, intended more to prove our undying love.

"Would you love me if I talked funny?"

"What if I had no arms?"

"What if I smelled bad?"

"What if I broke my neck, was paralyzed, and couldn't move?

Neither of us had ever thought to ask the last question. I wonder what our answers would have been.

I also thought about how much I hated this injury. It had hardly been a year, and it had already taken what seemed like everything from me. Gone was my independence. Gone was my physical prowess, the physique and strength I was so proud of. Gone were my finances and personal equity I had spent years working to save. And now, worst of all, gone was my wife, love of my life, and best friend. So much had been taken from me.

Yeah, this injury sucked.

# TWENTY-THREE
# BREAKTHROUGHS

One afternoon at the nursing home, I sat in the courtyard with a former co-worker and discussed the research being done with stem cells.

I tried to stay current on the latest stem cell therapies and trials, but I also made it a point to remain even-keeled when I read about any scientific breakthroughs. I sought to find a balance between my interest in current medical research and acceptance of my current situation. I did not want to not put my life on hold waiting for a medical miracle. However, I admit it was tough not to get excited as I learned about some of the stuff that had occurred or was rumored to take place soon.

Before my injury, I was on the fence when it came to stem cell use. I tried to balance my religious convictions with my desire to see sick people receive the help they need. Since my injury, I have read a lot about stem cells and other new techniques being developed.

As I have educated myself, my position has changed to where I support adult stem cell use, which in most cases involves having only one's own stem cells introduced into a different part of the body. My views are not as liberal when it comes to embryonic stem cells, depending on how they are attained.

A few months after our conversation, the first human was injected with embryonic stem cells a few months later in a clinical trial at the Shepherd Center in Atlanta. Although it's a controversial subject for many, and the cells' success in restoring function needs to be proven, it's hard not to be fascinated by the possibilities that may one day exist.

People who live with paralysis spend their lives being told all the things they will never do again, and they must learn to adjust to a new way of life. While I agree it is essential to adapt to the changes one encounters, I have never felt those changes need to be accepted as the end-all-be-all. One must accept the fact that life will now be different, but one never needs to accept that what has been lost will never be regained. Although it is okay to be excited about the scientific and medical breakthroughs, that should not be a reason to stop working hard to keep the body healthy and strong. It's a reason to work even harder, to stay fit and stable, in the hopes that one day, if there is a cure, you will be ready.

Sometimes human will and nature's law don't always achieve the desired results and science and medicine can offer tremendous assistance and freedom. Like I witnessed in the hospital, a lot of scientists and doctors are of firm faith and believe in both God and the power of medicine. They are not in conflict. It is God who gives us the intelligence to discover these life-saving techniques. It is man who decides how to apply them–for good or for bad.

I was not the first person with a spinal cord injury to fixate on being made "whole again." In my dreams, I am always whole. I have never had a dream in which I am in a wheelchair. In most of my dreams, I function the same way I did before my injury. I am aware that I was injured, recovered, and now seem a bit more guarded. I am an SCI survivor who has been restored to complete health. I remember a dream where I sat in a chair at my parents' house. Suddenly, I began to move and flailed my arms and hands around. It felt so real. The first thing I wanted to do was touch Kristy's face and hug her. Afterward, I took her to the County Fair, where all I wanted to do was play games that tested my dexterity. I threw darts at targets, tried to throw hula hoops over blocks, tossed balls into baskets, and shot rifles at targets. I won every game I played and a lot of stuffed animals in the process.

Not a day went by that at some point I did not dwell on my desire to function like I used to. I longed for the independence I was familiar with once upon a time. Voice-activated software, Bluetooth cell phones, and sip-n-puff power wheelchairs offered a type of autonomy, but all fell short of my desire for true independence. Ultimately, I concluded it was more productive to face my current situation and focus on what I could do, not lament on what I could not do. I believed there would be medical breakthroughs at some point down the road, but realized I was better suited if I appreciated who I was and where I was in my life. It wasn't always easy, but it was a conscious choice I made and worked diligently to adhere to.

The medical and scientific breakthroughs I one day hoped for manifested themselves in other ways. I was invited to participate in a study at the local VA hospital to measure and record the brain waves of individuals with SCIs as they tried to move their arms and hands. The long-term goal of the study was to gather enough data so that a prosthetic device could be designed that the mind controlled.

I found myself a willing participant in as many research projects as possible, to allow doctors, scientists, and researchers to compile the necessary information that could be used to one day improve the lives of anyone living with an SCI. Some of the studies I participated in have already yielded advancements. Additionally, for several months I saw a man by the name of Dr. Issam Nemeh, a medical doctor who believed in the power of healing through Christ. Each week I went to his office for a healing session that involved prayer and other nontraditional procedures.

Late that summer, I received the incredible news that I had finally been approved for the spinal cough assist system and would soon be implanted with the device that would allow me to cough and clear my throat on my own again. I had greatly realized the benefits of the DPS, and I now hoped the same could be said for the cough assist system.

The day after Labor Day I underwent an extremely invasive procedure that lasted six hours. An incision was made in the middle of my back, and the surgeon drilled into my T9, T11, and L1 vertebrae, where he placed small electrodes on the dura mater, the outermost layer of membrane that surrounds the spinal cord. A small wire attached to the electrodes was wrapped around to my abdominal muscles. On the end of the wire was a receiver that was stitched to my abs.

I was the fourteenth person in the world to have the procedure.

Several hours later I was able to cough for the first time in over a year! The device worked by placing an external receiver, not attached to the body, against my abs, where the internal receiver was located. All someone needed to do was push a button, and a charge triggered my abdominal muscles to contract, which forced a cough.

The first time I tried the device I was unsure what to expect. The doctor pushed the button on the receiver as I took a breath, waited a couple of seconds, and then tried to time my cough with the jolt of the device. It triggered quite a contraction in my abdominal muscles that forced the air to be expelled from my lungs and generated a cough. It felt like a punch to the gut without the pain, in much the same way a typical spasm feels. I let out such a forceful cough that it even caused my legs to jump. *The Plain Dealer* was there to document everything for their story. I called Kristy, Lindsey, and my dad so I could cough for each of them since they could not be there. They were all amazed to hear me cough for the first time in fifteen months. Who would think so many people could get ecstatic about something as simple as a cough!

The device proved to be a literal lifesaver. Not only did it mean that I could have my trach removed, but it meant more independence.

Now I could go out with friends and not have to worry about needing to be suctioned. Furthermore, it reduced my chances of developing pneumonia, a leading cause of death among people with quadriplegia.

To aid in my recovery, I spent time in the courtyard enjoying the last days of summer and the beginning of fall. I began to meditate, trying to live in the proverbial now. I found it appealing, as well as challenging. I watched the leaves migrate through their autumnal progression of color and I was struck by the beauty that presents itself as a result of death. It was weird how beautiful dying looked. Of course, the Bible already told of this, even though people often found more pain than beauty in the death of something. I reflected on the parallels between my own life and the "death" of the life I once knew.

I struggled to not think of my life as pre- and post-injury. I was still learning to move forward. I told myself that the past wasn't going anywhere. It was always there when and if I needed it. However, my future was ahead of me, still unwritten and meant to be experienced. I was doing myself a disservice if I spent more time focused on the road behind me rather than the road ahead. The future, even with its uncertainty, was something to look forward to and to be excited about.

Over the next few weeks, whenever I was back at Metro for my post-op, I visited with the patients on 7A. I was all too familiar with the anxiety that presented itself during those first several weeks. I tried my best to listen to the concerns of people I spoke with and offer what hope I could from my own experiences. It is an exclusive group to be an unfortunate member of, but we can relate to each other and lean on each other in a way that those outside our collective cannot.

It seemed as if every week I learned of someone who had suffered an SCI. I don't know if more injuries were occurring or if I was just more aware, but before my injury, Christopher Reeve was one of only a few people I'd heard of who lived with an SCI. The others were Dennis Byrd, whose story introduced me to the passage from Romans that still inspires me to this day, and Ron Kovic, whose injury was chronicled in the movie *Born on the Fourth of July.* Now, I seemed to discover someone new each week and each time it was disheartening.

At the time of my injury there were roughly 307 million people in the United States, and approximately 12,000 new SCIs each year, half of which were complete injuries like mine. I had a 0.002 percent chance of joining that unfortunate guild. Better odds existed for me to win the lottery. Yet, I continued to learn of new injuries on a somewhat frequent basis.

Maybe society's awareness of spinal cord injuries and the devastating effect they have on all who are touched by them would increase in time. Perhaps that increase would prompt more funding and research toward finding a cure. And more assistance toward helping those who lived with these injuries every day. Unfortunately, because there are only 12,000 new injuries each year, it is considered an orphan affliction and does not receive anywhere near the level of funding needed to make the slightest dent toward any meaningful progress. Instead, it takes public and private organizations, activists, scientists, and others working on their own accord to raise awareness and funding.

The scientific and medical communities were abuzz about the possibility of finding a cure for paralysis over the next several years; however, more needed to be done in the near term to make that a reality. Those of us who had suffered an SCI could not go back and receive a brand-new start, but we could keep moving in the right direction, working to create a better, brand-new tomorrow.

I knew I wanted to do something to help those living with an SCI achieve a better tomorrow.

***

As Thanksgiving arrived, it was another opportunity to reflect on my life. I had learned that my perfect plans were not always God's plans. Although my life had taken a turn away from the predictable and headed down the path of the unpredictable, there was still much for which I was thankful. Mostly, I was thankful for my family, for their unconditional love and unwavering support.

When I got down to it, I was fortunate to be where I was in my life. I survived a horrible accident that should've killed me. Instead, I was still on this earth and able to enjoy time with those I loved every day. I developed an amazing support network and had the good fortune of meeting several new and fascinating people whose paths I might never have crossed. I had personally seen and experienced the good in my neighbors and been the benefactor of their generosity. Every day I had breath in my lungs and time to reflect and pray. I learned I didn't need to get caught up in petty details that had formerly consumed me. I appreciated a beautiful day more than I ever thought possible. I found myself in a position to help others appreciate their lives and what they had–a position more powerful than anything my former career path could have offered me. There was a lot for which I was grateful.

However, I am not a Pollyanna. I often grew frustrated with what I could no longer do, with what I no longer had, with what I no longer might have. At those times, it was vital for me to catch my breath, calm down, and try to take things one moment at a time. I reminded myself that how I chose to use the blessings I'd been given was the true measure of giving thanks.

Around the same time, I turned in my discharge notice to the nursing facility, my Medicaid application had been approved, and the details were almost finalized for the at-home nursing care, equipment, and other items I needed. My goal was to spring myself by mid-January, although it took a few months longer to leave than anticipated.

A few weeks later I spent my second consecutive Christmas as a resident of Rae Ann Suburban. Fortunately, I escaped for the evening and attended a party hosted by the Voegeles, who had been gracious enough to invite my family into their home for Christmas.

The holiday passed and it was the start of a new year. While I had designated 2010 as the Year of the Miracle, expecting one big breakthrough, what I learned was that not all miracles were grandiose in scope, nor blatantly obvious. Some miracles came quietly and revealed themselves in a subtle manner that could only be appreciated over time. Those were the miracles I had experienced over the past twelve months through my family, friends, and the power of prayer.

A new year often prompts talk of resolutions and new beginnings. However, I made resolutions every day, as I suspect most people do who face challenging situations with unpredictable futures. My most significant resolution had been to remain resolute. When faced with a challenge like mine, I discovered that determination, perseverance, and an unwavering will were more important than doctors, pills, and hospitals. The latter were great defense mechanisms, but the former were the foundation for miracles.

During an appointment with an endocrinologist, I discovered I had the beginning stages of osteoporosis. Although typical for an individual with an SCI, I found it disheartening. I had been an athlete who prided himself on staying fit and active. I missed lifting weights, running, breaking a sweat, and feeling spent after workouts. While in college, I had competed in and won powerlifting competitions and was proud of the physique I developed. Now, I was forced to watch my body atrophy and deteriorate against my will, and that was very tough for me. The reality was I had to focus more on my mental regimen than my physical regimen. Although the physical component was important, it was all too often out of my control. I did my best to stay flexible and in shape but knew it was mental fortitude that would keep me healthy and fit.

It was imperative to get my head strong–and work every day to keep it strong.

A great reminder that further drove home that edict was delivered by Dennis Byrd, the man who had already inspired my life in so many ways. The ordinarily reclusive Byrd spoke to the New York Jets in early January, the night before their playoff game against the New England

Patriots. The week prior, Byrd sent the Jets his tattered jersey that had been cut from his body on the day of his injury, along with an inspirational letter addressed to the team. Head coach Rex Ryan was so moved by the gesture that he invited Dennis to address the players before the game.

On the evening of January 15, 2011, Byrd told the team, "A man has a body, a mind, and a spirit. There are times in a man's life when his body will tell him it can't continue on. There are times his mind will tell him that the task set for him is too hard to accomplish. Those two don't matter. It's a man's will and his spirit, and in those moments and in those times, that will tell him, 'You can do it,' and it will make the mind and body follow along."

Greatly inspired by Byrd's words, the New York Jets carried his jersey to the coin toss and then proceeded to win the game.

# TWENTY-FOUR
# HER AGAIN

On the morning of Tuesday, January 18, 2011, Kristy arrived at the nursing home and loaded me into a brand-new Chrysler Town & Country minivan that had been outfitted for my needs. My family had been able to purchase the van thanks to the successful fundraising efforts of my sister, former work colleagues, and others.

We drove into downtown Cleveland, listening to the radio and talking about what we should do later that evening. For now, there was other business we needed to attend to, although feelings of melancholy and trepidation filled my mind.

Forty minutes later we arrived at the Cuyahoga County Courthouse. Shortly thereafter we were in a courtroom, in front of Judge Cheryl Karner, who was seated behind a wooden desk, the state seal affixed to the wall behind her. I positioned my wheelchair in front of the desk, with Kristy at my right and our joint attorney on my left.

It was a day I never envisioned in my life. A day I had pleaded, repeatedly, with Kristy to avoid. Unfortunately, she had wanted this day for several months now.

It was the day our marriage was dissolved.

The judge asked each of us a few legal questions regarding our names, ages, and where we lived. She asked if we had children or if Kristy was pregnant. She then asked each of us if we intended to proceed with what had been stated in the dissolution agreement drafted a few weeks earlier.

I didn't want to affirm it, but what choice did I have?

I was about to lose my wife, the one person I told myself I could fight for and the one person in this world I believed would be with me through sickness and health, till death did us part. In truth, though, I lost Kristy the day I dove into that lake and broke my neck. She no longer wanted to hold on or believe we could be happy with what she felt our relationship had evolved into.

With the heaviest heart, "Yes," I replied to the judge.

She then asked Kristy the same question, at which point Kristy began to sob; however, she still managed to get the word out that the judge needed to hear. Once I saw the tears in Kristy's eyes, I lost it. Even the bailiff, who had seen hundreds of marriage dissolutions over the years, cried for the first time in her career.

And then, just like that, the dissolution of our marriage was avowed.

Kristy took the pen in her hand and signed the paper. I bit down on a pen between my teeth and made a messy "X" where I was supposed to sign.

"Okay I'm going to grant this," the judge said, "Good luck to both of you."

Luck seemed like a foreign concept to me.

Our relationship, cultivated with deep love and thousands of promises for the future over the past six years, no longer existed. It only took six minutes to render it null and void.

Kristy leaned over and hugged me, whispered in my ear, kissed me, and rubbed my chest. I asked her to wipe the tears from my face.

Three and a half years after we said, "I do," we said, "I don't."

Over the next several weeks, Kristy and I continued to spend time together as friends, but it was difficult to ignore the fact that we were no longer husband and wife. I would struggle with that for a while. I still viewed her through the lens of a husband, and as a result, my actions reflected that. After I agreed to give her a divorce, I hired a joint attorney to represent us. I wanted things to be amicable, and for her to be taken care of, even though I was under no legal obligation to do so. We had managed to amass a comfortable savings in addition to our other retirement investments. I agreed to give her a significant portion of the savings that I had assigned to the Medicaid trust. I also waived my right to any alimony she was required to provide me with due to my disability. The only thing I asked for was to continue to be listed on her employee health insurance plan for six months.

There was an enormous amount of empathy I felt for Kristy, so much so that I probably allowed it to cloud my judgment. Upon hearing of the details of my accident and subsequent injury, several of my friends, as well as family acquaintances, urged me to seek litigation against the Coldwater Lake Homeowners' Association. They said there was a precedent for a claim since proper notification had not been posted of the shallow water levels.

Furthermore, the township was not correctly mapped for emergency services and that led to the forty-five-minute delay before the ambulance reached me. Who knows how much additional damage might have happened as a result of my being moved and jostled around while we waited for the paramedics to arrive. Even though the Costells themselves would not have been the subject of any litigation, Kristy felt that if I tried to sue the lake, it could indirectly impact her family. She implored me not to take any action, and so I didn't.

There was no shortage of opinions offered to me when it came to others' feelings toward Kristy. Her decision to leave me elicited a variety of emotions from both friends and strangers. There were those who were appalled; those who were saddened; and those who weren't sure how to feel. Several people took their cues from what I had to say about the issue.

Publicly, I tried to be diplomatic and put on a happy front when I spoke of Kristy to others, whether through my website or with friends and family. Although I did not agree with her decision, I respected her choice. She had been my wife and the love of my life. I wanted her to be happy. Of course, I would have preferred it to be with me but did not want to prevent her from seeking what she felt I could no longer give her. I wanted her to be "her" again. For the first time in my life, I appreciated just how deep love could run and what it meant to love another unselfishly. For that reason, and many others, I didn't want anyone to speak ill of her in my presence. I felt the need to defend her, honor her, and protect her, even if it was no longer my duty to do so.

Privately, I was deeply hurt by her decision, more so than I let on. My life had been torn apart, and any chance for some residual happiness had been ripped from me with her decision to leave. I felt Kristy had acted selfishly when she was unwilling to give our relationship a chance to see what being together might entail over the next year. When I had been in the hospital, doubtful as to whether I even wanted to go on, it was Kristy who told me about Christopher Reeve's wife, Dana, who told him to give it two years before he made any major decisions. After all, as the doctors had constantly reminded us, so much could and often did change during those first two years.

It felt like Kristy had a master plan as to how life was supposed to unfold at this stage, and I had upset the proverbial applecart. It was clear to me that she wanted to get on with her life and get back into the role she saw herself needing to be in as a thirty-something.

Whether or not this was an unfair assessment is arguable, but what could not be debated were her actions in the months following our divorce.

# TWENTY-FIVE
# GETTING BACK UP

Five days after my thirty-fifth birthday I was released from the nursing home.

For the first time in more than twenty months, I was no longer confined to institutional living and I was in my own place at last. A local organization, Linking Employment, Abilities and Potential (LEAP), helped facilitate my move from the nursing home to my apartment through a home transition program they offered.

My first night at home was different than what I expected. I had looked forward to the day when I would finally be in my own place. However, as I lay in bed, I was overcome with an incredible feeling of melancholy as I thought about how far I had come and how hard I had worked to get to this very moment.

*What is next for me, though?*

Since my injury, I had achieved several noteworthy goals that improved my health and strengthened my emotional and mental well-being. One of the biggest goals was to return home. I finally achieved that.

*But now what?*

I was alone. I was no longer married. I no longer had a job to go back to, nothing to wake up and do each day. Suddenly, I felt a gaping void in my life I had not planned on and was not sure how to address it. That first night home, I fell asleep blanketed by a suffocating sense of depression.

Although I technically lived alone in the apartment, there was always someone around. Medicaid provided sixteen hours a day of nursing services. The other eight hours needed to be covered out-of-pocket. While at Rae Ann, I developed a great relationship with one of the aides, Tanya, and asked her to come work for me full-time. Fortunately, she agreed and has been with me ever since. In addition to Tanya's eight-hour shift, I ultimately hired independent providers to work as nurses.

I enjoyed being in my own place, but strangely also found myself frustrated by it. There were constant reminders that things weren't quite the same as the last time I lived at home. Now, I slept on a hospital bed, unable to escape its humming motor as air shifted throughout the mattress to relieve pressure points from various parts of my body. Above the bed, stretched across the ceiling, was a Hoyer lift, supported on both sides with floor to ceiling poles. The lift moved me from the bed to the wheelchair, a cruel, ever-present reminder that I could no longer rely on my muscles to transport me from Point A to Point B.

Once in my wheelchair, careful maneuvering was required to squeeze through the narrow hallway and into the living room. The living room was sparsely filled with furniture so I could move around. A large workstation hugged one of the walls where I worked on my computer. It certainly wasn't the rich-looking mahogany desk and plush leather chair that used to sit in my home office. Instead, it was an adjustable table that looked like something out of an IKEA catalog. It was high enough to accommodate my wheelchair and provide the necessary clearance needed so my wheelchair could be tilted every thirty minutes to shift my weight and thus stave off pressure sores.

Next to the workstation was the standing frame. It could be an ordeal to get me into the machine that supported my weight and allowed me to stand on my own two feet for as long as I could tolerate, which was sometimes only twenty minutes. Off the living room was a small patio where I spent as much time as the weather allowed. No matter where I was, there was always someone else in the room with me. Sure, they were needed to ensure my safety and prevent starvation; however, I was never alone.

My new digs also brought with it a much more relaxed and comfortable environment. The apartment had a kitchen where my family and friends could prepare meals at our own pace. Meals that we could enjoy with wine, laughter, and plenty of relaxation. Meals that were much more delectable than the peas, cheese, and mayonnaise salad, beets and succotash, and spaghetti surprise that were frequently served at Rae Ann. There were comfortable couches, a large TV, and scented candles to provide all the creature comforts of home. Three cats ran around freely, perched on windowsills, or hid under beds. There was even the occasional yelling for each other from room to room. Yes, my new home also had plenty of features reminding me of my old home. I felt like a human paradox–a person unable to move who still felt he could; an individual who longed to continue with the way life used to be when it was ever apparent that it was more different than ever.

As the weeks went on, I continued to find my groove. I participated in another study to measure any discernible muscle activity below my knees. The encouraging news was that slight traces of muscle movement were recorded. The discouraging news was they were minor and inconsistent. I tried to view the fact that any movement was positive and something to build on.

I met with others who were considering the cough assist system and happily demonstrated my device and answered their questions as best I could. Ever since being implanted, I could not stop singing its praises.

Days before Easter I participated in an interview in front of a live studio audience for a DVD about clinical trials–in my case, the cough assist system. As I left the studio, a young man dressed like Jesus plodded past me on the sidewalk. He carried a large wooden cross, wore a crown of thorns, and walked hunched over from the weight of the cross. It was a sobering sight to behold and reminded me of the sacrifice Christ made for us when He died on the cross. I later saw a story on the news about the young man. He was twenty-three years old and walked with the cross to help remind people of the pain and suffering Jesus endured so that we could be forgiven and one day welcomed into Heaven. At that point, I wished I had been able to move, as I would have asked the man to let me carry the cross for a short while.

Seeing him made me think about the challenges everyone faces in their lives. Inevitably, everyone has their cross to bear. At times they carry that cross themselves, but there are times when they rely on others to help shoulder the burden. I always considered myself an independent person and took pride in my ability to do things on my own. My injury taught me otherwise. It helped me learn how important it is to allow others into my life to help, even though I might not have felt I needed the assistance. For a prideful person like myself, this was a challenging lesson to accept. However, welcoming others into my life and opening myself to receive the help provided allowed me to grow as a person.

Every grand narrative I've read about someone who accomplished tremendous things involved other individuals whose guidance and benevolence benefited the person along the way. The most important person who can help is God. Although religious, I don't feel the need to preach to others. Rather, I believe that if people want Christ in their lives, they will seek Him out. However, people sometimes need a reminder of the power that exists in helping others.

I knew that helping others was something I wanted to do.

While in the nursing home I experienced the unpleasant reality of how it felt to have insurance discontinue the physical therapy my body desperately needed. To say it was disheartening, would be a complete understatement. Fortunately, I was able to rely on the generosity of others to assist with some of those services. However, there were thousands of others in a similar situation who were not as fortunate. I gave a tremendous amount of thought about what could be done to help those individuals.

Additionally, I knew firsthand what it felt like to be stuck in a nursing home, in the prime of life, with a debilitating injury. The unfortunate fact was that more and more young people also found themselves in a similar situation. To be surrounded by people in constant decline while you try to rebound can drag you down if you don't maintain a healthy, positive mental attitude. I was fortunate enough to stay positive in part due to the constant influx of friends and family I had. Not everyone is as fortunate.

Even if nursing homes become more accommodating to younger folks, in my opinion, better alternatives are still needed. I pondered the idea of a group home equipped to accommodate others. A place where SCI survivors can cohabitate in a more comfortable environment specifically designed for their needs and could pool their resources to split the costs of care, therapy, and other living expenses. Most importantly they could draw strength from one another. I even had a name for this idea: The Quad.

I transformed my thoughts into actions and began the process to establish a nonprofit organization called Getting Back Up, or GBU for short. Its mission would be to offer exercise-based recovery services and adaptable products that improved individuals' physical and emotional well-being. Since insurance failed to provide tools needed to enhance the quality of life, my goal for GBU would be to try to help bridge that gap and offer goods and services that made an immediate difference.

Perhaps even one day the organization could also bring The Quad to fruition.

As I worked to establish Getting Back Up and secure its 501(c)(3) status, another opportunity presented itself to me. LEAP, the agency that helped make my transition from the nursing home smooth, approached me about serving on its board of directors. LEAP had been founded more than three decades earlier and served over 1,700 individuals in the Northeast Ohio area with a mission to advance a society of equal opportunity for all persons, regardless of disability. The organization provided education, training, employment, and independent-living services to people with disabilities and helped them eliminate barriers to employment and independent living. Additionally, LEAP advocated for social change and public policies that promoted quality-of-life improvements for people with disabilities. Since 2011, I have served on LEAP's board in a variety of capacities, including vice president as well as chairman of the advocacy committee.

Weeks after our divorce, Kristy started to look for a job in another city. She told me that she felt the best way to move on with her life was to start anew somewhere else. As painful as it was to admit, I also knew it was the only way I would ever be able to move on with my life, as it was difficult to watch her come and go from the apartment complex, clearly leading her own life without me. I supported her by encouraging her to look for an opportunity outside of Cleveland; however, I was shocked when she informed me that she had convinced her current company to transfer her back to Washington D.C.

Less than three years earlier, Kristy told me she didn't want to live in the D.C. metro area, so I worked extremely hard and made a lot of professional sacrifice so we could move back to Cleveland to start our family. Now here she was telling me she was headed back to the very area we left behind.

Honestly, it felt like everything I'd done for our future together was all for naught.

*If we had just stayed in the D.C. metro area and never left, would any of this have happened?*

I asked her to at least leave Kingsly with me, but she pleaded with me, telling me that she needed Kingsly since she would be alone. Once again, I relented and gave in to her wishes, although Kingsly remained with me for a few weeks until Kristy came back for the rest of her belongings. I enjoyed having the furball in the apartment. She spent her nights curled up in my bed and many of her days in my lap. I think she wondered why I wouldn't pet her anymore. She developed a habit of nudging her head underneath my hand, which led to a spasm causing my hand to slap her head for a few seconds. She just sat there, squinted her eyes closed, and took it, as if to say, "It's okay, I get it."

A week before Memorial Day, Kristy was back in town to finalize her move. We spent a few hours together before it was time for her to leave. I said goodbye to Kingsly. And then it was time to say goodbye to Kristy. Although there was talk of getting together each time she was back in town, neither of us knew if that would happen. After we said our goodbyes, she hopped in the car and drove away.

That would be the last time I ever saw her.

# PART THREE

# TWENTY-SIX
# BROKEN

In the wake of Kristy's departure, I found myself in a bit of a funk.

One afternoon I sat at my computer and made a Top 10 list about what I liked and didn't like about my injury and what I'd been through.

My dislikes:

1. Not being able to move–unable to scratch my itches, feed myself or raise my arms above my head and stretch while letting out a big yawn.

2. Lacking the ability to run my fingers through the fur of an animal and feel its softness against my hand and fingers.

3. Being single again. I miss being married.

4. I haven't gone swimming, dove into an ocean wave, or been in the water in nearly two years.

5. Feeling great and then suddenly feeling horrible as a result of the onset of autonomic dysreflexia–a cruel reminder of how much my body has changed.

6. Lounging on the couch and falling asleep on a Sunday afternoon with a warm breeze blowing through the screen door and some random

golf tournament playing on TV.

7. Seeing how tired my family looks. I wish I could do more for all of them.

8. I can't just get up and go somewhere. Things take time, planning, and much more effort than I ever would've imagined.

9. I can't open a bottle of wine or light a cigar or refill someone's drink for them.

10. Missing "the old days" and wishing I could have them back.

My likes:

1. I'm proud of the adversity I've overcome and character I've built.

2. Having the ability (and responsibility) to help others in my situation, whether through talking to them, listening to them, or pointing out resources to benefit them. I am proud to be an ambassador for individuals with spinal cord injuries.

3. Warm, sunny days. I can't emphasize how much I appreciate the warm sun on my face and bright blue skies with fluffy white clouds hovering above me. It's good for the soul.

4. I can eat, swallow, and taste. I'm so fortunate to still have this ability.

5. Conversation. I have met many new and interesting people since my injury whose paths I otherwise might never have crossed. They have helped me and taught me so much.

6. I'm alive. It was very sad to be faced with the possibility of death. I can still tell people how much I love them and enjoy the beautiful things God intends for me to discover.

7. Being comfortable in bed. Sometimes it takes a while, but once I'm comfortable, I'm able to sleep soundly and dream more vividly than ever before.

8. A lot of new opportunities have been presented to me.

9. I have time to sit still, be still, meditate, and reflect. I had time before my accident but was always too consumed with what I thought

were things of "importance."

10. I can get into the movies for free. Plus, I get great seating at sporting events and concerts!

Over the next several months I continued my physical therapy regimen with Holly, a therapist I met, who volunteered her time each week to assist me with my exercises. One afternoon, I lay prone on a mat on the floor and was able to flex my trapezius muscles down to the T4 level. I typically didn't get excited easily, but this was a big deal. I constantly tried to move my shoulders and back muscles while sitting in my wheelchair. The effort seemed to have paid dividends. Not only was I able to flex the muscles, but the longer I lay there, the more they seemed to wake up. Holly was very encouraged and felt that I functioned at a C5 level, significantly better than the C3 level at which I was originally diagnosed.

It was a bittersweet revelation. I was thrilled with the progress I made but wondered how much further along I might have been had I received therapy on a consistent basis for the past two years.

I continued to partake in muscle studies at MetroHealth. During one session, activity was detected in my biceps. It was apparent something was trying to fire up. It had always been my belief my biceps would one day work again, and that test kept the fire aglow within me. That night, I lay in bed overcome with a genuine feeling of gratitude and happiness. I thanked the Lord for the ability I still had in my life. I prayed to Him, almost in a giddy manner, thanking Him repeatedly for how lucky I was. A very peaceful and serene feeling washed over me, and I was overcome with knowing that one day I would completely recover and walk again. It was a surreal, yet intense feeling of quiet reassurance imparted upon me as I fell asleep. The following day I still held on to that feeling of confidence and peacefulness God delivered the previous night. It was another reminder He was in charge, not the doctors who gave me a dismal prognosis and suggested that I forgo the use of the ventilator and allow myself to expire. I was elated that I refused to listen to them and, instead, I trusted in what God had in store for me.

A tremendous amount of positive news circulated that summer about paralyzed individuals who achieved remarkable feats. Stories ranged from an athlete who learned to walk again, to a woman who ascended Mount Kilimanjaro, to a man implanted with electrical implants that allowed him to stand and walk. It was fascinating to read of these accounts; however, I felt privileged to have met some other individuals who persevered in their fight each day, even though their stories didn't make headlines in the media.

One such individual was Alex Malarkey, a young man injured in a horrible car accident at the age of six. I first met Alex while at Rae Ann after his mother reached out to me through email. We began to converse regularly on Skype and still do so to this day. His story was chronicled in, *The Boy Who Came Back from Heaven*, a book embroiled in controversy, which Alex himself decried as "one of the most deceptive books ever."

Over the years that I have come to know Alex, I have been inspired by the strength and resiliency he continues to show. His journey has been extremely difficult, and it would be easy for someone in his situation to give up. However, I believe it is the relationship he has with God that has sustained him more than anything else. I am awed at how well he has accepted his situation and at the grace with which he lives his life. He also possesses wisdom far beyond his years, and I am proud to call him my friend. He is just one of several amazing individuals I have been fortunate enough to cross paths with as a result of the unfortunate injury we have in common.

On the second anniversary of my injury, I sat on the patio, surrounded by my strawberry and tomato plants, and again took stock of my life. A year earlier it had been a time for celebration, with a sprinkling of melancholy. Things were different this time around. I found myself overwhelmed with an incredible sense of haunting memories, and just a slight glimmer of celebration. I didn't feel sorry for myself; I just didn't know what to do with the feelings of sadness that still smoldered like the logs from the Coldwater Lake campfires I used to enjoy with Kristy. I missed her.

Overall, I felt healthy, in a decent place mentally and an even better place spiritually. I was genuinely excited about the road ahead, but a sense of loss and sadness was never far behind. The first year had been about recovery and healing; the past year was about rebuilding and getting back to work. I continued to discover things about myself, including my resiliency when it came to heartache and adversity. Hard times came and went and came again. And each time I was still standing at the end, so to speak.

That August, MetroHealth Hospital would host its 16th Annual Spinal Cord Injury Forum. The event attracted hundreds from all over Northeast Ohio and provided a day of education and the chance to connect with others. I was invited to give the keynote address, an opportunity I gladly accepted. I had worked with a gentleman from the Bureau of Vocational Rehabilitation to establish a business venture as a motivational speaker. The invite to speak at the SCI Forum came at the perfect time.

A week before my talk, I rested in bed at the apartment and reviewed my presentation with my sister, Lindsey. At one point I turned my head slightly to the side and suddenly heard a loud POP in my neck. It sounded like a firecracker had just gone off inside my head! The sound was anything but ordinary, and I immediately knew something was wrong.

For a few moments I remained perfectly still, hoping I had imagined the whole thing, but Lindsey also heard the unnatural sound and was concerned. We called 911. The EMTs arrived and slapped the dreaded hard Miami collar around my neck and transported me out of the apartment on a backboard. It was back to the hospital.

I spent the next two days in the hospital, during which time x-rays and CAT scans revealed that one of the titanium support rods anchored in my neck had snapped in half. All the vertebrae were still intact, and no damage to the skeletal frame could be seen. However, the sharp edges where the rod had busted now burrowed into the surrounding muscle tissue and caused constant, severe discomfort. I couldn't believe a titanium rod could snap in half as it did, but the x-rays didn't lie.

The doctors consulted with the neurosurgeon and decided the best course of action was to leave the broken rod in place and monitor it over the next several weeks. They assured me they did not see the potential for further damage to my spine; however, they couldn't do much for the discomfort other than pain medications. The most disturbing thing was that certain movements caused the two pieces to shift against each other, which re-created the horrible popping sound and triggered extremely painful muscle spasms.

I was relieved that no further damage had been incurred, but had a difficult time trying to adjust to the freaky sound of twisting metal that emanated from my neck. Furthermore, although the other rod was still in place, there was a good chance it too might snap at some point in the future. It certainly was not a common occurrence to have titanium hardware fail as it had, but I was told it happened now and then. That revelation didn't make me sleep any better. Unfortunately, while in the hospital, a pressure sore on my sacrum got worse and I contracted a UTI. Upon discharge, I was sent home with a cocktail of antibiotics and pain medications.

A few days later I delivered the keynote address at the SCI Forum to the largest attendance in its history. Despite the broken rod, pressure sore and UTI, everything went according to plan, and I felt grateful for the opportunity to share my story and hopefully encourage others who were facing similar challenges. Soon afterward I began to be approached on a regular basis about speaking to companies, schools, churches, and other organizations.

A few weeks later I returned to my alma mater and had the privilege of speaking to the students at Saint Ignatius High School. More than 500 people were in attendance to listen to my story and hear me recount the details of my accident, recovery and renewed faith in the Lord. Once again, I felt incredibly fortunate for having a forum to deliver my message and hopefully reach some of the students in a positive way.

The more I spoke to different groups, the more I realized it was something I felt compelled to do. I wanted to share my story and the lessons I learned, and communicate that everyone could rise above hardship, confront challenges that faced them, and discover a resilience they might not have realized they possessed. Sometimes people don't appreciate how strong they are until they are tested. Some people might need a nudge, but I believe everyone possesses the ability to pass the tests that life presents.

As fall approached, the colder weather accentuated the slightest nuances my body experienced and jacked up the level of discomfort. In particular, the busted rod in my neck continued to be a bother. Despite numerous massages and a steady dose of muscle relaxants, I found little relief from the constant soreness that pervaded my neck muscles. I consulted different doctors about what action to take. The broken piece of metal persistently cutting at my flesh led the doctors to be very conservative in their diagnosis. I hoped it might be possible to remove the broken rod entirely without adding any new hardware. However, some of the doctors did not share that sentiment and felt additional fusing might be necessary. Not in favor of that option, I continued to search out more viable alternatives.

One neurosurgeon I met with informed me that after consulting a colleague, he believed the rod could be safely removed without having to add any further fusion to my neck. He even thought I might gain extra degrees of lateral motion as a result of its removal. Furthermore, he planned to remove the screws from my skull, which might decrease the intense headaches I frequently experienced. X-rays showed that the rod had shifted, and the broken ends now overlapped each other, which explained the constant creaking and squeaking I heard whenever I moved my head. Although it would entail another neck surgery, I wanted the damn thing removed.

One last consultation was scheduled with a neurosurgeon who came highly recommended. Going into the appointment, I expected to hear a similar analysis. After an extensive Q and A session and detailed review of my x-rays and CT scans, the chief neurosurgeon and his team of doctors gave me their opinion. They believed the risk of surgery outweighed the benefit of removal and thought there was a 5 to 10 percent chance that I would not survive the surgery.

That was the last thing I expected to hear, especially since I had a serious surgery a year prior when I had the cough assist system implanted. However, that surgery was mostly done in the lower thoracic region, whereas this procedure would be a few centimeters below the brain stem. While I handled the anesthesia and venting extremely well last time, they felt there was no reason to tempt fate. Thus, after some reluctance, I decided to cancel the surgery and revisit the issue down the road.

In the meantime, I just had to live with the pain and discomfort.

In October I started to work out twice a week at Buckeye Wellness Center, the exercise facility for SCI rehabilitation and therapy that Chris Wynn worked diligently to bring to fruition. The gym mirrored the same therapy regimen as Project Walk, the pioneering facility in California it was modeled after, and employed a system known as patterned neural recognition, designed to retrain the central nervous system.

My initial workouts consisted of weighted exercises in which my trainers, Mike and Shannon, moved my legs in specific patterns as I tried to connect the movement with my brain, hoping that dormant nerve paths might reawaken. I lay on a table and tried to push my leg as they held it at a 90-degree angle with my foot against the palm of their hand. In other exercises I was strapped to the Total Gym piece of equipment and worked to connect my mind to the up-and-down leg press motion Mike or Shannon manipulated my legs to do.

As we moved through the exercises, I tried to activate and control my muscles. It didn't take many sessions before my muscles became more active and responded to the movements. Initially, my muscles fatigued quickly from being dormant so long; however, as my workouts progressed, they grew stronger.

Although my injury does not allow my body to sweat, I was still able to put it through a vigorous workout that left me exhausted after every two-hour session. I greatly welcomed the feeling of being spent due to a much-needed strenuous workout. Not to mention, the exercise also provided a great psychological boost, and I relished the way I felt when I finished.

During that first month in one of my biweekly sessions, I accomplished something I hadn't done during the previous twenty-seven months. I voluntarily lifted my foot a few inches off the ground on command! It was another small victory to celebrate and was a cause for great prayer and thanks to God. It was also a reminder that hard work still counted for something.

As Tanya and I drove home from the gym, I was filled with a sense of renewal. Once back at my apartment, I called my dad to share the good news. While talking to him, I yawned and ...

CRACK!

My head and neck jolted forward violently, and I immediately tensed up.

The other rod in my neck had just snapped!

Unfortunately, after an incredible therapy session where I accomplished a milestone that had eluded me for two years, I skipped my next session due to the pain I was in. I remained in bed and tried to find a position that alleviated the discomfort.

No matter what I did, I could not get comfortable. My headaches worsened, and I prayed for sleep as I did when I was first injured. There were moments when the pain was easier to accept than the constant squeaking, creaking, cracking and popping of the metal that resonated from my neck. It was an unnatural sound for the human body to produce. I decided the risk of surgery was worth it, put my trust in God, and scheduled an operation to remove the broken hardware from my neck.

After a week in bed, I'd had enough and returned to the gym. The last thing I wanted was to lose the momentum gained from consistent workouts. However, there was no escape from the hurt, and at times it was difficult to remain positive after what seemed like a nosedive into a miasma. It took a conscious effort to remind myself I had persevered through tough times before and could and would do it again.

I also found myself in a self-reflective state.

I thought about the trajectory of life and how it forced you to take the good with the bad, the sweet with the sour, and the joy with the pain. It was easy to question God's will when I didn't understand it. Like most people, I struggled to find an answer that explained why bad things happened to good people. Why did kindhearted parents lose their children in an automobile accident, only to survive and be forced to live out each day without their children? Why did innocent children suffer, deprived of the opportunity to appreciate the beauty and greatness of life?

Life constantly bombards us with devastating reminders of how much pain exists around us, but if you look closely, you'll find a story of triumph and joy to match every tale of heartache and suffering. However, I didn't believe that one equaled one. I grew excited when I heard of individuals who accomplished great things, but it didn't make it easier the day I received the news that a high school friend's son had inoperable brain cancer.

The jubilation of triumph does not always erase the anguish of suffering.

The fact remains that there is so much hurt and sorrow in this world and only God understands His plan.

At some point, everyone experiences the ups and downs life has to offer. Although we might not understand why things happen, we can control how we choose to let it affect us. We can also decide whether to accept God into our lives. I hate living with an SCI; I hate the ups and downs, the unpredictable and uncontrollable. But I would hate to think how much worse it would be if I were going through this alone without Him in my life.

I was once asked how I could still believe in God after what had happened to me. My response was, "How can I not?" I worked hard because I saw how much it mattered. It's the same reason I prayed. Faith doesn't make the pain and suffering disappear, nor does it provide all the answers I seek. But it brings the promise of something better, some reward extraordinarily unfathomable. And with all the hardship and heartache in this world, why would I not want to believe in something far greater than anything I have yet to experience? Faith doesn't cost anything, but I believe it will give me everything.

We are forced to play the hand we've been dealt. How we choose to play it is one of the few things in our lives we still have the power to control. That sentiment became a mantra of mine in every talk I delivered.

Focus on what you can control.

I am the first to admit that I didn't practice it as diligently as I wanted. At times I wondered when things would get better, as I imagine most individuals with an SCI do. To wonder does not mean one is disgruntled or not living a productive life. One doesn't have to be paralyzed to seek self-improvement. However, when paralyzed, self-improvement is often sought in a physical sense: movement, breathing, stable blood pressure, regular body temperature, etc. As much as I tried not to define myself by the physical, it was still a challenge.

It is just as vital to seek self-improvement in a mental, emotional and spiritual sense. Obstacles remain–finding meaningful activities to keep sharp, letting go of past relationships, accepting God's plan–but in some ways these obstacles, once overcome, will make you a stronger person than being able to walk to the mailbox or toss a tennis ball to a playful dog would. Having your physical faculties intact, but struggling to find a happy place mentally, emotionally and spiritually, is more paralyzing than sitting in a wheelchair.

At times, the same thing can be said for hope.

During a conversation with another quadriplegic, I was struck by a statement he made.

"I am waiting and hoping for a cure."

On the surface, it seemed like a completely reasonable statement from someone living with an SCI. However, it reminded me of something a respiratory therapist once told me at 3 a.m. as I lay in a hospital bed receiving a breathing treatment.

"Hope is just a bunch of hot air."

Hope cannot be seen, held, or created, at least not enough to make it into something tangible. Hope is something we conjure up in our hearts and heads to help us confront or cope with situations that arise in our lives. I am a strong believer in hope and feel it is vital when dealing with a traumatic situation.

But hope alone is not enough.

Every individual must constantly work toward bettering his or her situation instead of sitting around "waiting and hoping" for circumstances to change. Sometimes things do change for the better by themselves, and that is great and something to be thankful for. But usually, things don't change without some exertion behind them.

For me, hope was just a part of my daily recipe for living. My belief in myself played a much more significant role. I certainly welcomed all forms of serendipity, but also realized I was the catalyst for my own change.

# TWENTY-SEVEN
# ACCEPTANCE

Two days before Thanksgiving 2011, I underwent surgery to remove the broken titanium rods from my neck.

I found it ironic that just a few years earlier the idea of surgery would have scared the crap out of me. Now I found myself voluntarily signing up to have my neck and skull sliced open as if it were a routine occurrence. It was just another reminder of the new "normal" my injury brought with it.

The neurosurgeon I chose for the procedure was the same doctor who implanted my cough assist system a little over a year prior. During the procedure to remove the rods, he took out two separate pieces, each three-and-a-half inches in length, from each titanium rod, as well as the three-screw bracket on each side that attached the rods to my skull. He also removed some excess pieces of metal to hopefully alleviate the muscle and nerve agitation.

The surgery went well. The recovery was hell.

When I awoke after the surgery, I was immediately welcomed back to consciousness by severe, agonizing pain that rivaled anything I had encountered up to that point. That first evening, I was hooked up to a morphine drip around-the-clock, but was still in rough shape. It was a challenge to find any respite from the hurt I felt, and I spent most of the night praying for an escape from the pain.

A tremendous amount of discomfort remained over the next several days, however. I was sent home Thanksgiving afternoon after I convinced the doctors my pain level had subsided to a manageable state that could be treated with oral medications at home.

But I had an ulterior motive for wanting to leave.

It was the first Thanksgiving in three years I wouldn't have to spend in a hospital or nursing home. Although the celebration itself was low-key, the symbolism of being home with my family was enormous for me.

Over the next week, my pain decreased exponentially each day. Most of the discomfort I felt was due to the nerve pain. The entire back of my skull was numb and filled with a burning sensation. I hoped it would resolve itself in time. Eventually, after several months, the back of my head once again felt normal. However, the scars on the back of my neck continue to itch relentlessly to this day.

I had accumulated quite the collection of scars. The largest is a ten-inch line of scar tissue that runs down the middle of my back. There is a two-inch scar on my left waistline, a four-inch scar across my abdomen, and several others scattered across my chest from the feeding tube, chest tube, DPS, and cough assist system. The crown jewel is the six-inch zipper-like line that decorates the back of my neck. The latest addition, from the removal of the rods, lay across the scar that had already been there. At least the surgeon had a guide to follow when he made his cuts. I resemble a human voodoo doll but am proud of my collection. It serves as a reminder of what I have been through and where I am today. They are the souvenirs I will never lose.

The day I traveled to the hospital to get the staples removed from the back of my head, I was struck by a sight that caused me to pause and reflect on my good fortune. A homeless man stood on the side of the road holding a sign that asked for help. Right then and there I thanked God for all I had in my life: a roof over my head, access to food, people who loved and cared for me. I was paralyzed and unable to move in the way I desired but was willing to bet there were people in the world who would rather be in my situation than what they found themselves in. At that moment, my life didn't seem so difficult.

Unfortunately, the harsh reality of the variables that exist with an SCI reared their ugly heads minutes later. In the hospital parking lot, a paralyzed man was flat on his back behind the transportation van, his head against the pavement. His wheelchair had rolled backward off the motorized lift and fallen several feet, smacking on the hard asphalt below. He lay motionless on the pavement, his body strapped to his wheelchair. I felt sick to my stomach knowing it could have happened to anyone in our situation.

In less than a half an hour I witnessed two different sights that profoundly affected me. Each reminded me how unpredictable and unfair life can be, and how we should focus on all the good in our lives, appreciate it, and find our happiness–because it could all change. It may change slowly over time, or in the blink of an eye, but there's never a guarantee that tomorrow will be as good as today.

Fortunately, the holidays were spent in the cozy confines of my own place surrounded by loved ones. Father Damian stopped over to celebrate mass Christmas morning, and my family spent the evening at the Voegeles' annual Christmas party.

A few hours before midnight on New Year's Eve, I called Kristy to wish her a happy new year. It was extremely emotional, as I still loved her and thought of her as my wife, whereas she now only loved me as a friend. Time and distance had already shown their effect. We had a long conversation laced with a search for answers and filled with more heartache. I still struggled with how her feelings for me had changed so much and why nothing could have been done to bring them back. I needed an explanation that made sense to me.

Kristy told me she was overwhelmed after my accident and she felt isolated. My injury was not her fault, but she blamed herself for what had happened and felt others did as well. The pressure she placed on herself in those subsequent months sent her to an unhealthy place, filled with panic attacks and extreme depression. She never opened up about any of this because she felt she needed to be strong for everyone. She admitted, in hindsight, that she could have handled things better.

I was slightly miffed, as she made it sound like I had to suffer because of her lack of foresight. Her answer still didn't explain why her feelings for me changed. I needed more, and after some prodding, she admitted she felt the active life she wanted spent traveling and having children could no longer exist, thus she allowed our relationship to become platonic. She convinced herself that I could no longer give her the romantic love she craved.

Her words cut deeply, but I needed to hear them. She said it boiled down to the fact that the life she said "I do" to was gone and there was no longer anyone to support her. She told me one day she would fall in love again, and while she cherished the time we had, she was not coming back. She said she was a friend who loved me dearly; however, she felt I was still trying to be her husband instead of her friend.

Of course, I was. For me, it wasn't as easy to flip the switch.

Before we hung up, she admitted she was seeing someone. I wasn't surprised, but I still found her revelation to be surreal. I had suspected it for some time, but obviously, had hoped I was wrong. I'm not sure what I expected; we were divorced, no longer husband and wife. However, hearing her tell me another man would kiss her at midnight was a helpless and sickening feeling that left both my heart and head in a frenzy for which I had not been prepared. I wondered how long she had been seeing him, and even wondered if it was the same guy from the picture that had slipped from her folder.

I spent New Year's Eve by myself, engulfed in a feeling of

isolation.

The next several weeks required a tremendous amount of mental fortitude on my part to stay focused on my physical therapy and not allow myself to wallow in self-pity. Sure, things were difficult, but it was important for me to maintain a positive mental outlook on my future situation.

I was determined to make this my best year yet, a feat easier said than done when living with an SCI. My neurosurgeon cleared me to resume workouts at Buckeye Wellness Center, and I continued to amass small victories each week during my sessions. My hip flexor and quadriceps muscles had grown stronger from the repetitive exercises. After a strong table workout one afternoon, I moved to the RT300 FES bike–a stationary bike with electrode pads affixed to my legs and arms that delivered an electrical stimulus and forced my muscles to contract.

I rode the bike for a couple of miles using my muscles that were being electrically stimulated. As I headed to the van afterward, I experienced a tingling sensation throughout both of my legs, something that had never happened. I took it as a sign that the nerves in my legs were thanking me for a great workout.

Nerve regeneration in the spinal cord is a tricky and delicate undertaking. In general, human nerves regrow at the rate of a millimeter a day. However, there exists debate on whether the spinal cord nerves can regenerate. There are those who operate under the school of thought that regeneration is minimal at best and unlikely to lead to any recovery or function. There is another school of thought that believes that repetitive exercise and patterned neural activity can help "wake up" dormant and damaged nerves.

I believed the latter theory. However, patience was mandatory since it could take several years of constant repetition of the same motion to restore any function or sensation. Nonetheless, I persisted and was extremely grateful for those who continued to donate funds that allowed me to do so.

Most people move through their days in search of new adventure. Those who are paralyzed might spend a lifetime seeking to repeat things they once did. I was not ashamed that I now had to put all my effort toward trying to replicate a task that never seemed like an achievement in the past. Progress comes in all shapes and sizes. To some, progress might be renovating a room in their house or getting that big promotion at work; for me, it meant a tingling sensation in my legs. Progress is relative. And like the Scottish author Samuel Smiles said, "Progress, of the best kind, is comparatively slow."

I continued to be inspired by personal stories of perseverance and triumphs. That was the case when I read the story of Dan Millman, a gymnast at U.C. Berkeley, who was in a horrible motorcycle accident and recovered to become an NCAA champion. In his book, *Everyday Enlightenment: The Twelve Gateways to Personal Growth*, he said:

"Pain is a relatively objective, physical phenomenon; suffering is our psychological resistance to what happens. Events may create physical pain, but they do not in themselves create suffering. Resistance creates suffering. Stress happens when your mind resists what is ... The only problem in your life is your mind's resistance to life as it unfolds."

I struggled for a long time to accept my paralysis because I thought doing so equated to giving up. However, when I read Millman's words, they made me realize that only after I accepted the situation at hand would I be in the best position to confront the challenge in front of me.

I wish I had released the reins of resistance a bit sooner that first year after the injury. However, I was grateful to now be in a better place as a result of accepting my reality and working hard toward charting a new course.

Let me be sure to clarify that I don't accept that what I lost will never be regained. Rather, I accept the fact that right now I am paralyzed and must continue to work hard every moment to have a chance at getting where I want to be. Acceptance does not mean quitting. As Mark and Simone said in their TED talk, "Acceptance is knowing that grief is a raging river and you have to get into it, because when you do, it carries you to the next place, and eventually takes you to open land, where it will turn out okay in the end."

In addition to the consistent workouts, I poured myself into more advocacy work. Individuals across the country who were affected by SCIs, either reached out to me or I contacted them. I made myself available to listen to their concerns, answer their questions, and reinforce the fact that no one was alone in their battle–we could all learn something from each other. I still learn from others.

People often ask me about Complete vs. Incomplete injuries. The medical community is quick to assign a classification to an injury so it fits neatly into a specific compartment they can treat accordingly.

If only it were that easy.

In many cases classifying the injury limits the type of care, physical therapy, and other medical treatments the individual receives. Much worse, classifications may limit the willingness of the individual to push forward. Doctors told me I suffered a Complete injury since I did not have sensation at the base of my spine. Doctors also told me my injury was Incomplete because I had sensation in my biceps, which is below my level of injury. I focused on what I could do and continued to get stronger through hard work. I listened to myself and my body and not doctors when it came to my limitations.

The human spirit cannot be seen with x-rays and MRIs. It can only be seen in the actions of the individual who chooses not to give up and keeps pushing forward, regardless of the obstacles he or she has been told lay ahead.

The point at which the physiological and psychological intersect is perhaps the most crucial moment in any survivor's journey. It is at that moment one must choose to confront their plight, accept the present, and decide if they want to give up or get back up. Thus, the behavioral and individualistic questions are the questions that need to be answered by the individuals themselves. If I had a dollar for each time someone asked me how I adapted so well to my situation, I might have enough money to seek out some experimental treatment that would restore movement.

There are no one-size-fits-all answers.

Some of the ways I overcame my hurdles were to celebrate each event that allowed me to gain a little more independence. No matter how small a victory, it's still a victory. The more autonomy I gained back, the stronger I felt, and the more I was able to work toward gaining even more independence. Additionally, I garnered an appreciation for the little things that provided comfort and learned to appreciate them.

Unfortunately, some people never experience the victories found through physical therapy, adaptive equipment, and an incredible support network of friends and family. That is why I founded Getting Back Up, to provide individuals with the tools needed to improve their quality of life. A lot of time and effort has been spent to make the support the foundation offers accessible to others.

No one should ever stop doing the work, lose hope, or stop believing in miracles and the power of faith. Everyone has the choice to either give up or get up.

A great example of this philosophy is embodied in the work done by the Adversity 2 Advocacy Alliance. A2A, as it's referred to, exists to inspire, educate, and facilitate the process of turning personal challenges into service to others facing similar challenges. Its founder, Jeff Bell, invited me to become an advocate member of the Los Angeles based nonprofit. As he explained it, A2A is an all-volunteer group of dedicated men and women committed to promoting and fostering the power of turning adversity into advocacy. Its ranks include leading researchers, nationally-known health and wellness advocates, established and student journalists, doctors, teachers, attorneys, and other professionals–all individuals who turned their life challenges into service to others with similar challenges. Although each person brought a unique perspective to the project, everyone shared a passion for the A2A concepts of service, purpose, empathy, and resilience. I felt honored to have been invited to be part of such a dynamic community working to help others.

Unbeknownst to me, my sister, Lindsey, entered me in a search that *Cleveland Magazine* conducted to find the "Sexy Singles" living in the area. I found the whole thing to be rather comical, but I was honored that my sister would even think to submit me. During my interview, I was asked what I was passionate about. Naturally, my response was, "Helping people overcome adversity, including myself. It's something that's evolved as my life has evolved."

# TWENTY-EIGHT
# GOD BLESS YOU

In April 2012, Bruce Springsteen and the legendary E. Street Band brought their *Wrecking Ball* tour to Cleveland, home of the Rock & Roll Hall of Fame and birthplace of rock 'n' roll.

I had been a fan of The Boss since I first started listening to music. He was my all-time favorite, the one whose music had reached me from the moment I first heard it. I had always found a tapestry of messages in his music and the characters through which he conveyed those stories.

I had seen The Boss in concert several times, most recently in November 2008, two days before the presidential election, when he performed at a Barack Obama speaking event on the mall in downtown Cleveland. Kristy and I had just left First Energy Stadium after watching the Browns lose to the Baltimore Ravens and stopped on the mall to watch him perform. His most recent visit to Cleveland before now was in 2009, but I missed that show, as I lay in a hospital bed fighting for my life.

There was no way I was going to miss seeing him this time around.

Fortunately, I was able to secure tickets for myself, Damian, Kevin, and Mike. It seemed apropos that the four of us would go together, as they had been the guys who sat at my hospital bedside and jammed Springsteen songs on their guitars in the hopes it would make me feel better. Since my accident, I have listened to Bruce more than ever to motivate, relax, inspire, and invigorate myself. His songs help me appreciate how music can reach one's soul and encourage someone to dream and achieve things they previously thought unattainable.

It was Springsteen who once said, "You can change someone's life in three minutes with the right song."

On the eve of the show, I sent an email to the PR firm that handles Springsteen's publicity. I conveyed what Bruce's music had meant to me throughout my life, especially the past few years. In my message, with a childlike naïveté, I asked if Bruce could dedicate a song to me, and even included the section where I would be sitting.

Damian and I were especially excited because we had seen Springsteen together twenty years earlier at the old Richfield Coliseum. I expected this show to be somewhat bittersweet–a chance to see Bruce again, but from a wheelchair and on a different journey than I had been all those years ago.

The electricity in the air at the arena was palpable, and I could sense the adrenaline that coursed through the veins of the nearly 20,000 fans in attendance. Something just seemed special, and Damian and I both noted we were in for an incredible night. Springsteen is known for his marathon concerts, which usually eclipse the three-hour mark, unheard of for most performers today. One of his longest concerts was in Cleveland on New Year's Eve, when he and the E. Street Band rocked out for more than five hours. And his 1978 show at the Cleveland Agora was career-defining and arguably one of his greatest.

Bruce and the city have always had a special bond.

Early into his set I already knew I was witnessing the best Springsteen performance I had ever seen. But it was something he said into the microphone before starting one of his final songs that will forever make the night the most memorable show for me. After performing "The Rising," which is itself a prophetic song for me, the band started into the opening chords of their new song "We Are Alive," a song about triumph over death, of resurrection and hope.

It was then that Bruce leaned into the microphone and uttered four words I won't forget:

"For my friend, Scott."

I thought I might jump out of my chair!

My buddies immediately turned to me, with huge smiles on their faces, and shouted "Dude, that was you!"

As excited as I was, it was a surreal moment.

*Could that really be for me?*

But then again, how many Scotts were in the audience that The Boss felt compelled to dedicate a song to? After all, it wasn't something he typically did.

The answer would soon be made clear.

Upon the show's conclusion, the house lights came on, and a member of the event staff approached our seats to ask if I was Scott Fedor. He then had us follow him out of the arena, across the concourse, and into a large service elevator. My first thought was that we were getting a personal escort out to the parking lot.

It was then that I whispered to Damian, "Could this really be happening?"

"I just keep praying to the Holy Spirit," he replied.

Seconds later, the large elevator doors clanged open, and we were behind the stage. We watched roadies and crew members scramble around to tear down the massive stage. A woman introduced herself to me as Bruce Springsteen's manager, Barbara Carr. She informed me that my e-mail had been forwarded to her and Bruce wanted to meet me!

Shortly after that, Max Weinberg, the band's drummer, struck up a conversation with us and talked about the band's experiences in Cleveland, and what it's like to play with Bruce. It was another surreal moment, as we casually conversed with each other. I even asked him about the stuffed cabbage that a local restaurant, Sokolowski's University Inn, had provided for the band. After about fifteen minutes, he posed for a few pictures and then casually left on his way.

A minute later, Bruce Springsteen sauntered over, looking every bit the legendary rock star that he was while munching on a soft pretzel. It was a moment twenty-eight years in the making, ever since I heard my first Springsteen song. However, there were no handshakes. Instead, he walked right up to me and placed his hand around my neck and kissed the side of my head.

"God bless," were the first words one of the greatest rockers of all time said to me.

At that moment, there was not a doubt in my mind of how blessed I was. I was at a Bruce Springsteen concert. And I was now talking to the man himself!

Springsteen had an incredible presence about him. He was one of the greatest and loudest rock icons in the world and at the same time an extremely gentle and caring man who was genuinely interested in what I had to say. We talked about how great the show was, even Springsteen himself commenting on what a powerful performance it was.

I told him how much I loved one of his more obscure songs, "Zero and Blind Terry."

"That almost made the album," he chuckled.

That evening he played "Racing in the Street" a song that has much emotional and spiritual meaning for me. I was thrilled to have been able to hear it live an hour earlier and was now beyond words to be able to talk about it with Springsteen.

"I gotta tell you," I said, "I love your '78 version of 'Racing in the Street'".

He looked at me, and with that gritty and gravelly voice of his, and a proud and glowing look in his eyes, replied, "No man, tonight ... That was it tonight."

It was quite apparent to see how emotional the show and that song had been for him as well. As he posed with us for pictures, he noticed a medallion around my neck–the Miraculous Medal of Mary–the same one he wore around his neck.

"Ah, a Catholic boy," he smiled.

"We gotta stick together," I said.

One of my friends handed him one of my awareness bracelets, which he quickly put on his wrist before I finished explaining what it was. After a few more pictures it was time for him to board his plane back to New Jersey.

He leaned over and kissed my head again. "God bless you."

And then he sauntered away.

Over the next several days, my encounter with Springsteen went viral. I wrote about the evening on my blog and a multitude of news outlets around the world referenced the story. It was re-posted, re-tweeted (including by Springsteen guitarist, Nils Lofgren), mentioned on numerous other blogs, and featured in several newspapers. It was also the topic of church sermons the following Sunday. Strangers from different parishes across the country sent me messages informing me that my story was the subject of their priest's homily. I even listened to an audio recording of a sermon given by the pastor at a church in Brooklyn, New York.

Additionally, I received a tremendous outpouring of support from Springsteen fans around the world. I am still in contact with some of the amazing people I met as a result of what transpired. I also benefited from their generosity through donations, purchases of my awareness bracelet, and heartfelt gifts, including a relic of the Blessed Francis Xavier Seelos.

I was humbled by the attention my encounter generated but excited about the awareness it raised for individuals living with an SCI. The buzz surrounding my meeting with a worldly rock star eventually dissipated, but the reality of spinal cord injuries did not. Thus, I continued to do what I could to maintain an awareness and focus on SCIs.

Getting Back Up allowed me an avenue for that focus. On May 23, 2012 I received notice that GBU had officially been granted tax-exempt status and designated as a public charity. It was time to get to work. Chris Wynn and Will Voegele were both invited to join the board, and we soon had our first planning meeting. Our stated mission was clear and outlined what we wanted to accomplish, but the challenge existed to raise the necessary capital to realize that mission.

That first year we raised a little more than $3,000, not exactly the level needed to deliver on all the ideas I envisioned. However, as word spread and public and private grants were received, more money rolled in, and the concept of GBU started to take hold. Today, the organization has helped nearly one hundred individuals across the country receive the exercise-based therapy and adaptable products needed to improve their lives. I am extremely proud of what GBU has been able to achieve and continue to look for ways to expand its reach and grow its resources.

By law, I couldn't benefit from the services GBU provided, so I continued to rely on the generosity of others for my therapy regimen. My workouts at Buckeye continued to advance, and my trainer, Shannon, was not afraid to try new things with me. We developed my core to the point where I could sit unassisted on the edge of the table for several minutes. On occasion, I was even able to wiggle a toe and voluntarily induce a spasm. It usually took several minutes of intense concentration to get the slightest flicker, but I could replicate it a few times before I grew exhausted. It might not have seemed like much to an outsider, but it was something to me. It was something to build on; I could tap into the momentum it provided. The mind is a powerful instrument, and where the mind goes, the body often follows.

Unfortunately, spinal cord injuries don't get enough support from the healthcare industry, mainly insurance companies. The importance of exercise seems to be lost on them. Not only does exercise benefit a paralyzed individual in the same way as an able-bodied person, but it also provides a myriad of secondary improvements many fail to appreciate. For instance, someone who gains enough trunk control could transfer themselves from their bed to a wheelchair and not require assistance as often. Consistent exercise improves blood flow, which could help reduce the chance for a pressure sore, which can require extended hospital stays and surgeries. Millions of dollars in healthcare savings would be realized if these were reduced. A specialized mattress, which might cost a few hundred dollars, could end up saving thousands down the road. Proper exercise can even help someone get back to work, earn money, pay taxes, and shed their reliance on government care.

Granted, not everyone will experience these types of improvements, but the fact remains that most insurance plans won't pay for exercise-based therapy that maintains health. A blind eye has been turned on secondary and indirect complications. The healthcare industry employs a reactive thinking structure rather than a proactive one, and the mentality that exists today is one of stepping over dollars to pick up dimes. More enlightened thinking is needed.

***

In September 2012, I welcomed someone new into my apartment and my life. A twenty-nine-year-old Capuchin monkey named Melanie.

While I was at Rae Ann, I saw a story about a Boston-based organization called Helping Hands that trains monkeys to help paralyzed individuals with everyday tasks. As I learned more about the incredible intelligence and dexterity of the Capuchin, and what they were able to assist with, I became more intrigued. Capuchin monkeys are well-suited to a home environment and adept at adapting to new surroundings and new people in their lives. But perhaps more importantly, the monkeys use their hands to perform functional tasks that no other assistance animals can accomplish. They are natural tool users and have an active curiosity and a natural enjoyment for manipulating objects.

Using a monkey puppet, Lindsey assisted me with my application video. The skit we put together was a hit with the employees at Helping Hands and earned me the moniker, "Scott Fedorable." My application was approved, and I opened my home to a six-pound primate.

The first few days were spent forming a bond so that Melanie could get comfortable with me. A strong emotional bond is important since the relationship is one of unique companionship which can last for years. Capuchins typically live more than forty-five years in a home environment.

Melanie was trained to flip a light switch, insert a DVD, unscrew a water bottle top, and even reposition a limb that might have shifted from a spasm. The biggest thing I wanted her to do for me, though, was to wipe my face when it itched. Finally, a way to solve the frustration that itches brought with them.

Melanie had a lively personality and was fascinated with TV. She got excited each morning when the boob tube was turned on. She also loved food, as most animals do, and had an incredible internal clock when it came to meal times. She was sure to let everyone know when it was time to eat. Even a few minutes of deviation from her food schedule, and she was quick to fill the apartment with her animated vocals.

For a while, Melanie complied with most of my requests, provided I had a reward for her. Originally, I satisfied this demand via an apparatus attached to my wheelchair. However, it eventually proved too clunky and inefficient. There was a period where I rewarded her with verbal praise, but she soon tired of hearing how great she was, and instead preferred that I proved it with a tasty treat. Eventually, she assisted less and less. Today she is an entertaining pet, but unlike other animals, she will rummage through drawers and cabinets if left unsupervised.

Her cage has a spring door that I open by gripping a rubber knob with my teeth and giving a slight pull. Each time I position my chair in place to open the cage, she clings to the side and watches me intensely. She cheers me on by pursing her lips together and pretending to also pull on the knob. It often takes two or three times before I get the cage open since I start laughing when I see her bright little eyes bearing down on me. But once I get it open, she climbs out, hops up on my chair, and starts making her happy, cooing noises. She will still gladly assist me when needed, but I better have one of those tasty treats at the ready!

***

Over time, Kristy and I talked less frequently.

Her family visited on occasion; however, she never did. I discovered that she had gotten engaged earlier in the year. As I had celebrated the third anniversary of life since my accident, she had celebrated the promise of a new beginning with someone new. I remembered what she told me Christopher Reeve's wife said to him about waiting two years before making a major life decision. On my second anniversary of the accident, Kristy had already divorced me, moved away, and started a new relationship. A year later, she was engaged. I couldn't help but feel that she had some timeline she felt compelled to meet to return to the life she desired.

During one of our conversations, she admitted that she left fast. She felt she couldn't be strong enough for both of us, so she thought it best just to leave. Kristy also said she carried a lot of guilt about her decision and knew I would've handled it differently had our roles been reversed. It hurt me to hear her say this, as I still loved her and didn't want her to live with the guilt. I wanted her to live the life she wanted. However, the whole situation just plain sucked.

Three days before the end of the year, *The Plain Dealer* featured a four-page photo essay which chronicled the three-and-a-half years since my accident. To my dismay, the paper decided not to print the eight-part series that was to accompany the photos. However, Diane, who had written the story, read it to me over the phone. I found it to be very powerful, emotional, and cathartic.

I called Kristy and asked her to hear it as well. After all, it was also her story. However, she did not want to hear it. She had tried to accept the past and move forward, and she felt hearing it would suck her back into a dark hole that had consumed her for too long.

I couldn't help but think about the tremendous guilt Kristy had experienced with the death of our cat, Jack. I wondered about the similarities between Jack's situation and my situation and how they had affected Kristy. Perhaps she harbored feelings of guilt that made her eager to move on and try to forget everything about the past.

# TWENTY-NINE
# NEW TOMATOES

As another year greeted me, I continued to spend a great deal of time speaking to companies, schools, churches and other organizations about perseverance through difficult times and the power of a positive attitude.

I relished every talk and the chance to reach people in a way that might cause them to reflect on how they could live a better life in the face of any kind of adversity.

Although I found myself busier with each passing day, there was no escape from the physical doldrums that plagued my body. I would feel great for days only to suddenly be hit with the onslaught of issues that were always waiting on the periphery. The constant discomfort I battled in my neck and shoulders had worn on me and sent me to an orthopedic specialist to see if anything could be done to relieve the pain.

My muscles were so tight and spastic at times that I had zero range of motion in my neck. The slightest move left or right felt like pushing against a brick wall, and the never-ending tightness left my neck feeling like it was encased in concrete. The doctor suggested I cease my workouts, but I hated that idea since my body had grown stronger. I compromised and took a couple weeks off to rest my neck muscles but didn't find much relief. As in the past, I maintained a steady diet of heating pads and ibuprofen. Some days were just more manageable than others, par for the course with an SCI.

Despite my pain, my sister and I organized a surprise sixty-fifth birthday party for my mom. She had been there for me and continued to be daily, and the party was just one small token to thank her. Surprised by family and friends, she cried when she entered the room. Seeing the emotion on her face filled me with happiness.

Unfortunately, a few weeks later, her mother, affectionately known as Nani, passed away peacefully after a long battle with dementia. My mom was able to be at her side when she slipped away from us and into the loving arms of God. I was able to say goodbye via phone to let her know how much I loved her and that it was okay for her to leave us. Because Nani's mind had started to slow down, my family and I made it a point never to tell her about my accident. I'm pretty sure she closed her eyes for the last time remembering me as the strong, able-bodied, mischievous grandson she always knew me to be.

Two years after her passing, my grandfather also passed away and was able to reconnect with his bride in heaven. She and my grandfather, Popop, had been married for almost seventy-two years. To me, they embodied the meaning of marriage. It was entertaining to watch how they would often pick on each other in their own sweet way, or how Popop reached out to grab her and pull her into his easy chair as she walked by. He would squeeze her, kiss her, and embarrass her, and she tried her best to pretend she didn't enjoy it. Their banter was full of genuine love. I was fortunate while at Lehigh to be able to spend most of my Thanksgivings and Easters in Philadelphia with them.

***

It was a warm spring afternoon when both the president and principal of Saint Ignatius High School visited me. They were accompanied by the executive director of the Northeast Ohio chapter of Boys Hope Girls Hope (BHGH), an international organization centered on cultivating youth empowerment through the foundation of education and holistic support. The organization annually recognized leaders in the community who embodied BHGH's mission and values.

I had been nominated to receive the "Rising Pillar of Hope" award, which was given to an "individual who steadfastly sees possibility and hope despite the obstacles and is meaningfully dedicated to service for others." I was extremely humbled and grateful to have been selected to receive such an honor, and later that year accepted the award at a dinner and ceremony accompanied by friends and loved ones.

A few of the neighborhood kids had also begun to visit me on a frequent basis. Each day, Marcus, his brother Marcello, and their friend Wissam stopped over to hang out. They were all under the age of eleven, but for some reason eager to hang with a thirty-something quadriplegic.

I first met Marcus after he jumped from the second-floor landing and crashed into my bushes. Some girls were chasing him, and he decided to escape by leaping from the floor above into the landing pad of bushes below. Funny enough, he had a cast on his forearm, having broken it in an earlier accident. After he brushed himself off, he politely apologized and asked if he and his friends could hide in my yard so the girls wouldn't find them. I had no choice but to say yes, and a friendship blossomed.

After that they visited me every day and if I was busy, they would wait on my patio until I came out. On the days I was occupied I'd let them in briefly to say hi to Melanie. On several occasions, they offered to help clean her cage. Their mother, Jen, seemed envious of the chores they were willing to do for me, to which point Marcus reminded her that I was in a wheelchair.

It didn't take long for them to make me a member of their crew, which they aptly named the WOMP gang, even though no one knew what it stood for. I was told that I would be the "P." We even had our own flag. The WOMPers always wanted to help me out. On one occasion, they organized a neighborhood carwash that raised money for my organization, Getting Back Up. I was very moved when I discovered they even passed out air fresheners with a GBU business card stapled to them. They might have been still learning their multiplication tables, but they were already marketing experts.

Marcus and Marcello's parents, Rob and Jen, also frequently visited. Usually, after Jen took the boys home, Rob and I relaxed with a few of his world-famous margaritas and enjoyed some of my fifteen-year-old single malts. The family later moved to Florida. However, we remain in touch, and they still visit when in town.

***

I received an email from Kristy on July third.

It had been a while since we last spoke. She had recently remarried, less than a week after what would have been our six-year wedding anniversary. In her email, she wrote how proud she was of me. She said she couldn't believe how far I had come and how much I had accomplished in such a short time. Her email was bittersweet, as I loved to hear from her, but she was no longer my wife.

Furthermore, I was disheartened by her words. I appreciated the spirit of them, but thought, of course, she hadn't expected me to come so far; otherwise, she might not have left. Then again, perhaps it was inevitable and there was nothing that could have been done. Either way, I stared at the screen and debated whether to reply.

In the end, I chose not to respond and have not had any contact with her since.

It's difficult not to feel as if Kristy gave up on me way too soon. She is not a terrible person by any means. She is someone who was put in a horrible situation that would certainly have caused anyone torment. Years have since passed, and I have had plenty of time to reflect and pray long and hard about our situation. I can honestly say had our roles been reversed, I never would have left. She did what she felt she had to do so she could heal. I still love and pray for her and want her to be happy.

For me, there will always be unfinished business with Kristy, so many chapters of our life never written, reams of empty pages void of words and pictures. However, as this injury taught me–our plans are not what matter; rather, it's God's plans for us that matter. His plans don't always make sense, perhaps because I seek an easy explanation. I do believe, however, that explanation will reveal itself in time, but until it does God has given me something to sustain me ... Faith.

That Independence Day marked four years since my accident. Each anniversary started to serve as a new guidepost and replaced my birthday as a more significant measure of time. That morning on my patio I stared at the tiny green tomatoes that had started to grow. I thought back to the days following my accident when, with barely a whisper, I inquired as to how my tomatoes were doing. I had just broken my neck and yet I was worried about the tomato plants left alone on my apartment balcony. For a few moments in time, those tomatoes were the most important thing on my horizon. I never got to enjoy them, and never will; they're gone. But each year I could get a new tomato plant and enjoy the taste of the tomatoes.

New opportunities were just as sweet as new tomatoes.

# THIRTY
# THANK YOU

According to studies, statistics, and a slew of other data points, the mean age at which I should "expire" is in my mid-fifties.

In this case, the mean is represented by an equal number of people to the left and right of a data point. I want to think I lean toward the right and have some more time on my hands. The reality is, just like everyone else, my time on this planet is finite. It's easy to be lulled into the illusion that plenty of time remains to accomplish what's been written down, desired, or established in the mind. Therefore, I made it a point to stay productive and work each day toward my goals. However, living with an SCI also requires a steady dose of moderation and patience. Too much time in a chair, overextending oneself, believing the body can handle things like it used to, can lead to serious setbacks.

Even something as harmless as a new pair of shoes can kill you.

I tried out a pair of sleek-looking Nikes that caused a nasty blister to surface on the bottom of my left foot. Unaware of the intense pressure the shoe applied, I kept the new kicks on too long and discovered the result after it was too late. Although I did my best to keep pressure off my foot, the wound (and myself) proved quite stubborn and eventually led to osteomyelitis, a bone infection, that required a PICC line to be inserted into my upper left arm to administer antibiotics. After several weeks the infection cleared, and the line was removed.

I was back to feeling relatively good, except for the nagging soreness in my neck and shoulders. However, the first Saturday in June, Tanya drove me to the emergency room, as I struggled to breathe normally. I felt like I had run wind sprints while breathing through a straw. I hadn't slept a wink in days, up all night coughing and trying to control my breathing.

As soon as I entered the ER lobby, I asked for some oxygen. It was obvious something wasn't right, and I was ushered into a room for further examination. My blood oxygen level was 84 percent, prompting five liters of oxygen, which had to be increased to ten liters to maintain an oxygen level above 90 percent. An x-ray revealed cloudiness in my lower right lung. The doctor wanted to admit me; however, I did not want to stay in the hospital, so I contemplated going home. Fortunately, my good sense took over. I relented and was admitted to the ICU.

Things got worse.

The fluids I received had not increased my blood pressure, which hovered around 75/45. The doctor insisted he put a catheter in my neck to stabilize my pressure, but I was opposed and did not grant permission. Although his intentions were good, I felt we should give it more time, especially since SCIs typically cause the blood pressure to run low (my normal blood pressure is 100/60). I would consult with Dr. Nemo if it got to the point where something that drastic was needed.

I took an even firmer stance when he mentioned he might want to intubate me. Furthermore, he warned a tracheotomy might be needed to assist my breathing. Absolutely not! I am fully aware of how devastating pneumonia can be for someone with an SCI, yet I made it clear that under no circumstances was he to perform a tracheotomy. I had confidence in my ability to breathe on my own, even with the assistance of oxygen, and was not about to go back on a ventilator.

The following day there was even more cloudiness in the right lung, as well as some in the left lung. After not having as much as a sniffle for the past four and half years, I now had double pneumonia. The revelation threw me. I worked out regularly, ate well, stayed active, used my cough assist when needed. *How could this have happened?*

A few weeks prior I had attended my twenty-year high school reunion and found it ironic that I was now in the hospital since I broke my neck a few weeks after attending my fifteen-year reunion. The jury is still out on whether I attend any future reunions!

After four days in the ICU without sleep, I was given a double dose of a sleeping aid, which only elicited hallucinations of the clocks around me melting, as if trapped in a Salvador Dali painting. The drooping clocks were complemented by visions of my cat running around the floor. I made sure I hadn't been slipped a Haldol concoction.

On Wednesday afternoon I was visited by Sisters from Incarnate Word Academy, my former grade school. I asked them to pray for sleep. If I didn't get sleep soon, my body would not be able to keep up its fight against the pneumonia, and things could spiral down to a much worse place. Fortunately, the prayers worked. I finally slept. My blood pressure also stabilized and thwarted off any discussion about other assistive measures that might be needed.

After six days the antibiotics had done enough that I was moved to the step-down unit. The nuns visited again, and I was sure to thank them for their prayers. Marcus, Marcello, Rob, and Jen also visited me to say goodbye before they moved to Florida. Marcus gave me a beautiful shark made from crystallized sand, and Marcelo wrote me one of the best cards I had ever received.

I was finally released from the hospital after ten days.

A few months later I found myself back at the hospital, only this time a different hospital, and this time by choice. One of the West Michigan Air Care flight nurses who was with me on that July third flight to Bronson Methodist Hospital in Kalamazoo invited me to speak at the annual Air Care Fall Conference. I was eager to accept and had envisioned the day I might return to thank everyone for what they did for me.

One October afternoon I made the trek back to Bronson accompanied by Jeff and Helen, two of my nurses, as well as my mom and our family friend Lucy. Before speaking, I took a stroll down memory lane and visited the Air Care hangar, where I saw the actual chopper that transported me more than five years earlier. I also visited ICU room E-130, the epicenter of the disturbing hallucinations and extreme discomfort I experienced in the aftermath of my injury. The first thing I did when I wheeled into the room was check the overhead light to make sure there were no remnants of the giant, coiled anaconda that had tormented me as I lay in bed below. Fortunately, there was no snake.

However, I did see some of the nurses and a respiratory therapist who had taken care of me. They were amazed at how well I looked. Even though I don't remember them, it was rewarding to hear their comments about how far I had come and the expectations I had exceeded. I told them I wouldn't be where I was had it not been for them.

The following day I was the final speaker of the conference. I was preceded by Dr. Shelton Maltz, one of the attending doctors who took care of me. He had prepared my family and Kristy for the worst. I can't say I blame him, considering the extent of my injuries. His presentation was a case study of my injury and the subsequent trauma that ensued. He shared the x-rays, medical reports, and prognosis for recovery with the audience. It was sobering to hear him describe my prognosis in detail.

As I listened to him recount the situation, the severity of my injury hit me hard, like a prizefighter's punch. By all accounts, I should've died. I told the audience I felt sorry for the poor sap Dr. Maltz had described, and joked, "I'd hate to be that patient!"

Some in attendance had also been involved with my care and told me afterward how rewarding and gratifying it was to watch me tell my story in my own words, not knowing if they would have ever discovered what had happened to me.

I had no idea what type of emotions I might experience if I ever went back to Bronson for a visit, but surprisingly, there was no sense of sadness, apprehension, or even wonderment. And there was no sense of closure. But that's okay, as I wasn't in need of any closure. Unfortunately, some of the emotions did return for my mother, which didn't surprise me. Although I might not remember any of it, she was forced to consciously endure all of it, along with the rest of my family.

For me, though, the trip was extremely rewarding as it afforded me the opportunity to finally do what I had wanted to for some time: visit with all the EMTs, nurses, doctors, social workers, respiratory therapists, and others who took care of me. At last, I had the chance to say what I had wanted to say for five years ...

Thank you.

# THIRTY-ONE

# WANTS AND NEEDS

There is a litany of things I will always desire. They are simple things, yet their pursuit is unbelievably complex: a splash in the ocean, followed by a nap on a lounge chair, my toes sunk deep in the sand and a piña colada in my hand; grass stains on my clothes from chasing nieces and nephews around all day; a few minutes spent trying to catch my breath after breaking into a spontaneous backspin at a wedding reception; my fingers saturated with the smell of seafood from all the peel 'n' eat boiled shrimp I peeled myself on a lazy afternoon.

I give everyone living with paralysis, or other serious health issues, credit for dealing with the fact that the "want list" may always be just out of reach. It's not easy, or natural, to accept the cardinal tenant of an SCI: life has changed and no matter how hard one may try, wish, or pray, things will never be the way they once were.

The wants have been replaced by the not-so-glamorous needs: someone always nearby to assist with the most mundane of tasks; closets stuffed with items one is more apt to find at a hospital; wide hallways; doorways equipped with ramps; an accessible vehicle, which is usually a jacked-up minivan or large conversion van.

At first glance, the wants and needs may seem unfair and misbalanced toward the practical. However, a beautiful metamorphosis can occur and leave one with those things others might spend a lifetime hoping to add to their want list: loved ones always close at hand; friends and strangers who continuously go out of their way to offer help and support; the ability to reach others through words and actions in a positive way; an appreciation for the little things that we may one day realize were actually the big things.

In the end, there will always be things we want, just as there will be needs that are required. We must choose to exist in the space where we can focus on the wants that will better us as individuals, which is what we really need.

In the movie *Sympathy for Delicious*, a paraplegic on skid row discovers he possesses an ability to heal everyone he lays his hands on. The irony, though, is he is unable to restore his own health. After I watched the movie, I pondered the opposite notion:

*What if I could heal myself, but in doing so, could no longer offer hope or health to those around me? If given a choice, would I choose to heal myself or choose to fulfill the dreams of others by healing them?*

I can honestly say I don't know which option I would choose. Given my current state, sure, of course, I would love to get up, walk, dance, and jump around again. But at the same time, all things considered, it would be difficult to forgo the ability to help others and instead just focus on my own needs.

I'm not sure I would give up my new wants for something that is no longer a genuine need.

There is one thing I would give up in a heartbeat, though: Northeast Ohio weather.

Cleveland offers a very comfortable summer climate and provides its residents with four unique seasons that can each be enjoyed in their own way. However, the winters are brutal. The cold sucks. There is no other way to put it. That's especially the case when the body's thermostat is broken, which is the frustrating reality everyone living with an SCI must endure.

Ask anyone who has a busted spinal cord, and you'll probably get the same answer, "I'm always cold. I'm always hot. I never quite feel comfortable."

Such is the result when the body's central nervous system is unable to regulate temperature. The slightest chill in the air or barometric pressure change wreaks havoc on my joints, muscles, bones, and just about every other part of my body.

The perpetual soreness throughout my shoulders only worsens when the temperature drops, and sometimes my shoulder and neck muscles tighten to the point it hurts to talk. The muscle fibers spasm nonstop and ache to the point it causes my jaw to quiver and my teeth to chatter as if I were naked in a snowstorm.

When the days get shorter, the realization sets in that winter's challenges are close at hand. That's when it's time to battle frozen pavement and impassable sidewalks with mounds of snow, navigating my wheelchair through biting wind gusts, wearing layers of clothing that cause me to overheat, and subjecting others traveling in a vehicle with me to riding with the heat cranked up. There are other idiosyncrasies always with me that are amplified in the colder months, things like skin rashes and feelings of clamminess.

I keep a dry washcloth on my lap so I can have someone wipe my face every few minutes because it always feels clammy, like my skin is being doused by an ever-present spray bottle just a few feet away. But my face is dry as a bone, no sign of moisture. It just feels that way. It always feels that way. Sometimes I wear a hooded sweatshirt while inside to fool my mind into thinking my body is warm and dry. But it doesn't always work, and it's back to fidgeting with the house thermostat as if playing a game of temperature roulette.

One time I sat so close to the fireplace that I developed burns on the side of my hand, which I didn't realize until hours later. When I want to warm up, I place a hot beanbag-type wrap across my forehead and around my neck and shoulders. It works great until after repeated sessions in the microwave, the insides start to burn and stink. I've bought so many of the damn things I should own stock in the company.

The reality is that it is much tougher to get comfortable as the mercury drops. I long to be somewhere warm and salty, back to some beach once discovered in a previous life when I used to leave footprints instead of wheel tracks. I like it hot. I crave a warm weather environment, which is why I often wonder if Northeast Ohio is the best place for me. However, it's where my support network is. It also boasts world-class healthcare facilities and a low cost of living. I've also learned to navigate the state's Medicaid system.

So, I decided to build my home in Cleveland.

I found a lot I liked in an area I loved, demolished the existing house and cleared the land. I hired a builder I trusted to construct the home, which I designed, and reached out to several individuals and companies about my plans to hopefully incorporate the house into a pseudo-version of The Quad. Several organizations, as well as extraordinary friends, contributed products, cash, and other forms of goodwill to the project. Most of the expense was covered through the catastrophic insurance policy I received from Halex after my injury. I still fantasize about spending a few months each year somewhere below the thirty-fifth parallel, but for now I am comfortable in my home and feel grateful and fortunate to be able to live in such a place.

The move into my new home proved quite eventful.

The week I was scheduled to move I struggled with stomach spasms that had me feeling "off" my usual game. A trip to the ER on Monday turned into an admittance for sepsis due to a kidney infection. It could not have come at a worse time. My apartment needed to be packed up and ready for the movers by Wednesday. Unfortunately, the timeline was non-negotiable since the apartment had already been leased to a new tenant.

There are some moments when all you can do is place your faith in God. This was another one of them, and He delivered a few angels in the forms of my mother, Lucy, and Tanya, who got everything packed up in time for moving day. By the time Wednesday evening rolled around, I still couldn't get confirmation on a discharge date from any of the doctors. Not only was the new house an absolute disaster with stuff strewn everywhere, but the stress was also beginning to take its toll on others.

Lindsey was scheduled to get married in less than forty-eight hours.

I had joked the previous weekend that her pending nuptials were interfering with my impending move. However, now the situation was serious, as my pestilent kidneys were interfering with what should be the happiest day of her life. Not to mention, she had asked me to give a special speech, so there was no way I could let her down. Thursday afternoon I was finally discharged and allowed to head home. As I wheeled into my new home for the first time, Lucy and others were busy trying to make sense of the chaos. I left them to it and headed straight to bed for the rest of the day. Unfortunately, I awoke Friday morning and still felt awful, and grimaced as I wondered how I would struggle through the entire day. Fortunately, through the grace of God, I enjoyed a wonderful evening with family and friends and witnessed my sister marry her best friend, AJ, during a beautiful ceremony.

A lot of highs and lows transpired that first year in my new home. On Father's Day, I watched the Cleveland Cavaliers win the NBA Championship, finally turning the city into *Believeland*, and in the process putting an end to a Cleveland sports title drought that had plagued its beloved and diehard fans for decades.

A month later, my mother, who had sacrificed so much for me, had a knee replacement surgery that to this day still hasn't healed right.

In October, Lindsey and AJ gave birth to a beautiful girl they named Perry Eleanor, her middle name in honor of my paternal grandmother. Two years later they welcomed a son, Miller Anthony.

Not only did I become an uncle, but also a godfather, twice. I wrote both my niece and nephew a letter with a few thoughts on what this world has taught me:

"Welcome to the world. It's a great big place that gets smaller every day, and its unpredictability should be expected. Choose to live how you want but accept that things will be out of your control. Go at life with reckless abandon and give it everything you've got, making sure you proceed with caution. And always strive to do the right thing, but never be afraid to make mistakes."

An innocent and precious new life had arrived in my niece. Two weeks later, one was taken.

As I watched the Ohio State football game one Saturday evening, a ticker scrolled across the bottom of the screen with a terse six-word update.

Dennis Byrd killed in car crash.

Earlier that morning, Byrd and his twelve-year-old son had been in an automobile accident, and Dennis died from the massive injuries he sustained. He was fifty years old. Dennis Byrd was my Superman, my Christopher Reeve, the one I looked to for inspiration in the face of a spinal cord injury. We both shared a love of God, football, and the same Romans 8:18 Scripture verse that hung above our beds after our devastating injuries. The strength, courage, and faith Dennis exhibited throughout his life will always inspire me.

***

There is a long list of ongoing issues that are always with me, like a silent passenger in a car, ready to scream out at any moment without warning.

Serious matters like autonomic dysreflexia, pneumonia, decreased bone density, pressure sores, urinary tract infections, blood pressure and body temperature issues, and a whole host of other uncomfortable complications that are par for the course with an SCI. There are also the idiosyncrasies, things like nerve pain, a constant feeling of clamminess, skin rashes that appear for no reason, nausea, and vertigo.

Sitting in a chair all day is the easy part.

Living a productive life while guarding against the unseen circumstances that are always ready to pounce is the challenging part.

However, I don't let the challenges stop me. I rely on education, competent nurses, and rational thinking to deal with the day-to-day challenges of this injury. It's most likely the same for anyone who lives with a broken neck. But at times that's not enough. There is always the risk of a severe setback, infection, and even death, that comes with the territory. And science has proven that an SCI shortens one's lifespan. There is no retreat from the stark fact that finality is never far away, an ever-present reality when someone lives with an SCI.

The callous verity of that notion rocked my world one August when I lost two friends in two weeks, both from complications due to their spinal cord injuries. Five days after she celebrated her twenty-ninth birthday, Paris Adams passed away. She was a beautiful, young, and energetic woman who worked out with me at Buckeye Wellness Center.

Unfathomably, just seventeen days after Paris passed, Ryan Housholder passed away at the age of thirty-three. He was one of the first individuals I met after my injury, when he visited me at MetroHealth Hospital and introduced me to the cough assist system. The day he wheeled into my room he had such a welcoming smile on his face. He was stuck in a wheelchair yet exhibited such a youthful enthusiasm and positive presence. Ryan served as an example to me and was someone I looked up to as a reminder of how strong the human spirit is and how much difference faith can make in the face of adversity.

A year and a half later I lost another friend due to complications from an SCI, Alexandria Reese, a beautiful and kindhearted soul. She was thirty-four years old.

The community of SCI survivors is a tightknit bunch, an exclusive group that has suffered and endured tremendous hardship. It's very difficult even to begin to appreciate what living with an SCI is like. We rely on one another for camaraderie, support, knowledge, advice, levity, motivation, and so much more. When we lose one of our own, it hurts. Losing three young and amazing individuals in such a short span was extremely painful and disheartening.

I subscribe to the school of thought that we honor those we've lost through the way we choose to live our lives.

There is a Latin phrase, *Memento Mori*, whose literal translation means, "remember that you will die." I spent more time thinking about dying before I broke my neck. Now, my focus is on living. Once upon a time I lay in a hospital bed and wished for death. Now, thankful for life, I dwell on what I want to do and how much time I have left to do it. I wonder if I will achieve my goals before the ones I love have moved on, as I feel that would be the best way to show my gratitude to those who have supported me. As the years have progressed, I have reflected more on my mortality and how I might die–whether I will succumb to old age or some ailment related to an SCI. But for the most part, I don't look too far into the future anymore. Instead, I focus on a few days at a time. There is so much uncertainty, sometimes anxiety, that it's easier to not overwhelm my mind with far-off thoughts and worries that I can't control anyway. Things are more manageable when taken in small chunks.

One chunk at a time. One day at a time.

About five years after my injury, I experienced a feeling of appreciation and wonderment while at the Cleveland Browns home opener with my Dad and my friend Eric. As I sat in the sun's radiance, I hearkened back to the fact that five years earlier I doubted I would ever attend another Browns game, let alone make it out of the hospital.

But that afternoon at the game I didn't focus on being paralyzed, but rather on the fact that I had survived and had come out stronger as a result. There were many moments throughout the afternoon that I felt an overwhelming appreciation for my life.

What is remarkable, though, is that I later found out that Eric had also reflected on the very same concept. A year prior he had been diagnosed with stage IV non-Hodgkin's lymphoma, a devastating diagnosis that unfortunately often gets the best of those diagnosed. He made a miraculous, cancer free recovery, and was also able to appreciate that afternoon for what it was: a reminder of how precious life is and how grateful we should feel to be alive.

When I was in the hospital years earlier, Eric made a trip from Paris, France to visit me. As we discussed my future and the new life that was in store for me, he gave me some great advice I've never forgotten. He told me the road would be tough and challenging and I was facing a whole new kind of ballgame that would include some big home runs as well as missed shots. But there was one objective: to win!

He reminded me that I had no choice but to get up each day and "win the day!"

One day at a time.

# THIRTY-TWO
# I'M GOING TO LIVE

"You suffered a heart attack."

That's what the doctor told me in May 2017. Not exactly what I expected to hear two months after my forty-first birthday.

For several weeks I had noticed blood clots in the Foley bag that collected my urine. Potential causes were investigated and eliminated one by one, yet clots continued to amass. My nurse became concerned one morning when the entire Foley was filled with more than 800 milliliters of dark, crimson-colored urine. My blood pressure was an astounding 220/150, and I had an excruciating headache, all signs of autonomic dysreflexia. The headache reached the point where it hurt to be conscious, and the paramedics were called to transport me to the hospital.

Once in the ER, my blood pressure still hovered in the danger zone. I asked for some Nitro paste, but the doctors were unsure if they should administer it since my troponin levels were exceedingly high and indicated that damage to the heart had occurred. I continued to demand it until it was finally administered and lowered my pressure into the mid-hundreds–still elevated, but my head no longer felt like it was ready to burst. I was sent for x-rays and CAT scans and then transferred to the cardiac ICU.

More bloodwork was ordered to examine my troponin levels. Troponins are proteins found in the heart and are usually present in very low levels in the bloodstream. However, when damage to the heart occurs, they are released into the bloodstream at a high rate. All my tests indicated my heart had undergone serious trauma. Additional tests showed a baseball-sized hematoma in my bladder. Continuous irrigation was started to cycle saline through the bladder to break up the hematoma.

Fortunately, after several days the clots disappeared, and my troponin levels significantly decreased. I was released and urged to follow up with the urologist and cardiologist. The urologist did a bladder scan, which eliminated any signs of cancer or other conditions. Ultimately, they never concluded what had caused the consistent bleeding, but fortunately it disappeared. A second cardiologist concluded I had suffered a myocardial injury, different than a heart attack, but still reason for concern and advised I follow up for more tests.

The funny thing about a spinal cord injury is that it can desensitize someone to issues such as a myocardial injury. Having been through a gauntlet of ailments, surgeries, and hospital stays, I was not overly concerned with what the cardiologist told me and saw it as a one-off incident rather than a chronic situation.

There are a lot of changes that I have become accustomed to because of this injury. However, the permanence of some of the changes I've endured is something I don't know if I'll ever get used to. Gone is the spontaneity from many activities in my life, including getting ready each day. Every morning after I awake, the routine begins. Urine is drained from the Foley bag that hangs off my bed. I'm rolled onto my left side and a digital stimulation is performed to help me move my bowels since I haven't been able to go to the bathroom on my own since being injured.

Next, I'm ushered from my bed into the bathroom and lowered onto a shower chair utilizing an overhead ceiling lift. After I've been cleaned and rinsed, I usually close my eyes and relax under the hot water for several minutes–my version of a "quad spa." Afterward, I'm ushered back into bed and dressed for the day. My stretching routine depends on how sore I feel. Once dressed, I'm transferred into my wheelchair, which sits next to the bed. It takes almost two hours before I'm ready to begin my day. Gone is my ability to get up and go. Everything requires planning.

Another change I haven't welcomed but have been forced to adapt to is my sex life. Sexual pleasure is still possible; it's just different. I can still get aroused, though a pill is needed to assist. Although I have no feeling in the areas I'd like to, the immediate area below my level of injury is hypersensitive, and the proper touch can prove extremely sexual. I still enjoy sex, but sometimes it's not worth the effort it takes, unless it's with a partner who keeps an open mind and is willing to try different things. Again, everything requires planning.

I'm not the only one who has been forced to endure changes. People tend to lose sight of the magnitude to which others are also affected physically and emotionally. Parents, siblings, spouses, and others are forced into a daunting journey they never envisioned. It's not easy to watch someone you care for dearly and love deeply struggle with the daily grind that comes with paralysis. It takes a special breed of person and strength to accept that change.

For the paralyzed individual, there's no choice but to confront it. However, everyone else can choose the extent to which they will be involved in the journey. For an extraordinary few, though, it's not a choice, but rather a calling from God or a personal mandate that, in some cases, can be as challenging as paralysis itself.

It would be wrong to gloss over the fact that my family's plans were also derailed. They have continued to make tremendous sacrifices and have been there to help me through the adjustments in my life. On several occasions, as I've told my story to others, I've glimpsed my mom and sister from the corner of my eye and watched their eyes swell with tears. It's something I don't think I will ever get used to.

It's especially difficult to see the toll my injury has taken on my parents. I have witnessed them physically age faster than biology intended. Although they have unselfishly accepted the challenge my injury has delivered, it's impossible to not feel like a burden to them. I should be taking care of my parents as they grow old, it shouldn't be the other way around. I will never be able to repay them for what they have sacrificed and given up on my behalf.

***

Living in a wheelchair has taught me valuable lessons that don't just apply to someone living with a disability. These lessons prove valuable when confronted with moments of challenge and despair. However, I seek to apply them to my life daily and incorporate them into my everyday psyche.

"It all starts with the right attitude."

I used to have the word ATTITUDE written under the brim of my baseball hat. Every time I ran onto the diamond, it was right there to remind me: Attitude equals altitude. Attitude is everything. Without the right attitude, it is tough to accomplish anything significant. We are not in control of what happens to us. But we are in control of our attitude and the way we choose to respond to what happens to us. My attitude is what has kept me going stronger than a pack of Energizer batteries ever could.

Human resilience is a powerful thing that I never fully understood until I was faced with incredible adversity. I believe everyone's spirit is just as strong, but unfortunately, not everyone chooses to accept that. The power to change one's mindset, take on a new perspective, and focus on positivity is a gift most will never fully appreciate. I am still learning to appreciate the power my attitude can have over my life. Determining your attitude is something that's left up to you. You can be in control of your attitude. Or not. It's your choice. Tough times will still find you. No one is immune from the storm. But the rains don't last forever. Choose the right attitude. Make that last.

The scars on my body, and the chair I spend my days in, are always there to remind me that life can be unpredictable and unfair. Life doesn't reconstruct itself to accommodate our plans. We need to adapt our plans to accommodate what life hands us. Staying positive is a choice. And if that choice is cultivated into a habit, it becomes ingrained in the psyche, and ultimately becomes part of your behavior.

"Do not let adversity define you."

Cursed. Deadened. Decrepit. Inadequate. Invalidated. Screwed up. Weakened. All those words are synonyms for the word DISABLED. Those are offensive words to me, and certainly not words I would use to define myself. I may have a disability, but I am not disabled. I believe I still have a lot to offer. I still hope to achieve a lot; I just might need to do it from a chair for the time being. Regardless of what you are going through or have been through, your adversity does not define you. How you choose to live in the face of adversity is a much better definition. Do not let adversity define you.

"Inch by inch is a cinch, yard by yard is awfully hard."

I first heard the maxim when my dad read it to me in *Mind Gym: An Athlete's Guide to Inner Excellence* by Gary Mack and David Casstevens. Sometimes it helps to break things down and compartmentalize. Almost nothing is insurmountable when you break it down into its smallest parts. It's a lot easier to focus and see results when you are not overwhelmed by the bigger obstacle in front of you. While we'd all like to do great things and see great things happen right away, it doesn't just happen. It doesn't work overnight. Things take time. And sometimes, really great things take lots of time. But we need to invest the time if we want to improve. Stay the course and stay patient. Even if you only gain an inch at a time, those inches will soon add up to yards, and those yards to miles. And more importantly, change will happen.

"There'll be good days, and there'll be bad days."

I had good days and bad days before my accident, so I shouldn't be surprised if I still have bad days. The important thing is what is taken from the bad days. There's no one-size-fits-all recipe to rise above hardship. A lot depends on how we have lived life up until that point when adversity strikes. The collection of experiences and outcomes endured throughout our lives become the tools and instructions needed to deal with what comes next. Once you learn to move through tough times, you begin to accumulate more tools in your toolbox for the next tough time you encounter. Sure, you will encounter bad days in the future, but apply the tools garnered, and they won't last as long. And soon you'll find yourself stringing together more good days than bad days, and you start to realize, "Yeah, I can do this."

Like it or not, at some point all of us will face a daunting challenge that can cripple our psyche if we let it. It's during the times we find ourselves tested that we discover just how resilient the human spirit can be. More times than not, we make it through and come out the other end a stronger person as a result, even though we might not always appreciate it.

When it comes to adversity, there's no such thing as a free pass. Just because you have endured hardship and faced down what seemed like an impossible challenge in your past, that does not exclude you from having to do it all over again in the future. Adversity isn't a final exam where once it's done, it's over and you'll never have to repeat it. You should expect bad days will still find you. However, take solace in the fact that you have gotten through them in the past, and there's no reason you can't get through them again. We are much more resilient than we give ourselves credit for and need to remember that each time we encounter a new and uncertain challenge.

"It's all relative."

No matter how bad you have it, there is someone far worse off than you. The same can be said for how good you might think you have it. For the longest time after I was injured, I compared myself to others with a similar injury. Even though everyone told me that every spinal cord injury is unique, if I saw another person making more progress than me, I would wonder what I was doing wrong. Even though I felt I was working just as hard, if not harder, I didn't see the same results. Finally, I was able to accept the fact that my situation was not for lack of effort; instead, that was just the way it is.

The same can be said for a lot of the situations we find ourselves in. Don't compare situations, because everyone chooses to deal with things differently. A few things that have helped me: I focus on the now; I celebrate every victory, even the small ones; I incrementally work to get back what I lost; and I appreciate the simple things that provide comfort.

"Keep the faith and believe."

Whenever I need a reminder to keep the faith, I recall the Romans Scripture verse I first learned of when I read Dennis Byrd's story, and how that same verse was placed above my hospital bed. It reminds me that God does have a plan and I need to trust in it.

At times we might feel as if things are too much, pressing us and wearing us down, with no end in sight. And then a quick minute later we find ourselves in a completely different situation and mindset. What may have seemed insurmountable one second now seems like a distant memory. There are times when the challenges at hand require a significant amount of mental fortitude and perseverance to push on through. At times it's much easier to accept the role of victim rather than believe we are the master of our destiny. However, we are the masters of our attitudes.

We must adopt the proper mindset to confront the storms we

encounter. Make the active decision to do so. It's not always easy, but I'd venture to say it's better than the alternative of focusing on the dark clouds.

It's been said that adversity builds character. I think adversity builds gratitude. Anyone's situation can change in the blink of an eye, and sometimes the change can be as extreme as a relentless hurricane. It's just as easy to slip and fall on an ice patch as it is to dive into a lakebed hiding under shallow water. Some things are just as uncontrollable as the weather itself. What is controllable is how we react to our situations, how we choose to appreciate our blessings, what we learn from our hardships, and what we thank the good Lord for at the end of every day. At the end of each day, I am grateful for a tremendous amount.

A lot has happened to me since my injury: some bad things, some good things. But I am very grateful that there's been more good than bad. It's easy to look back on that fateful day and wonder what might have been. But I have had beautiful experiences since then: personal growth, incredible friendships, amazing opportunities. I thank God every day for my life. For the life I had before my accident. For the life I have now. He has instilled within me a spirit of resilience as well as a sense of appreciation I might not otherwise have ever discovered. He has allowed me the opportunity to reach others, whether through a conversation or a grant from Getting Back Up, and hopefully pass along something that might one day help someone else when they need it most. He has brought me through whatever has confronted me and brought me to this very moment. Today. Here, right now.

We all have a past written and etched on the walls of the soul. Those experiences, whether emotional, physical, or spiritual, make us who we are. A conscious effort must be made to apply past learnings to influence future choices. After my injury, I clamored for a "do over" for a long time. It took a conscious effort to transition my outlook from one of despair to one of happiness. It didn't happen overnight, but it happened, and it has made all the difference in my road to recovery.

In some ways, our past can serve as a dress rehearsal when it comes to creating our happiness. Recall the happiest moments of your life and what created that happiness. Perhaps there is an opportunity to re-create that attitude. Every passing moment is another chance to turn it all around. If we choose to accept that, then each passing moment might be the closest we ever get to a "do-over" and the chance to find what it is that makes us happy.

Where you find yourself at this very instant is the direct culmination of every single moment you've experienced right up until now. The good, the bad, the ugly, the uncertain, whatever it may have been, shaped who you are and where you are in the present. Our lives are happening in the present. The past is over. Life moves on, and we need to move with it. However, it's important to remember how you arrived at where you are. I don't live in the past, but I'm also not afraid to look back on it, learn from it, cry a little, laugh a lot, and smile because I'm here in a brand-new moment.

When I was growing up, my dad had a pale-yellow 1970 Buick LeSabre convertible. That steel boat on wheels sat dormant most of the year, and it was often a challenge to get its four-barrel engine to turn over. However, my father kept turning that key, gently pressing on the gas pedal, until eventually, he'd succeed in getting it started. But once started, that car could drive all day. Momentum is a lot like that old Buick. You must want to start. You must want to take that ride. You must visualize the enjoyment and satisfaction that awaits. It might not always be easy to get started, but once started it gets easier and easier to keep going. The ride is worth it.

The word "recovery" is a moving target, often shrouded in the misconception of tangible results. I have come to define recovery as a relative term. It's a juxtaposition of different goals and aspirations, and the journey I am on is the recovery, a learning experience that teaches me something new with every milestone I reach. As such, I am always rewarded with discovery. The Fourth of July used to be my favorite holiday. I always loved the celebration and pageantry that surrounded Independence Day. It marked a time for revelry. And then came July 3, 2009. The day I lost my independence. Each year on my anniversary I used to think about what my life might have looked like had I not been injured.

A lot of questions have been answered since I broke my neck. A lot remain unanswered. There are moments I wish I could answer all the questions that arise in my mind. It's the lucky ones who learn to be happy and content with unanswered questions. I consider myself a lucky one. I should have died all those years ago, and perhaps part of me did, but another part awakened and was given another lease on life. I embrace July third for what it is–a new beginning. I have learned to adapt. It's an adaptation that I vigorously fought all those years ago. Today, that same adaptation is something I embrace and work hard to parlay into something worthwhile. Adaptation has given me perspective. The Fourth of July is still my favorite holiday.

***

Someone once asked Christopher Reeve if it was easier to live with his injury as time went on. He replied it was the exact opposite.

After my injury, a tremendous mental adjustment was required. The physical part was easy. However, as the years have progressed, it's the physical aspect of my injury that wears me down. The constant muscle soreness, nerve pain, clamminess, and overall feeling of discomfort that never leaves has become my albatross. The monotony of the daily routine is a grind, leaving me sick and tired of feeling sick and tired.

I am fully paralyzed. I cannot move any part of my body other than slight head rotations and shoulder shrugs. Occasionally I have spasms, involuntary muscle jerks triggered by an external stimulus, such as touch. Other than that, I sit still in my wheelchair, unable to feed myself, brush my teeth, or wipe my face. I can't feel much below my shoulders. You can put my hands in a pot of boiling water or a bucket of freezing ice, and I would not know the difference. If I closed my eyes and you touched my body or moved an arm or a leg, I'd have no clue. It's been this way for years, and sometimes I am still amazed that I've managed as well as I have.

I can no longer ride a bull, bench press over 300 pounds, or hit a fastball. Gone are the days when I obsessed about gross margins, inventory turns, and sales data. Tasks I used to deem meaningful have been replaced by more critical issues, such as maintaining bone density, skin integrity, and pulmonary health. I've lost my physical prowess, but I am still Scott. I still have my personality, my intellect, my humor, and my great hair. I am still just as stubborn, if not more.

Life is a challenge at times. Life can be unfair, cruel, and unforgiving. But life is also beautiful. Every day I thank God for my life. Life doesn't owe us anything. It's us who owe life our best. These days, my best just happens to be from a wheelchair, and I carry one thought with me as I move through every day:

*I'm going to live.*

# EPILOGUE
# MY STORY

It took me a long time to write this book. I struggled as I wondered if I had a story to tell.

I'm not a professional athlete who defied doctors by walking out of the hospital, or even a collegiate athlete who inspired a nation and once again led his team back onto the field–and I'm certainly not a Hollywood celebrity, a real-world Superman who did more to raise awareness and research for spinal cord injuries than anyone could ever imagine.

My story is nothing special.

It's no more special than the family whose lives were wrecked by a drunk driver when their young daughter was killed and toddler son left paralyzed; or the young man whose neck was broken when a tree branch fell on him and killed his girlfriend; or the beautiful young woman who drove a drunk friend home and was the victim of a random bullet that shattered her neck and her dreams.

My story is no more special than that of any of those other individuals.

My story is just different.

Like a spinal cord injury itself, all our stories are unique. They are ours, and we own them. And sometimes, it's up to us to tell them, not so much for us, but for others.

I have shared my story while speaking to different groups and audiences, it's effect often not fully appreciated by me. However, those who thanked me afterwards remind me that my story can affect others. Sometimes for the better.

Although I might never know exactly what it was that resonated with them, it still gave them reason to pause and reflect. It served as an impetus to spur them to make some type of change.

This is extremely humbling. Sometimes even intimidating.

I've been encouraged by others to continue to tell my story.

This is me telling it.

I have tried to be as transparent as possible, sharing the highs and lows, the good and bad, the pretty and ugly. I have tried to be sensitive to others while doing my best to be truthful and sincere.

I can only hope that I have achieved what I set out to do–to tell my story as best I can, and hopefully reach someone who is moved to act. Moved to do something great that can help others as well as themselves.

Moved to do something that enriches their own story.

# ACKNOWLEDGMENTS

Although my name is on the cover, this book would not have come to fruition were it not for a myriad of individuals.

Mom and Dad, without both of you none of this would have been possible, literally and figuratively. Thank you for instilling in me the fighting spirit that helped carry me through the darkest time of my life. You have given me a life full of love and support, as well as those teachable moments I would not trade for anything. You also gave me a beautiful and supportive sister.

Lindsey, I know you received quite a few headaches from me (also both literally and figuratively) growing up. You have always had my back. It's been a privilege to watch you evolve into a strong woman and amazing mother. You picked a great partner in your husband. AJ, I am proud to call you a brother.

The amazing doctors, nurses, staff, and Air Care flight nurses at Bronson Methodist Hospital, MetroHealth Hospital, University Hospitals, The Cleveland Clinic, Regency Hospital, Rae Ann Nursing Home, and my fantastic nurses and caretakers: Jeff Gedeon, Michelle Hastings, Tanya Hullum, Shaquille Hullum, and Helen Kosko. Thanks for keeping me here.

My late godmother Faye Ratner, once gave my mom a plaque that read: "What good is having a friend if you can't use them." I have been blessed with the support and generosity of many friends whom I will never be able to repay for everything they have provided me. I'm especially grateful for the friends (and strangers) who have offered me prayers, support, and encouragement, whether through social media, an email, a phone call, or a visit. To my friends, all I can say is thank you.

My deepest gratitude to the special individuals who helped turn my manuscript into a book: My editor Laurie Chittenden, for her invaluable insight and guidance in helping me tell my story; Katie Bradesca, Susan Drabik, Dawn Johnston, Steve Luttner, Jody Toohy, and Will Voegele for agreeing to read and critique; Brooks Becker for the copyediting; Kate Voegele for writing the Foreword, as well as for your awesome music that continues to inspire me; those who had a kind word to say and offered their endorsement; Sara Kornokovich for the Freddie hook up; Eric Mull for the fantastic photography. And, of course, all those who encouraged me to write this book and tell my story. I hope you find it worth reading.

Additionally, thank you to John Kuntz, Dale Omori, and Diane Suchetka from *The Plain Dealer.* Lucy Simm for the unselfishness she has provided to my entire family, as well as all the home-cooked meals.

My sincerest gratitude and appreciation to those who have donated to my discretionary trust fund. Without your support, I would not be able to benefit from the vital therapy services necessary for someone with a spinal cord injury. It is that therapy that has helped me grow stronger.

Thank you, Dennis Byrd for your constant source of inspiration. And thank you Bruce Springsteen for the companion you have given me through your music.

Finally, and most importantly, thank you to God. You're the reason.

# IF YOU WOULD LIKE TO HELP

Breaking one's neck and facing a future full of daunting odds is not something anyone can do alone. I am extremely grateful for the prayers, support, and assistance I have received. Special thanks to those who have contributed to my Discretionary Assistance Trust. I have come so far, yet I have so much further to go.

To get involved or learn more, visit scottwfedor.com.

To learn more about Getting Back Up, visit gettingbackup.org.

# SUGGESTED READING

If you would like to read some other books that have influenced my life and attitude, here are a few I think you might enjoy:

Brown, Jr., H. Jackson. *Life's Little Instruction Book: 511 Suggestions, Observations, and Reminders on How to Live a Happy and Rewarding Life.* Nashville: Rutledge Hill Press, 1991.

Byrd, Dennis and D'Orso, Mike. *Rise and Walk: The Trial and Triumph of Dennis Byrd.* New York: HarperCollins, 1993.

Ferguson, Howard. *The Edge: The Guide to Fulfilling Dreams, Maximizing Success, and Enjoying a Lifetime of Happiness.* Cleveland: Howard E. Ferguson, 1982.

Krakauer, Jon. *Into Thin Air: A Personal Account of the Mt. Everest Disaster.* New York: Villard Books, 1997.

Mack, Gary and Casstevens, David. *Mind Gym: An Athlete's Guide to Inner Excellence.* New York: McGraw-Hill Education, 2001.

Paulus, Trina. *Hope for the Flowers.* New York: Paulist Press, 1972.

Saint-Exupéry, Antoine de. *The Little Prince.* New York: Reynal & Hitchcock, 1943.

Springsteen, Bruce. *Born to Run.* New York: Simon & Schuster, 2016.

Stanton, Doug. *In Harm's Way: The Sinking of the U.S.S. Indianapolis and the Extraordinary Story of Its Survivors.* New York: Henry Holt and Company, 2001.

***

And for your viewing pleasure:

*Joe Versus the Volcano.* Directed by John Patrick Shanley, Warner Bros., March 9, 1990.

# ABOUT THE AUTHOR

Scott Fedor is an inspirational speaker and disability advocate who has inspired others across the world. He is the founder of Getting Back Up, a nonprofit that assists individuals with spinal cord injuries, and is an advocate member of the Adversity 2 Advocacy Alliance, which promotes turning personal challenges into service to others. Throughout his remarkable journey he has continued to find strength in his faith, family, and positive attitude. He currently resides in Cleveland, Ohio.

scottwfedor.com
@scottwfedor

CPSIA information can be obtained
at www.ICGtesting.com
Printed in the USA
LVHW051945181119
637697LV00010B/461/P